THE EXPLORERS CLUB

THE EXPLORERS CLUB

A VISUAL JOURNEY THROUGH THE PAST, PRESENT, AND FUTURE OF EXPLORATION

EDITED BY JEFF WILSER

TEN SPEED PRESS
California | New York

Why climb Everest?
"Because it's there."

—GEORGE MALLORY, 1923

Seeker

Why Go?
Because I can
It is what humans do
We explore, We observe, We learn
Seeker!

—DR. SIAN PROCTOR, 2021

CONTENTS

3—CURIOSITY IN ACTION

The New Golden Age of Exploration

THE EXPLORERS CLUB
NORTH POLE
SOUTH POLE 1911
EVEREST
CHALLENGER DEEP
MOON

INTRODUCTION

The sign itself isn't flashy. It's easy to miss. At 46 East Seventieth Street, just two blocks from Central Park, hangs a plaque that says THE EXPLORERS CLUB.

Most people stroll right past this humble sign. But some are curious. They might notice a mysterious flag by the doorway—a flag not linked to any nation or city or state. Or they might spot the stained glass windows above, which look like they're from Windsor Castle. (They are.) Or perhaps they see that the door itself is made of heavy wrought iron, the kind of imposing entrance that's fit for a fortress.

Then they open the door.

And the moment you set foot inside The Explorers Club, you leave the streets of New York and enter a world that seems to exist in another dimension. It's a place of history and adventure. A shrine to science and wonder. Over six creaky floors of this Neo-Jacobean mansion—impossibly larger than you would guess from the street—you'll find a never-ending collection of treasures from the past: sixteenth-century maps, the books of Napoleon, flags from the Apollo astronauts.

And as you roam the halls, you might assume the Club is a kind of museum or dusty monument focused on old glories. There's a bit of truth to that. The Club is proud of its past and its "Famous Firsts," as its members have been the first to the North Pole, the first to the South Pole, the first to summit Everest, the first to the deepest point in the ocean, the first to the moon.

But look closer. And step further into the Club.

In the Members' Lounge, perhaps at the bar, you'll find something altogether different: modern-day explorers who are laughing, telling stories,

The charter members of The Explorers Club, 1904.

exchanging ideas, collaborating, brainstorming, and plotting future missions. These are some of the Club's 3,400 (and counting) active members—from more than sixty countries—who push the boundaries of human knowledge. They're the true heartbeat of the Club. Which raises the question, "Just what, exactly, are modern explorers doing? What's left to explore?" After all, the world is now well-mapped. We all carry a GPS in our pocket. As *The Explorers Journal* once put it, "Every so often someone asks us, 'Isn't exploration a more or less dead profession nowadays?' "

That was written in 1937.

At the time, to many, it seemed that exploration had indeed reached a cul-de-sac. The globe was complete. Even the North and South Poles had been discovered. What more could we possibly learn?

If explorers had then decided to close up shop, we never would have landed on the moon. We would not understand the scope of the galaxy. We would not have developed much of modern technology. We would not understand climate change.

Exploration wasn't dead in 1937, but it did evolve. Since the Club was founded in 1904, exploration has shifted from a reckless streak of exploitation to a push for conservation, from a drive to conquer to an eagerness to collaborate, from a celebration of "adventuring" to a commitment to hard science, and from the gates of exclusion to a culture of inclusivity.

This book tells the story of that evolution across three eras of exploration:

> Expanding the Maps: Chasing the Dragons
> Breaking the Boundaries: Climbing Higher and Diving Deeper
> Curiosity in Action: The New Golden Age of Exploration

For the name of the first era, we can thank an Explorers Club member who knew a thing or two about Famous Firsts. That would be John Glenn. In 2013, at the Club's annual black-tie dinner, the astronaut gave a speech about exploration. He noted that back in the days of old-timey maps—the ones that showed the "known world"—the maps had dark edges on the sides, along with boiling pots of oil and warnings such as "There be dragons here."

It was the explorer's job to expand the map and push back the dragon. "Our whole history has been one of dragon-pushing," Glenn said to his colleagues. "Pushing dragons back off the edge and filling in those gaps on the maps. And that is a key role that The Explorers Club has provided."

By the 1920s, most of those dragons had been chased and pushed off the map. The globe was complete. Explorers switched their focus to daring experiments in manned balloons, airplanes, submersibles, and finally to rockets and space shuttles. They climbed higher in space, dived deeper in the ocean, and dived deeper into the science. Thus, the second era of exploration: breaking the boundaries by climbing higher, diving deeper.

And now it's evolving once again.

"We're entering a new golden age of exploration," says Richard Garriott, the Club's forty-fifth president. It's an era in which Nina Lanza, a NASA scientist, uses a laser-shooting rover to search for life on Mars. For Lanza, exploration is not dead: "To me, exploration is almost synonymous with discovery, and it's learning about our universe." She notes that while exploration can still be physical—whether on other planets or deep in the ocean—it can also mean a deeper understanding of how the universe ticks. "Through exploration, we get to broaden the scope of our existence."

In the new golden era, conservationists like Jane Goodall, Laurie Marker, and Callie Veelenturf study and protect endangered species. Other anthropologists, such as the linguist K. David Harrison, work to preserve indigenous cultures that are rapidly vanishing.

These are just a few of hundreds of examples. By crossing the vertical length of Africa on foot—from Cape Town to Cairo—eco-explorer Mario Rigby highlights cultures that are often misunderstood or overlooked. Justin Dunnavant, an "underwater archaeologist," dives in the ocean to search for

A bust of Lowell Thomas, the legendary writer and broadcaster who introduced the world to Lawrence of Arabia. For decades, Thomas was a staple at the Club. The headquarters is now known as the Lowell Thomas building.

sunken slave ships, exposing truths about our past that help us understand our present. And Ed Lu, a former astronaut, is developing a defense system against extinction-level asteroids.

Exploration is needed for humanity to survive. And in some ways that has always been the mission. "Exploration has always been a survival tactic for human beings. It's how to find shelter. It's how to make fire," says Edith Widder, an oceanographer who's plumbing the depths of the sea. Her work suggests that bioluminescence—those brilliant underwater displays of fireworks—could be the key to unlocking the mysteries of the carbon cycle, a crucial link to global warming, and what she calls "a big part of the story of life." It's a story we need to better understand.

And exploration, ultimately, is how we do more than just survive—it's how we thrive. It's how we learn. How we grow and even how we think. The Club defines exploration as "curiosity acted upon," and this curiosity is part of what makes us human. "Curiosity is our binding theme," says Ted Janulis, a former Club president. Every explorer is curious about something and

The Explorers Club flag. They often endure wear-and-tear from expeditions in the field; each imperfection speaks to its history.

they're driven to understand it. "It could be butterflies. It could be caves or mountains or valleys or the moon."

All of us are curious. True, perhaps we haven't been so consumed by curiosity that we climbed into a volcano or circumnavigated the globe in a hot-air balloon, but we all have the instinct. And it's a trait that can be kindled.

That is why, finally, at its core, this book is meant to awaken the explorer in all of us. The stories of the people in this book can instruct us, teach us, inspire us. Whether a harrowing journey in the Arctic or a perspective-tilting trip to Tanzania or a voyage that could help bring us to Mars, the stories can nudge us to think differently, to restore our childlike wonder, and even to remember what it's like to dream.

"Everyone is an explorer," says Milbry Polk, a longtime Club member and author of *Women of Discovery*. "It's in our genes. It's part of the essence of being human."

All of us are explorers.

So welcome to The Explorers Club.

1—EXPANDING THE MAPS

CHASING THE DRAGONS

The earliest roots of exploration, of course, go back thousands and even millions of years, to a time when our distant ancestors left Africa and fanned out to Eurasia and beyond. The Explorers Club is old but not that old. So, with a few exceptions, we'll limit the scope of this section to the era of the Club's existence, and that era is heavy on the Arctic. After all, the Club began its life as the "Arctic Club."

In this first stage, there's a heavy emphasis on the word "first." First to the North Pole. First to the South Pole. First to plant a flag and claim victory. At its best, that hunger to be first can kindle our competitive spirit and launch us into the future (exhibit A: the Apollo space program). Yet especially in this Heroic Age of exploration, the obsession with being first—that raging ego—can endanger expeditions, cost lives, and exploit indigenous people. There are heroes, yes, but also villains.

This era is full of bravery and brutality, science and scoundrels, heroes and hubris. We won't flinch from these realities, and these stories can serve as cautionary tales. Exploration has a complicated past. Let's dive into it.

THE TWO GREELYS: A TALE OF ARCTIC ANGUISH

On the second floor of The Explorers Club, in a library of rare and treasured books, your eyes are drawn to a large painting by Albert L. Operti (see detail, opposite). It depicts a scene from the Arctic—cold, gray, bleak—and a row of bodies on the ground. Maybe the bodies are dead, maybe they're alive; it's hard to tell. Bundled in dark winter coats, men work to carry even more bodies on stretchers. The sky is the color of smoke. The painting tells a story that most history books have forgotten, or perhaps chose to hide from children. The painting, in a sense, tells the first story of The Explorers Club.

And our story begins in the Civil War.

ARCTIC MOON

A young abolitionist wanted to fight for the North. He was only seventeen years old. He tried to enlist but was rejected—too young. He tried again, denied again. Then he was rejected a third time. Could he lie about his age? He considered this, but his integrity gave him pause, so as a compromise, he wrote "18" on the bottom of his shoes; now he could tell the army with a straight face, "I am over eighteen." This did the trick.

In the battle of Antietam, the bloodiest day in American history, the teenager was shot in the jaw. He lost four teeth and was knocked unconscious. Moments later he awoke, scrambled to escape, and was shot in the leg. Somehow he lived. He was soon promoted to sergeant, then lieutenant, and then he led one of the North's first Black infantry units.

The soldier's name was Adolphus Greely.

Greely spoke Latin. He enjoyed literature. When his fellow officers played cards or drank whiskey, Greely devoured books. The army noticed his curiosity. After the war, Greely joined the US Signal Corps and crisscrossed Nebraska, Utah, and Wyoming to help install the nation's network of telegraphs.

In 1881, the army tapped Greely to lead a daring mission: a three-year voyage called the Lady Franklin Bay Expedition. The very name was ominous. Lady Franklin Bay, an icy chunk of northern Greenland, was named after Jane Franklin, the wife of the British explorer Sir John Franklin, who, in 1845, led two ships to the Arctic and was never heard from again.

Greely's job? The mission was scientific. Greely and his team of twenty-four men (most from the army) would journey north with crates of barometers, chronometers, thermometers, magnetometers, galvanometers—basically all the meters. They would record measurements as close to the North Pole as possible. The expedition was part of the International Polar Year, a grander global project that sought to better understand the climate of the Arctic. The idea was visionary. Eleven nations participated, from Norway to France to Russia, in a joint scientific effort that foreshadowed the International Space Station.

The journey also had a second, sneakier mission. Greely, like most explorers of the nineteenth century, was lured by that greatest prize of all: the North Pole. In today's world, it can be tough to understand this obsession with the Arctic. But put yourself in the 1880s. The world's maps had been filled in to the east and west, but the north and south remained a tantalizing dark unknown. These Arctic expeditions were like going to Mars.

The trip was so important that President James A. Garfield invited Greely to the White House. The president took in Greely's almost regal appearance—six feet tall, trim, sharp eyes, glasses, crisp pointy beard. The man had gravitas. "Under your leadership, I am confident that the work will be a success," the president told him. "The honor of our nation will be maintained in this scientific contest with other civilized nations."

In another omen, President Garfield would soon be assassinated.

Greely and his crew of twenty-four embarked for the Arctic in the summer of 1881. The men were well provisioned. They lugged thousands of pounds of coal, pork, cod, salmon, canned vegetables, beans, rice, potatoes, syrup, and rum. As Greely made his way north, he studied the customs of the Arctic's indigenous people, realizing he had much to learn. "Greely observed that the Inuit houses were built of stone and turf, lined with wood, so low that he could hardly stand up inside. He was impressed by their ingenuity in using stretched seal intestines for windows," writes Buddy Levy in *Labyrinth of Ice*.

Adolphus Greely. The explorer was known for his penetrating eyes (which were often behind glasses) and his dark beard, which hid a scar from a Civil War gunshot.

This would become a recurring theme for savvy explorers: you are more likely to succeed when you learn the customs and cultures of indigenous people.

Their ship reached Lady Franklin Bay on August 11, 1881. Greely was pleased with the progress. In a clever feat of engineering, the crew traveled with a roomy prefabricated shelter—more than 60 feet long—that they erected by the bay. They called it Fort Conger. Sturdy and warm, the fort had a potbellied stove, a kitchen, and bunks for each of the men. Greely even brought hundreds of his beloved books, which he could read at night in a rocking chair.

The men sprang to work. They broke out their instruments and collected hundreds of readings per day, freezing their hands to measure the region's wind speed, temperature, and ice depths. Greely recorded all of this in neat, orderly, nineteenth-century versions of spreadsheets. They collected flowers and plants and bird eggs. Greely made duplicate copies of everything, obsessed with cataloging and organizing the data. He ordered the doctor, for example, to create "six complete sets of botanical specimens so arranged that they could be securely stored and transported." When the doctor completed his homework, Greely deemed the work sloppy and had it redone from scratch. They would get the science right.

On October 14, 1881, the sun would set on this cozy scientific outpost and it wouldn't rise for another three months. The Long Night of the Arctic had arrived. So Greely kept the men busy. Under moonlight and the dazzling northern lights, which Greely found to be "the most exquisite tints of violet running into the deepest blue," they continued collecting scientific measurements, they did calisthenics in the bracing cold, and they amused themselves with snowshoe races.

He created what was essentially a Greely Academy (although he didn't call it that), giving classes on subjects like grammar, mathematics, and the nature of magnetism. The doctor taught a French class. The men played chess and read novels; they even cranked out a newspaper that presaged *The Onion,* called the *Arctic Moon,* that contained satirical essays and misadventures of the "anti-swearing club."

On Thanksgiving, Greely was thankful for "success in scientific and geographic work," and they feasted on oyster soup and lobster salad. The chef outdid himself on Christmas, serving an eight-course meal that included "spiced musk-ox tongue," coconut pie, and plum pudding.

When the sun finally rose again, Greely focused on what he called the "mystic north." He knew he lacked the resources to reach the Pole, but he dispatched his most trusted crew, including an Inuk, for a daring push to reach the "Farthest North," an honor that the British had claimed for centuries.

(Whether there had been Inuit who had gone even farther north, of course, is an open question.)

Greely's crew chased the dragon. For weeks, using teams of dog sledges, they roamed the mystic north and mapped new terrain. When the team reached a latitude of 83 degrees, the senior-most enlisted man, Sergeant David L. Brainard, proudly unfurled an American flag knitted by Greely's wife, Henrietta, and later gushed, "We have reached a higher latitude than ever before reached by mortal man, and on a land farther north than was supposed by many to exist."

Year 1 of the Greely Expedition, by any standard, was a rousing success. They collected a staggering haul of scientific data, they remained in good spirits, they were all in fine health, and they even reached the hallowed Farthest North. Greely had done it. "I am of course delighted beyond measure," he wrote to Henrietta.

Now the rest of the mission should be a cakewalk. Soon their resupply ship would deliver more food, and after another round or two of snowshoe races, gluttonous Thanksgivings, and cheeky issues of the *Arctic Moon,* they'd return home as triumphant heroes.

What could go wrong?

"VESSEL RETURNED SAFELY"

Any expedition is only as good as its backup plans, logistics, and overall team. "When you look at the 'Famous Firsts,' I now see them all as team sports," says Ted Janulis, a former Club president. "You don't get to the moon on your own." Greely couldn't get to the Farthest North alone, and to complete his mission and return home, he was critically dependent on the larger team of the US Army.

And that team botched the job. This had been the plan: one year into Greely's three-year mission, a ship would steam to Fort Conger and deliver another cache of food. But the resupply failed. Thanks in part to bureaucratic dithering, the ship was delayed and the weather was colder than expected, freezing the shipping lanes. No food would reach Fort Conger.

However, the men did have one key ally who could prove their savior: Greely. No, not Adolphus Greely, but his wife, Henrietta. Well-read and independent, she thoroughly studied charts and maps and the history of Arctic exploration. "It turned out that she knew as much about the high northern regions as—and in many cases more than—the politicians in Washington who had sent her husband there in the first place," notes Levy.

The mission officially began as "The Lady Franklin Bay Expedition," but it would later become known by a new name: The Greely Expedition.

The irony is that Henrietta, who showed more foresight than her husband, had strongly urged Adolphus to bow out of the expedition. She had a clearer sense of the risks. "I would rather be your wife as you are, than your widow as the most revered man that you could become," she explained before he left, hoping to check his ambition. Citing a fact that seems iffy at best, Adolphus assured her that the "mortality [rate] among Arctic explorers for the past twenty years has really been less than [that for the] men remaining at home." Ultimately, Henrietta gave her blessing, as "I love you too well to mar your life, to interfere with your life dreams." Not only would Henrietta not "interfere," she also gave birth to twins just before Adolphus left on the expedition: a boy and a girl; only the girl survived. Henrietta would raise the girl on her own.

So Henrietta had every right to think *I told you so* when she received this gutting telegram from the US Army after the bungled resupply: "Failed to reach Lady Franklin Bay. Vessel returned safely." That was it. That's all they told her.

Henrietta could have chosen to wait by the telegram, but she went the other route. She prodded the US government to make a second, more urgent resupply attempt. Henrietta struck up friendships with military generals, she lobbied politicians, and she coaxed the editors of newspapers—from the *Chicago Tribune* to the *Atlanta Constitution*—to write front-page stories about Greely's abandonment in the Arctic. The world began to listen.

Fast-forward to the summer of 1883, in Year 2 of the Greely Expedition. This was the next possible window for sending a ship to Fort Conger. (The narrow shipping lanes are frozen for much of the year.) Henrietta was now in regular correspondence with the commander of the resupply ship, Lieutenant Ernest Garlington, who assured her that "every effort possible will be made to reach Fort Conger."

The ship headed toward Fort Conger . . . and hit an iceberg and sank to the bottom of the sea.

Greely was doomed.

ICE PRISON

Fort Conger. Year 2. Every day the men took turns climbing to the top of a lookout point, cast their eyes south, and hoped to see their resupply ship. "If no vessel comes, I consider our chances desperate," Greely wrote in his journal.

No vessel came.

So Greely stuck to his orders and led the men south, toward home, in a daring attempt to reach food and shelter. While the resupply ship had failed to reach Fort Conger, perhaps, at the very least, it had dropped a cache of supplies along the way? (That was the backup plan.) Greely left Fort Conger in a humble flotilla of three small boats, carrying all the food they could.

But navigating a ship through the sea of fog, sleet, and floating icebergs was perilous. Soon it became impossible. It didn't help that the ship's engineer, Cross, was a drunk who stole alcohol from the boat's fuel supply. When Cross was boozy and insubordinate, Greely grabbed his gun and said, "Shut up, or I'll put a bullet through you!"

Now Greely made the agonizing call: they would travel on foot. Using ropes and sledges, they hauled 5,000 pounds of food, gear, and scientific records across the ice. They lugged so much gear they couldn't carry it all at once. They muscled half the gear forward, turned around to backtrack, and then returned for the second half.

Most of the gear was essential, like food and fuel. Then there were the scientific records—three tin boxes of journals—and something called the Peirce pendulum, which weighed 100 pounds, that was used to measure the precise shape of the earth. By now, as Levy notes, it had become a symbol of their scientific mission. Maybe they should ditch it? Greely, aware that his men were hungry and tired and pushed to their limits, put the question up to a vote. "Not one [man] would hear of abandoning the pendulum," Greely proudly wrote. The science would endure, even if it killed them.

The weary team, now more than two years into their northern hell, finally made it south to Cape Sabine—their best and final hope for food. It was here that Lieutenant Garlington and the army, if they failed to reach Fort Conger, would have delivered the lifesaving cache of supplies.

And sure enough, in a pinprick of hope, the team found a cairn from the US Army. Garlington had written Greely a letter, explaining how his ship had been "nipped" by an iceberg. (Garlington managed to abandon ship before it sank.) Greely eagerly read the letter, anticipating directions to nearby stockpiles of food. And he soon learned that, yes, just as he hoped, there was indeed a stash of nearby food. As one crew member wrote in his journal, "Glorious news!"

But Greely knew better. He did the math. The bulk of the rations had sunk to the bottom of the sea; they had only forty days of food. Even if they cut down to miserable quarter rations—just barely enough to keep them alive—Greely figured they could stretch this to April, tops. It was now October. The winter sun was about to set for three endless months, plunging the men into a ravenous darkness. In his journal, Greely confessed that this would mean "a winter of starvation, suffering, and probably death for some."

1882
A. Conger
Grinnell Land

Special Tidal Observations.

Tide	Time	Tide	Time	Tide	Time	Tide	Time	
Inches		Inches		Inches		Inches		Remarks.
130		103		76	1.41 am	49	3.36 "	
129		102		75	1.45 "	48	3.40 "	
128		101		74	1.49 "	47	3.47 "	
127		100		73	1.53 "	46	3.53 "	
126		99		72	1.57 "	45	4.1 am	
125		98		71	2.01 "	44	4.06 "	
124		97		70	2.05 "	43	4.12 "	
123		96	4th	69	2.09 "	42	4.18 "	
122		95	11.51 pm 5th	68	2.13 "	41	4.30 "	
121		94	12.04 am	67	2.16 "	40	4.43 "	
120		93	12.14 "	66	2.20 "	39	5.03 "	
119		92	12.24 "	65	2.23 "	38	5.24 "	Low Tide
118		91	12.30 "	64	2.27 "	37		
117		90	12.35 "	63	2.31 "	36		
116		89	12.41 "	62	2.35 "	35		
115		88	12.46 "	61	2.38 "	34		
114		87	12.51 "	60	2.42 "	33		
113		86	12.56 "	59	2.47 "	32		
112		85	1.3 am	58	2.52 "	31		
111		84	1.8 "	57	2.56 "	30		
110		83	1.13 "	56	3. am	29		
109		82	1.17 "	55	3.04 "	28		
108		81	1.21 "	54	3.08 "	27		
107		80	1.25 "	53	3.13 "	26		
106		79	1.29 "	52	3.20 "	25		
105		78	1.33 "	51	3.26 "	24		
104		77	1.37 "	50	3.31 "	23		

Meticulously recorded measurements of the tides. Under Greely's detail-obsessed leadership, the crew took thousands of measurements like this—of ice depths, temperatures, barometric pressure.

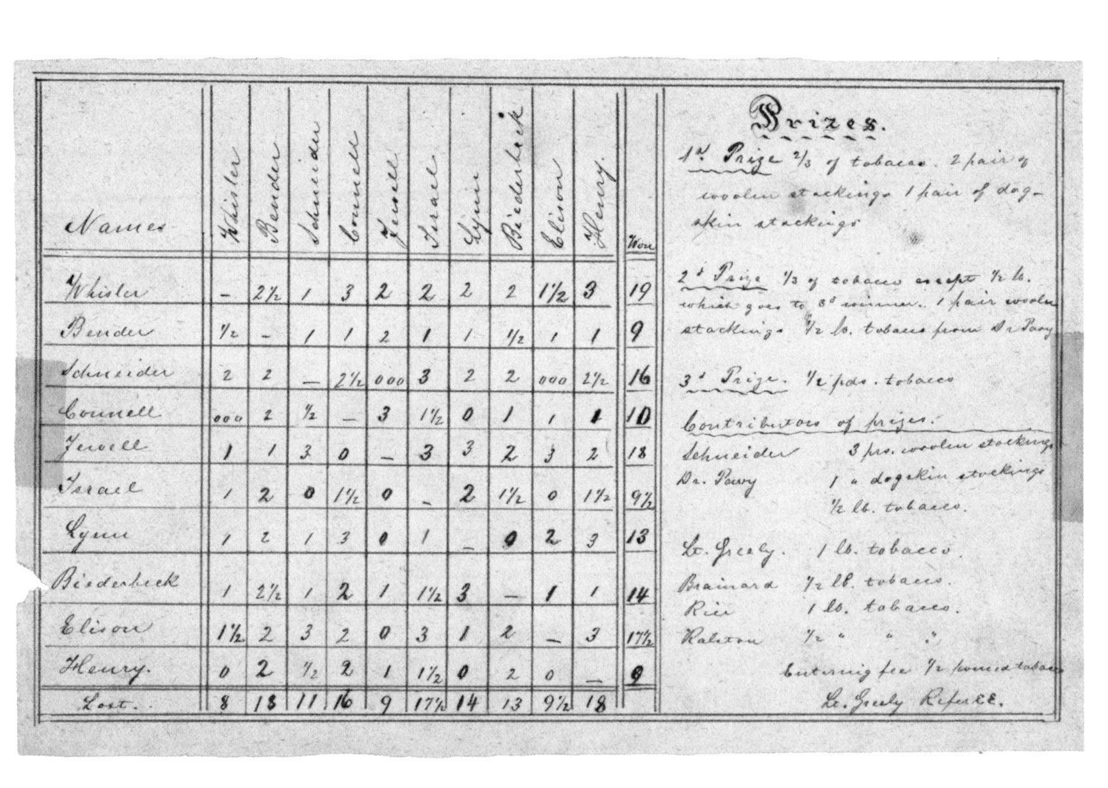

Names	Whisler	Bender	Schneider	Connell	Jewell	Israel	Lynn	Biederbeck	Elison	Henry	Won
Whisler	–	2½	1	3	2	2	2	2	1½	3	19
Bender	½	–	1	1	2	1	1	½	1	1	9
Schneider	2	2	–	2½	000	3	2	2	000	2½	16
Connell	000	2	½	–	3	1½	0	1	1	1	10
Jewell	1	1	3	0	–	3	3	2	3	2	18
Israel	1	2	0	1½	0	–	2	1½	0	1½	9½
Lynn	1	2	1	3	0	1	–	0	2	3	13
Biederbeck	1	2½	1	2	1	1½	3	–	1	1	14
Elison	1½	2	3	2	0	3	1	2	–	3	17½
Henry.	0	2	½	2	1	1½	0	2	0	–	9
Lost.	8	18	11	16	9	17½	14	13	9½	18	

Prizes.

1st Prize ⅔ of tobacco. 2 pair of woolen stockings 1 pair of dog-skin stockings

2d Prize ⅓ of tobacco except ½ lb. which goes to 3d winner. 1 pair woolen stockings. ½ lb. tobacco from Dr Pavy

3d Prize. ½ pds. tobacco

Contributors of prizes.

Schneider 3 prs. woolen stockings

Dr. Pavy 1 " dogskin stockings

½ lb. tobacco.

Lt. Greely. 1 lb. tobacco.

Brainard ½ lb. tobacco.

Rice 1 lb. tobacco.

Ralston ½ " " "

Entering fee ½ pound tobacco

Lt. Greely Referee.

Greely incentivized the men with games and prizes to boost morale. This is a scorecard that kept track of the winnings. (The prizes, of course, were heavy on tobacco.)

The men discovered something else in the meager cache of supplies: newspapers from home. And the papers contained a story about the Greely Expedition itself, meaning that the men could read about their very plight. "They cannot return to Fort Conger, and there will be no shelter for them at Cape Sabine," the *Louisville Courier-Journal* explained, almost like a Greek chorus. "They will then lie down on the cold ground, under the quiet stars, to die."

But the men would not go quietly. Using what he had learned from the Inuit, Greely ordered them to build a shelter out of ice blocks, stones, and wood that they stripped from their boats. Their new home was only 18 feet wide and 25 feet long—it made Fort Conger look like a palace—and only 4 feet tall. For months they would be unable to stand.

Before the Long Night set in, Greely had the foresight to carefully package all of his scientific records, photo negatives, and personal journals in waterproof cases. He stashed them at the summit of a small nearby mountain, with the gleaming pendulum on top. The science, as always, was paramount. "I am determined that our work shall not perish with us," Greely wrote in his journal. He left a letter by the pendulum that stated, "my party is now permanently encamped on the west side of a small neck of land. . . . All well."

All was not well. The wind howled, the temperatures reached –13 degrees, and their sleeping bags froze to the ground. The men had little to do but sit and wait. "We are so huddled and crowded together that the confinement is almost unbearable," Greely wrote in his journal. He dearly missed Henrietta, writing her letters that she would likely never read, promising that when he returned he would never leave her again, as "one such separation is enough for a lifetime."

They used tin cans to build a makeshift stove, and this let them cook their dwindling supply of beef and bacon. They hadn't bathed in months. Sharing just one mirror, they could watch as their beards grew and their bodies shrank. "I only wonder that we are not insane," Greely wrote. "I wonder if we will survive the horrors of this ice prison." With food running low, they began to eat dog biscuits. To break up the culinary monotony, every Sunday they looked forward to a pudding called a "son of a gun"—a mixture of raisins, canned milk, and seal blubber. That was the bright spot.

Their misery is hard to fathom. For perspective, consider just this one simple task that worked the same in 1884 as today: "If you want to go take a poop, you just dig a hole in the ice," says the Club's forty-fifth president, Richard Garriott, who has been to the North Pole. Even with modern Arctic gear, says Garriott, "It hurts. Your skin begins to frostbite almost immediately. And for the people doing it a hundred years ago, it would be even more miserable."

Frostbite was always a threat. On a desperate scouting mission to locate food, one member of the crew, Corporal Elison, contracted frostbite on his hands and feet. The frostbite was so agonizing that his teammates, themselves shivering, placed his frozen hands between their own naked thighs. The attempt was noble but futile. “Kill me,” begged Elison. “Please kill me.”

Elison was not killed. Instead, the men rallied to his cause, even voting to reduce their own paltry rations so Elison could eat more while he recuperated. Elison lost the use of his hands, so they fed him with a spoon. Elison couldn’t stand, so they helped him urinate in a tin can. “Never did rough-bearded men express more sympathy or tenderness for a crippled comrade,” wrote one starving man in his journal. Elison’s feet were so numb that one day, without any warning, they simply fell off his ankles. He didn’t notice for weeks.

In the midst of this darkness and misery and squalor, Greely did something extraordinary: he reopened Greely Academy. If the men were starving, he would nourish them with knowledge. Illuminated by the dim light of a blubber lamp, Greely gave daily lectures on geography, the “grain and fruit products of the United States,” and his own memories of the Civil War. He helped them keep their sanity. Even more extraordinary? They continued recording scientific measurements. Temperatures, wind speeds, ice depths—Greely insisted that the science would go on. The men had a purpose and they clung to life.

They survived days, weeks, and then months of this cooped-up agony. “To celebrate Christmas, a number of men saved up tiny bits of their rations in order to make a feast,” writes A. L. Todd in *Abandoned*. Together, huddling for warmth, they sang “O Tannenbaum” and “Silent Night.”

The Christmas spirit could only hold for so long, and food began to mysteriously disappear. Greely realized the crew had a thief, or maybe two thieves. He had long considered the doctor, Octave Pavy, a “mischief-maker,” and his instincts would be confirmed when the doctor began nicking Elison’s extra rations. But the real thief was Private Henry, who was caught stealing bacon, then caught a second time, then a third time. Further proof: Greely and twenty-three other men became so emaciated they were nearly skeletal, but Henry remained strong. Greely gave Henry a final warning: if he stole again, he would be shot.

On February 17, the sun finally returned but it would not bring them food. “We have used the last of our seal-meat in a fine stew,” Greely wrote with typical optimism. But soon they would eat the last of their dog biscuits. The men tried scraping black lichen from rocks. They ate moss. They fished for shrimp in the icy waters, but what little they could find lacked protein. They grew even weaker. The handwriting in Greely's journals becomes nearly illegible, as he forced himself to jot down the final memories of the doomed expedition. "To die is easy, very easy," he wrote with a feeble hand. "It is only hard to strive, to endure, to live."

Greely, somehow, had kept his crew alive for months longer than anyone had thought possible. But reality was cold and cruel. The first death was Cross, the drunken engineer. The men stepped outside their shelter and Greely read the rites and gave a funeral service. Then another death. Then another. Each time someone died, Greely recalled their strengths and praised their service, reminding them of happier and warmer times.

Now the men longed for the days of dog food. "I only eat my own boots and part of an old pair of pants," wrote one. "I feel myself going fast, but I wished that it would go yet faster." Another died. Then another. When Private Henry again stole food, Greely ordered him executed. (Every man agreed with the call.) And in one version of the story passed down through the ages, according to Will Roseman, the Club's executive director, Henry was so cold and miserable that he *wanted* to be shot, and when the rifle misfired because it was freezing, Henry blew on the gun to thaw it.

They shared sleeping bags for warmth. And toward the end, the men became so desensitized to it all that if their sleeping bag partner died in the night, they would remain in the bag until morning, lying next to a corpse.

Eighteen of the twenty-five men died.

The men lacked water. So Greely took on this duty himself, melting ice against the naked skin of his stomach, and then dripping it into their mouths. And when they had nothing else to eat, Greely ripped the seal skin from his sleeping bag and fed it to his crew.

After they had eaten the leather of their boots, their feet were exposed and felt like blocks of ice. They considered using a piece of fabric that would give them warmth: the American flag that Greely had brought on the expedition, the flag sewn by Henrietta. This is the flag that made it Farthest North. If they cut up that flag into strips, they could use it to warm their feet. Greely and his men considered the idea. Then they decided that rather than cut the flag, they would prefer to freeze to death. (Henrietta's flag now hangs in The Explorers Club.)

Somehow, even at the end, they kept their gallows humor. Eight days after they ran out of food, Greely wrote Henrietta that he was "perfectly well but weak," joking that when he gets home, he "shall take [a] long sick leave."

But there was nothing else he could do. "I think I am near my end," Greely confided on May 3. By now his entire sleeping bag was gone; they had eaten all of it. Greely knew that he had cheated death in the Civil War, and he had cheated death in these three freezing years. Now his bill was due. He was too weak to even read his prayer book. Commander Adolphus Greely set aside his journal, he closed his eyes, and he lay down to die.

THE *BEAR*

There was one person who still carried the torch of hope. For the past year, Henrietta had not given up on her husband. She continued to send telegrams to army generals, asking pointed questions. "Can not a steamer if started immediately with stores reach Upernavik or Godhavn and winter [there], sending sledging parties north?" she asked one. "If on reaching Melville Bay no chance of helping party appears, cannot vessel return to Disko?" she asked another. In a letter to politicians in DC, Henrietta wrote, "I feel that the government has not kept faith with the party."

Henrietta was not messing around. "Her pen was busy daily as she urged every person among her large, scattered family and her many women friends, some [from] her schooldays, to help [save] the life of her dear one," writes A. L. Todd. Henrietta and her friends—a growing network of friends—continued to urge newspaper editors to give the story more coverage.

And they did. The Greely Expedition, thanks in part to the efforts of Henrietta, became the biggest story in the nation. STILL HOPE FOR GREELY, blared one; GREELY MAY ESCAPE, announced another; and one fact-challenged paper led with GREELY'S MURDER REPORTED—SAID TO HAVE BEEN SLAIN BY MURDEROUS CREW.

Now the public demanded answers. *Where was Greely? Why had he been abandoned? Bring him home!* It's tough to imagine a modern-day equivalent; the closest analogy might be how in *The Martian*, the entire world rooted for the return of Matt Damon's astronaut.

Henrietta kept writing letters. They were so forceful that they eventually reached the desk of President Chester A. Arthur. Finally the government took action. Secretary of War Robert Todd Lincoln (son of Abe), who hadn't wanted to "hazard more lives" in a vain attempt to save a man who was already dead, now scrambled to solve the problem. (Lincoln himself was part of the problem; he had always considered the trip a waste of resources and his delay is one reason the first resupply failed.)

Lincoln promised Henrietta and the world, essentially, that *this time* it would be different! This time the US Navy would lead the charge. This time a rescue ship would leave earlier in the season, as soon as the ice thawed. This

The members of The Greely Expedition in happier, warmer, less frost-bitten times.

time they would bring the *Bear,* a retrofitted steamer ship that had a custom-made battering ram for smashing through icebergs.

Henrietta's response?

Not good enough.

She would take no chances. To boost the odds of someone finding her husband, she whipped up the idea of a global "Bounty Plan," suggesting a $25,000 reward (roughly $757,000 today) to any private whaler who found Greely. The bill went before Congress. And given the fierce public opinion now rallying behind Greely (both Adolphus and Henrietta), Congress had no choice but to pass it.

The Bounty Plan did two things: it summoned a small armada of private whalers to join the hunt for Greely, but just as important, it spurred the navy to redouble its efforts, lest they'd be embarrassed by a whaler beating them to the punch.

On April 24, at the Brooklyn Navy Yard, the *Bear* prepared to begin its search for Greely. "Its imminent departure was national news," notes Levy, and hundreds of visitors boarded the ship to inspect it, many of them leaving bouquets of flowers. Thousands of New Yorkers gathered to see the *Bear* depart, cheering and waving their flags.

The *Bear* headed north.

This time the crew made better progress. The *Bear* used its battering ram to crush through the kind of icebergs that felled the prior mission. The *Bear* and a second ship, *Thetis,* steamed toward Greenland. The men were burdened with the knowledge that at this point, realistically, they were on a mission to recover corpses. But even that would be a kind of victory—Henrietta deserved to learn how her husband had died. The nation deserved and demanded closure.

Most of the landscape looked the same—ice and rocks and more ice. As the ships traveled north, not far from Cape Sabine, a sharp-eyed ensign noticed something glimmering in the distance, something shiny that pointed to the sky. Greely's pendulum. The symbol of scientific discovery. Greely had always put his faith in science, and now, at the very end, science pointed the *Bear* toward his camp.

The rescue crew sprinted ashore, hustling to find the sad remains of Greely's team. The bodies, the journals, the flag, the chronicles of despair. Instead, a lieutenant from the *Bear* discovered something impossible. Something even miraculous. As the lieutenant later remembered, he saw "a dark man with a long, matted beard, in a dirty and tattered dressing gown . . . and brilliant, staring eyes."

The man looked like a walking skeleton. But he was alive. And in a whisper, the man confirmed his identity. Adolphus Greely.

"Seven of us left," Greely said softly. "Here we are, dying like men. Did what I came to do—beat the best record."

By some accounts, Greely would have perished if the ships had arrived even hours later. His life was saved by Henrietta. Without her tenacious pressure, it's unlikely the ships would have made it in time. The survivors were given blankets and water and food. Some were carried out on stretchers, a scene memorialized in the bleak, gray, icy painting on the second floor of The Explorers Club. Now the painting has a different meaning. If you don't know the story, it's a portrait of despair, but the broader context reveals a scene of hope, grit, and improbable rescue.

The *Bear* wisely brought along two doctors, and they supervised a feeding regimen of beef extract and condensed milk. Aboard the *Bear* and *Thetis,* the men took baths and changed into warm flannel clothes. They ate oatmeal and were nursed back to health. Although . . . not all of the men. One of the seven who survived was Elison, now just 78 pounds, who had lost his hands and feet to frostbite. Now he had gangrene. The doctors decided he needed an emergency amputation of his legs; the operation killed him.

The *Bear* and *Thetis* headed south, toward home, and toward Henrietta. The *Bear* soon telegrammed the White House, and the story of Greely's resurrection electrified the nation. FROM THE JAWS OF DEATH reported the *Chicago Tribune.*

The ships made their way to a harbor near the border of Maine and New Hampshire. This is normally a quiet port. But on August 1, 1884, the harbor filled with a dozen navy warships, an entire fleet of civilian sailboats, and thousands of well-wishers who cheered the return of Commander Greely. Politicians lined the boats. A navy band played "Home Again."

Greely scanned the massive crowd. There was only one person he wanted to see . . . and then he spotted her. Escorted up the ramp by the secretary of the navy, she was the first to board the ship and then, finally, after a separation of more than three years, Henrietta and Adolphus embraced.

He would never leave her again.

MR. PRESIDENT

So how should history remember Greely? Some see him as a failure—a cautionary tale—who led nineteen men to their death. Many of Greely's decisions have been questioned, such as leaving the warmth (and food) of Fort Conger, or not searching for an Inuit settlement, or not involving more Inuit from the get-go. Or perhaps Greely was an inspiring leader who somehow, in the coldest circle of hell, after being forsaken by the world, saved the lives of five men. Was the Greely Expedition a success or a failure? "Was Greely a genius or an idiot?" asks Richard Garriott, who answers his own question: "Both."

Greely gave the world more than he knew, and certainly more than the history books acknowledge. For the rest of his life, Greely was proudest of reaching Farthest North—filling out the map and chasing the dragon.

But Greely was mistaken. For that's not his true legacy.

Think back to all of those thousands of scientific measurements, the ones that he meticulously categorized and waterproofed in sealed cases. Greely risked his life (and the lives of his crew) to bring these measurements home. Those records—hundreds of pages—were eventually read before Congress.

Then the records traveled farther. They traveled across the globe and they traveled through time. The measurements that Greely collected eventually fed into the larger apparatus of the first International Polar Year. They joined the data collected by scientists in ten other countries.

More data would follow. The International Polar Year of 1882 was the first chapter of a century-long project, a chain of scientific missions that includes Polar Years in 1932, 1957, and 2007. That work continues to this day. The very phrase "climate change," at heart, requires scientists to know the older temperatures of the earth. Greely helped give us that baseline. He was one of the world's first climate change scientists. Greely's expedition, while doomed, helped launch the scientific field that could be our planet's salvation.

And that's the story of Adolphus Greely, the man who would later, in 1904, become the first president of The Explorers Club.

Greely the Cannibal?

When the crew from the *Bear* recovered the eighteen dead bodies from the Greely expedition, one ensign noticed something chilling. In his report, he wrote that a few of the corpses "had been cut, and the flesh removed." And this ensign was no fool. "I refrain from details," he added, "thinking it best not to be put into writing."

Rumors of cannibalism would haunt Greely for the rest of his life, with some calling him "Eat 'Em Alive" Greely. "One of the cannibals probably was the doctor, for some of the partly eaten bodies had been carved with the skill of a surgeon," theorized former Explorers Club president Vilhjalmur Stefansson in 1961.

The evidence against cannibalism: Perhaps the carved flesh was used not as food, but as bait for their shrimp fishing. It's also possible, perhaps even probable, that *some* of the crew did indeed succumb to cannibalism, but not Greely or the survivors. In the final agonizing days at Cape Sabine, after all, Greely was so woozy that he lacked the strength to read his prayer book. It would have been easy for someone to snack on human flesh without being noticed. "If there has been cannibalism," Greely later said, "and there now seems no doubt about it, the man-eating was done in secrecy and entirely without my knowledge."

History will never know.

The Greely camp in its final, ragged, on-the-cusp-of-death incarnation.

Matthew Henson (center) and the Inuit team of Ootah, Egingwah, Seegloo, and Ooqueah.

FIRST TO THE NORTH POLE . . . MAYBE?

We begin in a place we have seen before.

1883. Year 2 of the Greely Expedition. When the resupply ship failed to reach Fort Conger, Greely ordered his men to pack up and leave. He was in a hurry. He sealed the scientific records, he folded the flag that Henrietta had sewn, and he supervised the loading of their escape boats. In a move that was frankly un-Greely-like, they left Fort Conger in such a rush that their beds were unmade, the dishes were unwashed, and biscuits were scattered on the kitchen floor. Then they nailed the door closed and headed south.

Fort Conger would remain empty for many years, a shuttered museum of Arctic anguish. Then, in 1899, nearly two decades after it was built, a man cracked open the front door. He lit an oil lamp and peered inside, eager to find warmth and food.

The man's name was Matthew Henson. He took off his mittens and looked around, surprised to see the spilled food, the cluttered dishes, the mess of boxes in the hallways. Perhaps he felt the ghastly shadow of Greely's crew.

Henson wasn't alone. He arrived with Robert Peary, by far the more famous of the two, along with a surgeon and four Inuit—Uutaaq, Iggiannguaq, Ukkujaak, and Sigluk. Henson and Peary were on a quest to reach the North Pole; they would use Fort Conger as a base for their next attempt.

As the men cleaned up Greely's mess, Henson spoke with the Inuit to translate. They settled into their comfy new beds, they lit Greely's old stove, and they could relax with the books and novels that had been left behind.

But their stay at Fort Conger would not be pleasant. Peary contracted frostbite on his feet; he lost most of his toes, and now he painfully hobbled on stumps. This meant that for the rest of his life, Robert Peary, nominally the leader of the expedition, would be forced to sit on a dogsled while others pulled him. He would literally lead from behind.

Henson's story was different. For starters, Henson didn't look like most of the "famous" explorers of the age. He didn't wear fancy suits in New York social clubs, he didn't give interviews to an adoring press, and he didn't hobnob with US presidents.

Henson couldn't do any of this because he was Black. His mother died when he was seven; his father died when he was ten. He would explore by necessity. In his early teenage years, as Henson puts it matter-of-factly in his memoir, "I shipped as cabin-boy, on board a vessel bound for China." He trained himself to become a seaman who traveled to Japan, Spain, North Africa, and the Black Sea. He later returned to DC and worked as a stock boy, where he met a man who said, "I need a boy to go with me to Central America, as a valet. Keep my clothes and quarters clean. Must be honest with regular work habits." Peary recruited Henson to be his "body-servant" on an expedition to Nicaragua. The two were inseparable for the next twenty years. As Peary later said of Henson, "I can't get along without him."

Now they were cooped up together at Fort Conger for eighteen months. Much of what happened there is a mystery, but we know two things for certain, both of which are seminal to understanding the race for the North Pole, which Peary considered the "prize of the centuries."

The first thing we know: Henson and Peary made big changes to Fort Conger. Back in 1881, Greely had brought a roomy prefabricated fort that could sleep twenty-five men. At the time the idea seemed inspired, but Henson and Peary, who had spent more time with the Inuit, realized the idea was flawed. The Inuit showed them a better way.

So Peary and Henson worked to rebuild the fort from scratch. They tore down the walls. They dismantled the wood. They built three smaller, subterranean structures that were connected by tunnels, and then they used a mix of earth, snow, and Greely's abandoned supplies for insulation. This reimagined design "recalls Inuit techniques of both siting and grouping dwellings close to one another and to the shore," concludes a research paper from the Arctic Institute of North America. "Semi-subterranean, small, and interconnected dwellings could be adequately heated with a minimal expenditure of precious fuel."

Peary might have been in charge, but the overhaul of Fort Conger was classic Matthew Henson. He would later embed himself with Inuit and learn their customs—they called him Mahri-Pahluk, "Matthew the Kind One."

Robert Peary and Matthew Henson, who collaborated
on seven Arctic missions over twenty-three years.

"For periods covering more than twelve months," Henson wrote, "I have been to all intents an [Inuit], with [Inuit] for companions, speaking their language, dressing in the same kind of clothes, living in the same kind of dens, eating the same food, enjoying their pleasures, and frequently sharing their griefs. I have come to love these people." It was Henson's genius to learn from the Inuit, says Lacey Flint, The Explorers Club's longtime archivist, explaining that "Henson said, 'Wait a second, we're not wearing and using what the Inuit are wearing and using. We should be.' "

Henson had a certain self-awareness. He sensed that interactions with the Inuit might harm the latter's culture, a complicated dynamic that haunts the legacy of exploration to this day. Henson observed, for example, that before their encounters with Arctic explorers, the Inuit had never used tobacco. "Today every member of the tribe has had experience with tobacco, craves it, and will give most everything, except his gun, to get it," writes Henson. "Even little toddlers, three and four years old, will eat tobacco." (Henson then adds, somewhat curiously, "Strange to say, it has no bad effect.")

Peary's relationship with the Inuit? He seemed to view them as a means to an end, a cheap body of labor that could propel him to the Pole. For the Pole was his ticket to fame. After one failed attempt that nevertheless gained

Hanging from the ceiling at The Explorers Club is one of the wooden sledges used by Henson and Peary. Bound together with seal-skin rope, it was pulled by up to eight dogs and could haul 1,200 pounds. The design was adapted by Henson after he lived with the Inuit and learned their innovations and technology.

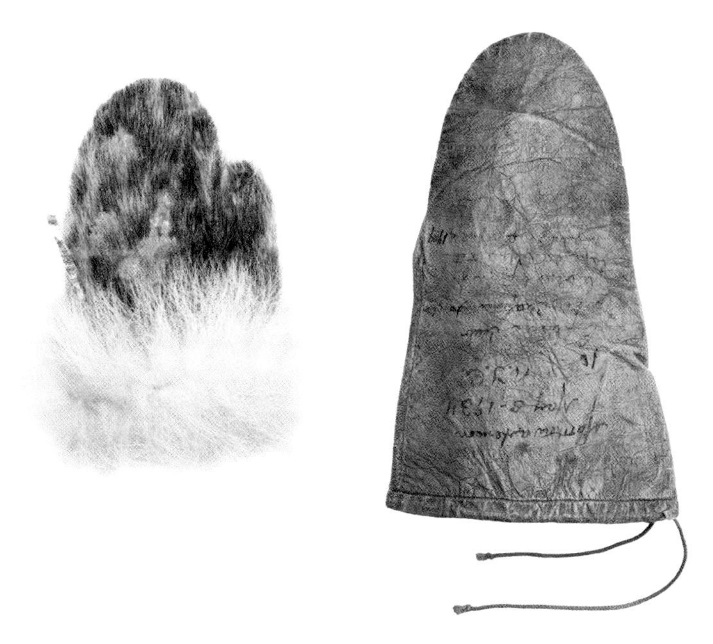

Henson's mittens, also at the Club. Made from seal skin and polar bear fur, they were created for him by Inuit women. The mittens were more elegant and intricate in design than usual, which speaks to his special and respected place in their community. In 1934, Henson signed the one on the right, "To the Explorers Club."

him press coverage, Peary wrote his mother to say, "My last trip brought my name before the world; my next will give me a standing in the world. . . . I will be foremost in the highest circles in the capital, and make powerful friends with whom I can shape my future instead of letting it come as it will. . . . Remember, mother, I *must* have fame."

The Inuit could help bring Peary that fame. He staffed his expeditions with local Inuit, for reasons both wise (they knew the land better than anyone) and cynical (they couldn't share the glory). Peary took and took. He fathered a child with a local Inuit woman* (Henson, recently divorced, did the same). He paid the Inuit little, he relocated them farther north to work as supply relays, and he dug up meteorites from Inuit land and essentially stole them as found treasure.

---

* Peary's defense of his Arctic extramarital affair? "It is asking too much of masculine human nature to expect it to remain in Arctic climate enduring constant hardship, without one relieving feature. Feminine companionship not only causes greater contentment, but as a matter of both mental and physical health and the retention of the top notch of manhood it is a necessity."

In Peary's most appalling stunt, he brought six Inuit back with him to the United States and delivered them to the American Museum of Natural History. As one Inuit remembered it, Peary had promised them "nice warm houses in the sunshine land, and guns and knives and needles and many other things." But the Inuit would not find nice warm houses. Instead, the museum kept the Inuit in its basement. A heat wave made them sick. Four of them died. The bodies were used as skeletons for display in the museum.

In 1899, in that winter refuge at Fort Conger, it's tough to know how much Henson knew of Peary's dealings with the Inuit. And it's tough to know how much credit (or blame) to give to each man for their joint work. But this brings us to the second thing we know for certain that happened in Greely's old fort: a fight between Henson and Peary.

Or if not a fight per se, then at least a tense exchange. It seems that Peary felt Henson was no longer being duly obsequious.

"I have a right to expect you will say 'Sir' to me always," Peary told Henson. "That you will pay attention when I am talking to you."

Lest there be any ambiguity, Peary spelled it out even more clearly: "Show that you hear the directions I give you by saying 'Yes, sir' or 'All right, sir.' "

This dialogue comes straight from the journal of Robert Peary. Henson omits the exchange from his own memoirs, so we are left only to wonder what he was thinking at this time. Perhaps, biting his tongue, he thought about how he had always been the one to do most of the work—the hunting, the training of the dogs, the constant repairs of broken sledges.

Or maybe Henson thought about how most of his contemporaries—his white contemporaries—thought it improbable or even absurd that a Black man could survive in the Arctic. The racism was not subtle. "When confronted in an offensive tone by a naval officer who suggested that no Negro could survive subzero cold, Henson expressed such confidence in his ability to do so that the officer promised to pay him one hundred dollars if he returned 'without any fingers or toes frozen off,' " writes Bruce Henderson in *True North*. Yet it was Peary, not Henson, who lost his toes. After returning from the Arctic, Henson happened to see the naval officer again. Henson held out his hands and said, "You see, my fingers are all here." The officer didn't remember the bet. When Henson jogged his memory, the officer demanded to see Henson's toes. "Henson sat down, removed his shoes and socks, and wiggled his ten toes," writes Henderson. The officer paid up.

And now in Fort Conger, even after all that Henson had contributed, Peary told him, "Call me Sir." We can only imagine that Henson said, "Yes, sir," loyal

A painting from Albert L. Operti, depicting Inuit with the meteorites that Peary eventually stole. Amazingly, Operti—an Arctic explorer himself (and an official artist for Peary)—painted this on Peary's work apron.

as always. And he would continue to be at Peary's side—or, more accurately, in the front, while Peary was pulled in a sledge—for expedition after expedition. Their dash for the Pole would fail that winter of 1899. Then it would fail again in 1905. And again in 1906. They made a total of eight attempts.

Each attempt cost money, and Peary needed capital. So he created an organization comprised exclusively of wealthy white men called the Peary Arctic Club as a means to raise funds. In the early days of both the Peary Arctic Club and The Explorers Club, Peary mingled with New York socialites in a quest to both gain clout and raise capital. By 1908, he had raised enough to build a ship, the *Roosevelt,* savvily named to flatter the president. And Teddy Roosevelt, an explorer at heart, did indeed climb aboard the *Roosevelt* to wish Peary and his crew of twenty-two men bon voyage, cheering them with shouts of "Bully! Bully!"

Aboard the *Roosevelt,* Henson served as a carpenter, a barber, a tailor, a dog trainer, and an interpreter. Meanwhile, Peary relaxed in a stateroom that included a private bathtub and a piano.

Josephine Peary and the Snow Baby

In an era when the conventional wisdom was that "women have no place in the Arctic," Josephine Peary refused to let that stop her. She joined her husband, Robert, on multiple expeditions. Incredibly, she gave birth to their "Snow Baby" only 13 degrees from the North Pole. Perhaps even more incredibly, she somehow kept her cool when meeting Robert's young Inuit mistress—and she even helped raise their son.

Josephine Peary had a gift for describing her adventures. "Hundreds and hundreds of miles away in the white frozen north, far beyond where the big ships go to hunt huge black whales, there is a wonderful land of snow and ice, mountains, glaciers, and icebergs," she wrote to begin her memoir *The Snow Baby*.

Years ago at Fort Conger, Greely's crew had to somehow amuse themselves during the dark months of the Arctic's Long Night. Now imagine doing this while raising a baby on your own. "Then the sun went away, and for days and weeks baby lived in the little room where a lamp was burning night and day," wrote Josephine. Her Inuit friends loved the baby. "They called her 'AH-POO-MIK-A-NIN-NY' (the Snow Baby), and brought her presents of fur mittens, little sealskin boots, walrus tusks, baby bear and seal skins, and many other things."

But Josephine wasn't always in mom mode. In the field she got her hands dirty. On one expedition, when their boat was surrounded and attacked by 250 walruses, she reloaded the rifles as they kept the "monsters" (her word) at bay. "I cannot describe my feelings when these monsters surrounded us, their great tusks almost touching the boat, and the bullets whistling about my ears in every direction," she later wrote. "I thought it about an even chance whether I would be shot or drowned."

Josephine Peary was not shot or drowned. And she outlived her husband by decades, passing away in 1955 at the age of ninety-two years young.

Once the ship arrived at the Arctic, Henson, as always, went ashore and traded with the Inuit for sledge dogs, food, and fuel. Henson says the real heroes of the Arctic exploration are the dogs who pulled the sledges, for without them, "the story of the North Pole would remain untold; for human ingenuity has not yet devised any other means to overcome the obstacles of cold, storm, and ice that nature has placed in the way." They took ninety-eight dogs on the final push to the Pole, feeding them double rations.

In March 1909, after months of trudging north in the icy darkness, as Henson described it, "the sun, a flaming disk of fiery crimson, shows his distorted image above the horizon."

As they closed in on the "prize of centuries," Peary had a decision to make: Who should accompany him on the final leg to the North Pole? He settled on the Inuit team of Ootah, Egingwah, Seegloo, and Ooqueah, in addition to the indispensable Matthew Henson. It is now generally believed that Peary chose this group because he did not want to share the glory with another white man.

On April 6, 1909, Matthew Henson, Robert Peary, and the Inuit team reached the North Pole—or at least what they thought was the North Pole. They unfurled an American flag. As Henson later remembered, "A thrill of patriotism ran through me and I raised my voice to cheer the starry emblem of my native land." Peary's reaction was a touch lighter on the patriotism: "The Pole at last. The prize of three centuries. My dream and goal for twenty years. Mine at last!"

Who was actually the *first* to physically step on the North Pole? This is one of history's great unsolved mysteries. Most textbooks say it was Peary. But as Henson told the *New York Times* in 1955, "I was in the lead that had overshot the mark a couple of miles. . . . We went back then, and I could see that my footprints were the first at the spot."

Henson led the way; Peary trailed behind in the dog sledge. Or maybe it was the Inuit who had first reached the Pole. Or it might have been Peary's former associate, Dr. Frederick Cook, who claimed to have conquered the Pole a year earlier. Complicating matters, a thorough examination of the evidence later suggested that Henson, Peary, and the Inuit all came a few miles short. One skeptic was Adolphus Greely, who by then was acknowledged as perhaps the world's foremost Arctic authority; he sifted through the records and concluded, "I do not believe that he reached the North Pole."

The Explorers Club now officially credits Henson, Peary, and the Inuit Ootah, Egingwah, Seegloo, and Ooqueah as "co-discoverers of the North Pole." But after years poring through the records and archives and evidence, Lacey Flint unofficially says, "Matthew Henson is the reason that the North Pole Expedition was successful."

This recognition did not happen overnight.

It took nearly a century.

Peary returned from the North Pole and became a celebrity. Henson returned from the North Pole to work as a parking lot attendant. Peary was taught in every textbook; Henson's name vanished. In 1909, Peary was elected president of The Explorers Club; Henson was not a member that year. Just a few of the countless examples of discrimination: The National Geographic Society gave its Hubbard Gold Medal to Robert Peary, and asked him who else in his party should receive the honor. Peary told them that Matthew Henson, his "colored assistant," should receive the medal. National Geographic responded, "No, we mean the other white man who came closest."

Peary was buried in a distinguished grave at Arlington National Cemetery, honored with a massive globe statue that heralded him as "Discoverer of the North Pole." Henson was buried in a random grave in the Bronx.

Over time, some of Henson's contemporaries demanded justice. In 1931, one of the men in the North Pole Expedition, who later became an admiral in the navy, asked Congress to award Henson a special medal. "Henson went to the Pole with Peary because he was a better man than any man in Peary's party," wrote Admiral Donald MacMillan to Congress. "In fact, he was of more value to Commander Peary on the Polar Sea than all white men combined."

Congress ignored the request.

Things improved a bit in 1937, when The Explorers Club awarded Henson a "Life Membership" and then upgraded this to Honorary Membership in 1948. (Henson aside, the Club remained all white.) The Club raised funds for Henson and helped him financially; Henson himself made donations to the Club, sending $5 here and there when he could.

In 1954, President Eisenhower welcomed Henson, then eighty-seven years old, to the White House. An Explorers Club member named Dr. S. Allen Counter, a Black neurobiologist, worked to further restore Henson's legacy. In 1986, Counter traveled to the Arctic and found the Inuit children of both Henson and Peary; now old men, they had never been to the United States or met any of their American family. Counter arranged for Anaukaq (son of Henson) and Kali (son of Peary) to travel to the United States and meet their relatives for the "North Pole Family Reunion." Counter also asked President Reagan to have Henson reinterred and buried at Arlington National Cemetery. Reagan agreed. The navy later named an oceanographic research ship in his honor: USNS *Henson* sailed to visit his grave at Arlington with twelve of his descendants. The world began to catch up.

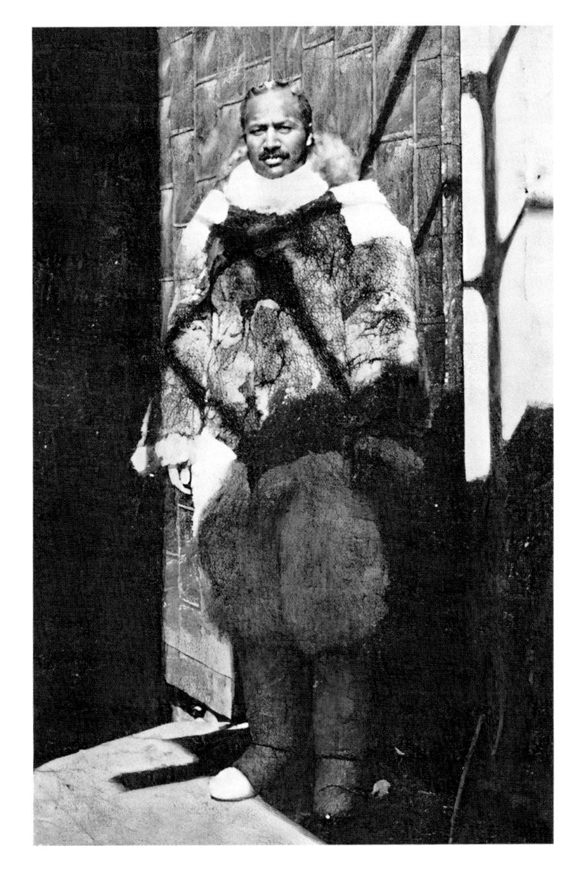

Henson in a fox fur coat made by Inuit women. Like the mittens on page 35, the coat was far more elaborate and even fancier than most Arctic garb of the time—another testament to the stature he held within the community.

The restoration of Matthew Henson's legacy is more than just an issue of righting a wrong, or "political correctness," or even getting the facts straight. Representation matters. "When I was growing up, I'd heard of Peary, but I had never heard of Matthew Henson," says J. Robert "J.R." Harris, the first Black member of The Explorers Club to sit on its board of directors. "They never mentioned a Black man. They just mentioned Peary. So you grow up thinking that explorers are white males."

But the narrative of "only white males can be explorers" is no longer true. It never was.

The Explorers Club Flag

It's a symbol. It's an honor. It's a link between the legends of our past and the promise of our future.

The Explorers Club flag is more than a century old. The red signifies courage; the blue conveys fidelity. The compass rose, dead center, symbolizes the worldwide circle of the Club's interests.

There are a total of 242 Explorers Club flags. Each one has its own unique history. Each one tells a story. Beginning in 1918, Club members have brought these flags to every corner of the earth—and beyond. The flag has been to the top of Everest, to the bottom of the ocean, and to the North and South Poles. Neil Armstrong and Buzz Aldrin brought a miniaturized Explorers Club flag to the moon.

There are currently 3,400 Explorers Club members, and roughly 8,000 in total since the Club's founding. Only a tiny percentage have carried the flag into the field. "It's an honor. Not everyone can take the flag," says Constance Difede, a longtime vice president and chair of the Club's Flag and Honors Committee. To apply for a coveted flag expedition, members need to demonstrate how their mission will be somehow beneficial to humankind. How will the expedition advance science? How will it improve our understanding of the world? What questions will it answer? Or as Difede puts it, "You don't want to be the ten thousandth person to climb Everest on the same route." But if you're conducting some groundbreaking medical experiment at high altitude, and Everest is a logical setting? Then it's a possibility.

Members know that when they bring a flag into the field, it's a solemn duty to return the flag in good standing. "We tell members that they can check all their luggage on a plane, but don't check that flag," says Difede, laughing. Sometimes flags are retired. This happens for one of two reasons: the flag is so tattered and frayed that it's no longer fit for the field, or the flag has been part of a mission that was so historic, it would be a crime to risk it on future missions.

Here's an example: In 1970, Club member Jim Lovell tried to bring a full-size Explorers Club flag to the moon. His plan was to plant the flag on the moon's surface, unfurl it, and snap a photo that would last for eternity. Unfortunately, a small glitch got in the way. Lovell, of course, was the commander of Apollo 13, and better known to many as "the astronaut played by Tom Hanks." Along with a handwritten letter to the Club, Lovell returned the flag and noted that his expedition's plans "were disrupted," but that "I thought you would enjoy having these two artifacts for The Explorers Club's flag collection."

The Apollo 13 flag is now displayed proudly in the Club.

Initial prototype of the Club flag.

The Lewis Cotlow Second Antarctic Expedition, 1963. Pictured with Cotlow (left) are RCMP Constable R.C. Currie (center) and Special Eskimo Constable Simon Akpaleeapik. They're holding Flag 116.

Members of the Scott expedition. Note the lack of fur—the kind of clothing worn by the Inuit and Matthew Henson.

Another work (this time a sketch) by Albert L. Operti. For most Arctic and Antarctic explorers, dog-sledding was the key to success.

DOGS OVER PONIES: FIRST TO THE SOUTH POLE

1904. The Explorers Club kicked off the weekly lectures that continue to this day; at the time they were called "smokers." As early member Horace Dade Ashton later remembered, even in its inception "it was far more than just a social club. Its goals were scientific in nature, and its members aimed to preserve the instinct to explore." The wooden walls of the Club began to fill with maps, flags, and mementos from far-flung places.

In 1905, the Peary Arctic Club merged with The Explorers Club. And by 1909, the Club had much to celebrate. After the discovery (or near discovery) of the North Pole, the map had now been filled in to the east, to the west, and to the north. The dragons had all been chased and pushed back.

With one exception.

There still remained one final mystery on the map: the South Pole.

And at this stage of exploration, the game was still very much about conquering, of being the first, of clinching personal and national glory. The man poised to reach this honor was Robert Falcon Scott, a captain in the British navy who hoped the mission would make him an admiral. Despite a mediocre record in the navy, Scott had political connections (thanks largely to his enterprising wife) and the imprimatur of the British government. And he felt certain that the South Pole was his and his alone, effectively warning other lurking rivals, like Ernest Shackleton, that he had "dibs."

Scott departed London in June 1910. Before he left, he spent two weeks with Robert Peary, who was still dripping with North Pole prestige. Peary had a one-word piece of advice for Scott: *dogs*. Peary knew that sledge dogs (and Matthew Henson's expertise) helped get him to the Pole. He urged Scott to bring dogs, good dogs, lots of dogs. As Peary remembered, "I talked dogs and dogs with him, but without results."

Scott's magnificent naval ship, the *Terra Nova,* departed from London with great fanfare, but one onlooker was unimpressed. "There were gold lace and cocked hats and dignitaries enough to run a Navy," observed Captain Robert Bartlett, an Explorers Club member who had been on Peary and Henson's team. He noted that "the basis of all Peary's work was application of [Inuit] methods. . . . In contrast to this, the British worked out their own theories." When Bartlett noticed all the fancy and elaborate British clothing, he realized that "none of it looked like the [Inuit] stuff that we were used to."

But none of this mattered to Scott. He had the full backing of the British Empire, he had no serious competition, he was steaming to his destiny, and by God he would get to the South Pole or die trying.

"A SCIENTIFIC STUDY"

At that very moment, another polar explorer was finalizing his plans to head in the opposite direction—up north, back to the Arctic, where he would embark on a multiyear scientific survey.

Enter Roald Amundsen, a Norwegian with twenty years of polar exploration chops. He claimed that all he cared about was the science. For example, in a 1908 speech at the Norwegian Geographical Society, Amundsen acknowledged that while he did have ambitions of reaching the North Pole, this was not his primary objective. "I want to make it absolutely clear that this—the assault on the Pole, will not be the aim of the expedition," Amundsen told his audience. "The main object is a scientific study of the Polar Sea itself."

This was a lie.

Soon after Amundsen gave that high-minded speech in 1908, he was startled to learn that the North Pole had been discovered *twice.* First (allegedly) by Dr. Frederick Cook, then by Peary and the uncredited Henson and Inuit.

For two years, he continued to prepare his expedition to the northern Arctic, training his crew and ordering supplies, raising capital, and giving interviews to the press.

But that was all an elaborate ruse. In one of the most audacious stunts in the history of exploration, once Amundsen realized he couldn't be the first to the North Pole, he secretly changed his plans and plotted a voyage to the south. When Amundsen's ship left the docks of Norway, not even his crew knew of the mischief. Amundsen only made his plans public after the ship was far enough at sea that it couldn't be recalled.

Scott was a charmer and looked dashing in his crisp uniform. Amundsen just wanted to wear what was most effective, looks be damned.

"If I were to maintain my reputation as an explorer," Amundsen later confessed, "I had to win a sensational victory one way or another. I decided on a coup." In those days, that's how one defined the success of exploration. He felt he had no choice, and in some ways he was right. "Aircraft and tractors were waiting in the wings. This was the last classic journey in the old style, and it was to end the era of terrestrial exploration that began with the explosion of the human spirit during the Renaissance," writes Roland Huntford in *The Last Place on Earth*.

Scott headed south.

Amundsen headed south.

The race was on.

A DOG AND PONY SHOW

If a casino could put odds on Scott versus Amundsen, the British captain would be the heavy favorite. He enjoyed a head start of more than a month. He had the larger team. He had the full backing of the British Empire.

What did Amundsen have going for him?

Let's start with the preparation. Amundsen, who had learned to ski as a toddler, had a sense that skiing would be the key to his mission's success. He trained for the expedition like an Olympic hopeful, determined to master the slopes. He even recruited an actual ski champion of Norway, Olav Bjaaland, to join the expedition and train the men.

Amundsen obsessed over the gear, he went on multiple trial runs, and he devoured the books and journals devoted to polar exploration. Amundsen spent more than two years preparing for this expedition.

Scott spent just nine months.

Amundsen was an effective leader. Just as Greely thought of clever ways to keep his men busy at Fort Conger, Amundsen strategized on how to boost the morale of his team. For example, when they arrived at Antarctica, once the men were sheltered in their portable hut, Amundsen created a daily contest of "guess the temperature." This incentivized his team to brave the cold and step outside each morning, guess the temperature, and then record the number in a log. Each month he gave a prize to the most accurate guesser.

Amundsen told the crew the contest was meant to sharpen their ability to gauge temperatures, just in case the thermometers broke. But the true purpose was psychological. "Because of the prizes, everybody insists on going out to look at the weather. And that's why the prizes have been put up,"

Amundsen wrote in his diary. "But nobody knew it. I find this little morning visit out in the open to be so beneficial," as it helps "wake a sleepy man and bring feelings into equilibrium."

Amundsen took his turn with unpleasant chores, he trusted his men, and he led with a light touch. The crew respected him.

Scott? Let's review just one anecdote. Years earlier, in his first expedition to the Antarctic with Ernest Shackleton, the two clashed. Despite being dangerously low on rations, Scott ordered his crew to keep pressing south with no margin for error. Shackleton thought this was reckless. Cooler heads prevailed and Scott eventually turned around, but not before an altercation that included Shackleton telling Scott, "You're the worst bloody fool of the lot."

Omens don't come any clearer. Prioritizing the safety of his men was a lesson that Scott would never learn.

Or consider logistics. For this journey to the South Pole, Scott put his faith in three modes of transport: motorized sledges, ponies, and the brute force of "man hauling" sledges across the ice.

Asking each man to lug 200 pounds across the ice is not ideal, but the notion appealed to Scott's sense of manly British stoicism. Relying on sledge dogs, by contrast, was almost cowardly. "In my mind no journey ever made with dogs can approach the height of that fine conception which is realised when a party of men go forth to face hardships, dangers, and difficulties with their own unaided efforts," he wrote. "Surely in this case the conquest is more nobly and splendidly won."

And now for the ponies. There are only a few problems with bringing horses to the Antarctic instead of dogs:

- Horses are not able to dig themselves into the snow for warmth.
- Horses sweat through their hide, so their skin gets wet and freezes (unlike dogs, who sweat through their tongues).
- Horses are more likely to trip and fall on the ice.
- Horses eat hay.

This last point is crucial. Dogs could eat food that's native to the Arctic and Antarctic, such as the abundant supply of seals. (This is why Inuit used them for generations.) Horses eat hay. While no one knew this with 100 percent certainty—it had not yet been discovered—there was a very good chance that hay does not grow at the South Pole. This meant that Scott would be forced to carry rations not only for the men, but also the horses.

"THE WORST JOURNEY IN THE WORLD"

Amundsen, like Peary and Henson before him, wore the furs of the Inuit and embraced their techniques for surviving in freezing conditions. He even wore Inuit-inspired ski goggles. Scott did not bother to do so, and he would often complain of poor visibility.

Deep into the expedition, when it was far too late to make changes, Scott had a "sneaking feeling" that the local Inuit fur clothing "may outclass our more civilized garb." One of Scott's crewmates was more blunt: "Our troubles were greatly increased by the state of our clothes. If we had been dressed in lead we should have been able to move our arms and necks and heads more easily than we could now," wrote Apsley Cherry-Garrard in the memoir *The Worst Journey in the World*. He found that once the fancy British clothes froze, they were "hard as boards and stuck out from our bodies in every imaginable fold and angle."

And finally, in a contrast that's instructive for every future explorer, Scott and Amundsen had radically different approaches to what was an acceptable margin of error. Amundsen planned for worst-case scenarios. He ensured he had ample cushion, he brought extra food, he factored in time for rest, he carefully measured the distance between his supply depots, and he padded the schedule to account for days with bad weather. Scott did none of this. He brought too little food and failed to keep track of the rations. (Many decades later, in the next phase of exploration, Amundsen's approach would be a bedrock principle for NASA.)

Scott's ship reached the Antarctic more than a month before Amundsen's *Fram*. But as the weeks and months ticked by, it became clear that Amundsen was gaining ground. The Norwegians glided on skis and pulled their sledges with dogs, as Amundsen found that the "sledges and skis glide easily and pleasantly." Meanwhile, Scott's ponies died (as many predicted) and his motorized tractors broke down (ditto), so the men had to haul the sledges themselves. Each mile was torture.

The skis, the sledge dogs, the superior planning, and the leadership of Amundsen brought the Norwegians to the South Pole on December 14, 1911. They took photos and unfurled the Norwegian flag. "So we arrived and were able to plant our flag at the geographical South Pole. God be thanked!" Amundsen wrote. (Bjaaland, the champion skier, simply noted in his journal, "The skiing was good.")

Scott eventually reached the South Pole, but was crestfallen to see the Norwegian flags. Now he would need to slog back to his base camp with a precariously low amount of food.

He had miscalculated the distance of his supply depots and he spread them too far apart, meaning that his team was out of food before reaching each restock. Finally, at the bitter end, Scott dispatched one of his men to the base camp and begged him to return with sledge dogs—only the dogs could save them.

The dogs would not arrive in time.

When Scott finally realized that he was doomed, he lay in a tent with his two surviving crewmates. (Two had already died.) He did have one thing going for him. A gifted writer, Scott summoned the prose that would turn him into a national legend. He cast himself as a hero felled by impossible circumstances, a glorious martyr. "We are showing that Englishmen can still die with a bold spirit, fighting it out to the end," Scott wrote in his journal, while starving to death because of his own blunders. "I think this makes a fine example for Englishmen of the future."

Amundsen, ironically, never garnered the same level of acclaim as Scott. The dead have gravitas. Scott's "unlucky" heroism was so ingrained in British culture that in 1979, when Huntford's meticulously researched book was published, the nation was shocked and scandalized when he concluded, "Scott had brought disaster on himself by his own incompetence."

And as for Amundsen? For decades, in some ways in Scott's shadow, he spent years lecturing and trying to lighten the load of his debt. He would become a member of The Explorers Club. And sometimes in his lectures, Amundsen would be asked, "Why go to the Poles?"

That very question, in a way, is a proxy for the larger question of this book, "Why bother with exploration?" Every explorer has a different answer. This is Amundsen's: "Little brains . . . have only room for thoughts of bread and butter."

Teddy and the Table

They call it "the Long Table." And it's exactly what it sounds like: a long wooden table that anchors the Board Room of The Explorers Club, flanked by a wall of books and maps and journals. This treasure was once known as the Long Table of Fellowship. For more than a century, it has been a tradition for explorers to sit around this table—fueled at times by ample drink—and swap stories from far-flung places. As George Plimpton observed, "Around the long table one hears the names Shanghai, London, Rio de Janeiro and Lima but only as stopovers on the way to Tatsienlu, Kuressaare, the Matto Grosso, or Machu Pichu."

Just one of countless examples: "I was driving across Mongolia, from Kalgan to Urga, with a friend who later was murdered in China," begins Roy Chapman Andrews, the paleontologist who served both as a Club president and as a director of the American Museum of Natural History. As he told his fellow Club members, "I was half dozing over the wheel, for the road was good. Suddenly five men appeared on the end of the promontory and, without the slightest warning, opened fire on our car." If this sounds like something straight out of an Indiana Jones movie, well, maybe it's not a coincidence that Andrews wore a fedora and brandished a whip—many believe him to be the inspiration for Indy himself. (Exhibit A: You can find his bullwhip in the Club's collections.)

The Long Table once belonged to Teddy Roosevelt, who sat at it to plan the Panama Canal. Roosevelt was an explorer. In 1914, he had nearly died when journeying to Panama to chart the "River of Doubt" through the Amazon rainforest. "The expedition must not stop," Roosevelt told his team. Feverish and unable to walk, he insisted that the exploration come first. "Go, and leave me here." He had lost 50 pounds and was delirious, repeating to himself lines from Samuel Taylor Coleridge's "Kubla Khan": "In Xanadu did Kubla Khan a stately pleasure-dome decree. In Xanadu did Kubla Khan a stately pleasure-dome decree." Somehow he survived. Teddy returned to New York and in 1915 applied for membership to the Club. Like all candidates, he had to fill out an application, a protocol that continues to this day. Under the qualifications section he wrote, "President of the United States." Amazingly, he only ranked this as his *fourth* credential.

Par M. B. Ingr. de la Marine.
1758
Baye de Gales
Henkes 1670
MER G
I de Jean Mayen
Rochers
Walsingham
Passage du Nord
Passo du Sud
C. Forbisher
Cap de Bonne Esperance
Cap Blanc
Cap Discord
Cap Farewel
Salten
Drontheim
ANGERMANIE
MEDELPADIE
HELSINGIE
GESARIKI
UPLANDE
GOTHIE
I. d'Oeland
BALTIQUE
POMÉRANIE

The Maps of Gertrude Bell

On the top floor of The Explorers Club—just next to an old shortwave radio station, where members once monitored expeditions in real time—you'll find a room with thousands of rare and treasured maps.

These maps include a sixteenth-century hand-painted rendering of the Polus Arcticus (North Pole) and Polus Antarcticus (South Pole). Or "La Louisiane," from 1718, the first detailed map of the Gulf of Mexico coastal region. And in a 2020 inventory of the collection, the cartography expert Tom Paradise was astonished to find something that eclipsed all of these: contemporary, hand-drawn maps of the legendary Gertrude Bell.

In the early 1900s, women were not yet allowed to become members of The Explorers Club, but Gertrude Bell could have led it. Bell was a writer, a traveler, an explorer, a war hero, a savvy political operator, and a British spy. Starting in the 1890s, Bell journeyed thousands of miles through west Asia. She drew maps. She climbed mountains. She often traveled alone and she learned the customs of the local people. The first woman to graduate from Oxford with a degree in Modern History, she cultivated friendships and trust at the highest levels of communities and governments throughout the region.

Paradise, who is also a geosciences professor and map historian, chuckles as he imagines how Bell must have confused and bewildered the people she would meet along her long journey. "This woman is in a skirt with boots, right? She's totally GI Joe. And she's talking to locals in Arabic. And she knows modern standard Arabic and local Bedouin dialects, a remarkable feat for a Westerner, let alone a woman," says Paradise. "She was a badass. She was fearless."

The *Endurance*, Shackleton's fabled ship that was lost for more than a century.

THE LAST DRAGON CHASER

By the early 1920s, much of exploration had shifted from the Arctic to warmer climates—to deserts and jungles—as the Club's "smokers" highlighted the discovery of scientific treasures. A 1922 issue of *The Explorers Journal,* for example, touts the exploits of Roy Chapman Andrews, whose "most spectacular find is the skull of the giant hornless rhinoceros *Baluchitherium.* This skull is nearly 5 feet in length and the animal itself equaled or exceeded in size the largest mammoths and elephants. The expedition has, in addition, secured complete skeletons of small Cretaceous dinosaurs."

In that same issue, the *Journal* notes that "Carl Akeley's noble memorial, the African Hall at the American Museum of Natural History, is taking tangible shape." (Akeley would die before finishing the job, but the work would be completed by his second wife, Mary Jobe Akeley, a fellow explorer.)

But the lure of the Poles remained. This was especially true for Ernest Shackleton, who, when giving a speech at a Club luncheon, once confessed that he had no idea why he kept returning to the Antarctic, as "it just draws me." With tropics-loving Carl Akeley in attendance, Shackleton joked that for him the cold was preferable to the heat, as "I know I'd die if I went into the tropics. . . . In the Antarctic all we have is cold and ice and weather. We do not have any germs. In the tropics you go to sleep, and something comes up during the night and bites your leg off, and when you wake up you are dead."

He enjoyed making this joke at The Explorers Club. The line got a good laugh.

There was less laughter in 1915, when Shackleton returned to the Antarctic. He sailed on a ship that might just be the most aptly named vessel in nautical history: the *Endurance.*

Ernest Shackleton, already an icon of exploration
by the time of the *Endurance* expedition.

"THE RITZ"

Shackleton had been to the Antarctic before. More than a decade earlier, during Robert Scott's first trip to the South Pole, it was a young Shackleton who was the voice of reason, convincing Scott they lacked the supplies to go farther. They wisely turned around and the men lived. In 1908, Shackleton came to the Antarctic a second time—nearly reaching the South Pole. He could have risked it, but he valued the lives of his men more than the glory of a Famous First, and as he later told his wife, "A live donkey is better than a dead lion, isn't it?"

On his third trip, in 1914, the goal was to cross the Antarctic by land, which he believed to be "the one great main object of Antarctic journeyings." He chose twenty-seven crew members to join the *Endurance* from a pool of five thousand applicants. This is widely regarded as the last expedition of the Heroic Age of exploration.

And it did not start well.

On the way to its destination in the Antarctic, in the unforgiving Weddell Sea, the *Endurance* struggled to navigate the shifting pack ice and became trapped. It wouldn't budge for days. Then weeks. Then months. Shackleton hoped the ice would eventually thaw and unclench the ship, so the crew simply stayed put, jokingly calling their new long-term accommodations "The Ritz."

In May, the Long Night of the sunless Antarctic winter had arrived. "In all the world there is no desolation more complete than the polar night," writes Alfred Lansing in the classic recounting of this story, *Endurance.* "It is a return to the Ice Age—no warmth, no life, no movement." To maintain their sanity, the crew walked circles around the ship in a ritual that they called the "madhouse promenade."

The good news is that over the course of several months, the ice did indeed begin to shift. The bad news is that the pressure of the ice began to crush the *Endurance,* filling it with water.

"She's going, boys," Shackleton told the crew. "I think it's time to get off."

They were several hundred miles away from rescue. The icy terrain was precarious to travel by foot, and at any moment they might reach the edge of an iceberg, or the ground beneath them might crack. But trying to sail through the icy water was even more dangerous, as the smaller boats they brought could get crushed. Shackleton decided they would go on foot and drag the boats with them. That meant they had to travel light. He gathered the men in a circle and told them to ditch everything that wasn't utterly essential, and to demonstrate, he took gold coins from his pocket and tossed them into the snow.

Shackleton brought sixty-nine dogs with him on the *Endurance*. They would serve him in more ways than he could have expected.

So they left the sad remains of the *Endurance*. And they grimly marched. They averaged only 2 miles per day, sleeping in crowded tents that provided little relief from the -2 degrees cold. They used dog sledges to help haul the gear. (Shackleton had learned from Scott's blunders.) "The dogs were wonderful," wrote Shackleton, who had spent months supervising their training. "Without them we could never have transported half the food and gear that we did." They hunted seals to augment their rations; to save ammo they killed the seals with wooden oars.

On January 13, Shackleton made an agonizing decision. It was unpopular with the men. And he hated the idea, considering it "the worst job" of the entire expedition. But he knew it must be done.

He gave a grim order: all of the sledge dogs needed to be killed.

They had brought a total of sixty-nine dogs to Antarctica, and then more puppies were born on the *Endurance*. The men had grown attached to them. "He is a fine little dog," a crew member wrote in his diary about a puppy named Grus. "I have had him, fed him, and trained him since he was born. I remember taking him out when he was a puppy in my pocket, only his nose peeping out and getting covered with frost."

But Shackleton did the math. He was always conscious of the rations—this sets him apart from Scott—and he knew that their supplies were limited; they couldn't afford to feed both the humans and the dogs. The wrenching business must be done. But before the dogs were shot, they were asked to do yet more sledge work, loyally straining to pull their masters forward. "My dogs will be shot tomorrow," a crew member wrote. Then they butchered the bodies and grilled the meat as steaks. Included was the little puppy, Grus, who one crew member thought "has a better flavor than the sea leopard."

AN "INHOSPITABLE PLACE"

The phrase "walking on thin ice" is now a cliché. But that is precisely what Shackleton and company had to do—and they did it while hauling three boats. Every night on the iceberg, when they shivered in their tents, they knew there was a chance that the ground could swallow them before morning.

Then in April it finally happened. The iceberg was about to crack. "Strike the tents and clear the boats!" Shackleton barked. The men sprang into action, quickly tearing down tents and staging the boats by the water.

"Launch the boats," Shackleton ordered.

And so they began rowing. Now the freezing water sprayed them and added to their misery, turning their clothes into icy suits of torture. "If a man shifted his position, even slightly, his skin came in contact with a new, unwarmed surface of his clothing," writes Lansing. "Everyone tried to sit still, but it could not be done. The weariness, the lack of food, the exertion, and the worry had weakened them so that the harder they tried to sit still, the more they shivered—and their own shivering kept them awake."

Somehow they all survived the first night, but the second night in their frozen hell was even colder. Water invaded the bottom of the boats and it kept their feet cold and wet. Shackleton ordered them to wiggle their toes to keep their feet from freezing. "Most of the men also had diarrhea from their diet of uncooked pemmican," writes Lansing. "And they would suddenly have to rush for the side. . . . Invariably, the icy sea wet them from beneath."

"The Ritz" before it slowly sank into the icy waters.

Through all of this, Shackleton kept a careful watch on the crew's morale, looking for the weakest link. When they began rowing the next day, searching for land, Shackleton noticed that one crew member—Blackboro—had frostbite on his feet, and was at critical risk of gangrene.

"We shall be on Elephant Island tomorrow," Shackleton told him. "No one has ever landed there before, and you will be the first ashore."

The next day they did indeed row to Elephant Island, ravenous and freezing and nearly four days without sleep, half dead. When they neared the shore, Shackleton instructed Blackboro to climb out of the boat. Blackboro wouldn't do it. Shackleton, exasperated, hoisted Blackboro over the edge. (He later realized that Blackboro couldn't move because of the frostbite on his feet, and felt ashamed.)

At first the men rejoiced. They were out of the freezing boats and on solid ground for the first time in more than a year. But the land was cruel. "A more inhospitable place could scarcely be imagined," wrote one crew member in his journal. "The gusts increased in violence and became so strong that we could hardly walk against them." Soon a blizzard arrived. As another wrote, "The driving snow rushed down one's throat as one breathed and choked one."

But at least they were finally able to sleep, and the next morning they feasted on a meal of pigeons. Now Shackleton had to make another tough call: he would need to split up the party.

Elephant Island was still more than 500 miles from civilization. If they all remained where they were, they would eventually die. But their three meager boats were not fit for a long sea journey. Only the strongest, the *James Caird*, had any plausible chance. Shackleton gave careful thought to who should go on the relief mission with him. In a surprising decision, he also chose to bring crew members who might cause the most trouble. The people left on the island would be stranded for months, figured Shackleton, and it was better to have any mischief-makers under his personal watch.

So Shackleton, his trusty navigator Frank Worsley, and a crew of four boarded the *James Caird* and returned to the icy waters. At night, it was so cold that the boat became frozen in ice; they chipped it away with an axe. Then they ran low on drinking water. As the days passed, their rations shrank to half a cup of water per day. Their bearded faces were covered in soot. They all had some form of frostbite. Chunks of their skin were missing.

Still they kept rowing, kept freezing, kept fighting. And weeks later, through the fog, one of the crew pointed and yelled, "Land!"

The rest of the crew was silent, unwilling to believe their luck had turned.

Finally Shackleton broke the silence: "We've done it."

Hotel Explorers Club

The physical location of The Explorers Club bounced around in its early years, starting with an empty loft at 345 Amsterdam Avenue.

No one particularly liked it. "It is generally agreed by the members that the present quarters of the Club at 345 Amsterdam Avenue are wholly inadequate and altogether too small for comfortable and effective meetings," the 1921 *Explorers Journal* reports.

"Beneath the present library and assembly room is a garage and machine shop, adding to the fire risk a constant din and gasoline odor that seriously interferes with the use of the library."

Happily, the Club would later move to a townhouse at 47 West Seventy-Sixth Street, not far from where it is today. "In 1928, both solvent and popular, the Club leased an eight-story building, hoping to pay off the investment by renting out five stories of bedrooms," explained George Plimpton in *As Told at The Explorers Club*.

So The Explorers Club became a hotel. If this quirky hotel—and even today's version of the Club—sounds like something out of a Wes Anderson movie, that's not entirely a coincidence. Wes Anderson was so charmed by the Club that he asked its then president, Richard Wiese, to be a consultant on *The Life Aquatic*.

And in 1929, The Explorers Club Hotel had its admirers. "I found the Club an ideal location," gushes one 1929 version of a Yelp review. "Explorers may be an odd lot, but those one meets at the Club are regular fellows." Alas, the hotel concept was not long for this world; as George Plimpton put it, "the membership turned out to be better explorers than landlords."

TOBOGGANERS

But Shackleton spoke too soon. Their destination, South Georgia, was guarded by an almost comically treacherous mix of storms, gusty winds, and deadly reefs. Somehow they found an opening into a cove, guided the *James Caird* to safety, and stumbled to a stream of fresh water. At last, they could drink.

After studying their maps, Shackleton realized they were still 29 miles from the whaling station. This was not a smooth hike on a gentle trail. As Lansing explains, "In the three-quarters of a century that men had been coming to South Georgia, not one man had ever crossed the island—for the simple reason that it could not be done."

Shackleton, against all odds, had just led the men on one of history's most improbable sea journeys. Now, with no rest or equipment, he would do the same across the mountains. Once again, he adapted and improvised. The men found 2-inch screws from their boats and attached them to their boots, creating makeshift climbing gear.

At 2:00 a.m., Shackleton led an even smaller party of three and began climbing the mountains of South Georgia. He walked fast and with purpose. Their feet sank in the snow, but they kept plodding forward. The terrain was so steep at times that they cut steps in the mountain with an axe. Yet soon they reached a paradox. The higher they climbed, the closer they came to their goal—the other end of the island. But higher was also colder. And daylight was fading. If they remained on top of the mountain ridge when the sun went down, they would freeze to death.

Shackleton led the men lower and toward the whaling station, scrambling down as fast as they could against the setting sun. Then Shackleton cut steps into the ridge, used rope to tie the men together, and they climbed lower in a sharp drop. In two hours, they descended 500 feet. This was taking too long—they would never make it down before dark.

Shackleton then made one of his most audacious decisions: they would slide down the mountain. There was a chance they could hit jagged rocks, slide off a cliff, or die, but they didn't have a choice.

The three men sat down on the mountain and each wrapped his arms and legs around the torso of the man in front. As Lansing describes it, "They looked like three tobogganers without a toboggan."

They were now at the top of a roller coaster with no guardrails, no seat belts, and no idea if there was even a track in front of them. In the twilight of the Antarctic sun, they pushed themselves over the edge of the world, held one another tight, battled their fear, and prayed.

LOST AND BOUND

Flash forward 106 years. Shackleton succeeded in reaching the whaling station and rescuing his men, becoming one of Britain's heroes. He was arguably the last titan of the Heroic Age of exploration. His legacy looms large. When the astronaut Mike Massimino trained to go to space, NASA used Shackleton as an example of how to lead expeditions. "If you look at Shackleton's example, and if you look at the science objectives and the exploration objectives, you'd say, 'Well, he never made it,'" says Massimino. "The ship ended up at the bottom of the ocean. But it *was* a success, because everybody came back alive." Think of Shackleton's expedition as the polar version of Apollo 13.

And for more than one hundred years, Shackleton's legendary ship, the *Endurance,* was lost to the world. The very pack ice in the freezing tempest of the Weddell Sea that doomed Shackleton felled search after search.

Then along came a Club member named Mensun Bound, a deep-ocean archaeologist. As he later shared at a Club luncheon, he first read a book about Shackleton when he was eight years old.

The story stuck with him. Over the years he discovered shipwreck after shipwreck, and in 2019 he led an expedition to find the *Endurance.* It was a "dismal failure," Bound told the Club, primarily because ice floes kept shifting and flummoxing the ship.

But he didn't give up; instead, he adapted. "We learned a lot of lessons from that," he explained, such as "using satellite photography to monitor the ice floes." Once they could predict where the ice was moving, they had an easier time maneuvering their ship for the search.

They searched for a full week, using remote submersibles that trawled the seafloor. Their sonar pings found nothing. Then they hunted for a second week—exhausting their budgeted time and resources. Then, on the final day, one of Bound's crew smirked at him. He held up a display that showed the deep-sea cameras from below. "Gents," he said, "let me introduce you to the *Endurance.*"

Mensun Bound, whether he knew it or not, had just provided closure to an era of exploration.

Mensun Bound, holding the Club flag after finding the *Endurance*.

SET 20 D
THEODORE ROOSEVELT

The Most Polarizing Room in The Explorers Club

When Teddy Roosevelt was president, he invited a man named Carl Akeley to join him for a dinner at the White House. Akeley was one of the early taxidermists. "I sat through course after course and did not eat a bite, for the President kept me busy telling stories of Africa," Akeley recounted. After dinner, as the two left the dining room, Roosevelt turned to Akeley and said, "As soon as I am through with this job, I am going to Africa."

The two became fast friends. And Roosevelt was a man of his word. As soon as he finished his "job," in 1909, the president joined Akeley in Africa. Their mission was to collect materials for the American Museum of Natural History, and it was sponsored by the Smithsonian.

In those days, of course, "collect materials" was a euphemism for hunting animals, killing them, and returning with the "trophies." Many of these animals would end up at The Explorers Club, in a room that was once called the Trophy Room but, for obvious reasons, has been rebranded as the Gallery. It's a complicated room with a complicated legacy.

In the Club's early days, taxidermy was thought to be the best way—really the only way—to preserve animals for education and research. This is why the room is packed with mounts of a rhino horn, an elephant tusk, Tibetan antelope, bison, the head of a wolf, black rhinoceros, elk, and a cheetah shot by Teddy Roosevelt. The room is off-putting for many. (Jane Goodall hates the room and refuses to enter it.)

On the other hand, the Gallery is the favorite room of Laurie Marker, the woman who has almost single-handedly prevented cheetahs from going extinct. The way she sees it, Roosevelt was "hunting and bringing things back for museums. We didn't know anything. So that was a museum study." And these old trophies still have scientific value today, for as Marker says, "You can always get a piece of the sample and do genetics on it." Ultimately, Marker views Roosevelt and Akeley as "some of our longtime conservationists. They were just maybe a bit misguided back at that point in time."

2—BREAKING THE BOUNDARIES

CLIMBING HIGHER AND DIVING DEEPER

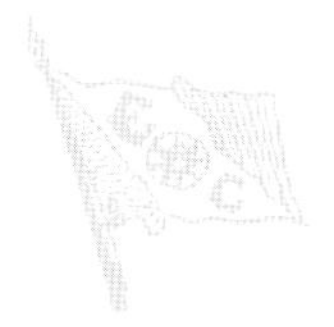

By the 1920s, all the maps had been filled in. The dragons had been chased and pushed back to the very edges. We had a good sense of the continents and the Poles.

But our curiosity was unquenched.

What lies at the bottom of the ocean? How deep can we go?

World War I sparked a boom in aviation. Could we reach the stratosphere? Get to outer space? Even to the moon?

You know many of the heroes who are featured in this section, so we won't belabor the obvious. But you might be surprised by who helped launch this era of exploration. And now it's time for the return of an old friend. . . .

He's back. Greely had a second—and sneakily important—chapter of exploration that history has largely overlooked. In 1935, he received the Congressional Medal of Honor at the age of 91. General Douglas MacArthur helped award the medal, making Greely a living link between the Civil War and World War II.

THE WINGS OF GREELY

1884. After being reunited with Henrietta, Adolphus Greely decided that he would no longer make any three-year treks to the Arctic. He had served his time. Greely resumed his old work at the US Signal Corps, quickly climbing the ranks and becoming the chief signal officer in 1887. (Along the way, Greely became the first volunteer private to be promoted to brigadier general in the history of the United States.)

He helped develop the weather service. He figured out how to lay oceanic cables to Alaska and the Philippines and the Caribbean, literally connecting North America. Always curious, Greely soon became fascinated by a new technology with enormous potential: aircraft. He was no stranger to the idea of flight. During the Civil War, at Yorktown, Greely happened to witness the launch of the first American observation balloon, which flew in the sky to glimpse the troop movements of the Confederate army. (The plan was not foolproof: the Union balloon flew over Confederate lines and the rebels tried to shoot it down; the wind changed just in time and the balloon escaped to safety.)

The memory stuck with Greely and decades later, as the leader of the army's Signal Corps, he harnessed a network of balloons to quickly and efficiently collect meteorological data. That was part of Greely's broader effort to gather data from all corners of the nation and make sense of it. "Greely connected the nation's telegraph companies and made them weather stations as well," writes the military historian Paul D. Walker. "At sunrise and sunset, they would telegraph his central office in Washington, DC, with their local weather. With this constant flow of information, he could make estimates of weather conditions or, as they later became known, forecasts." This is just one more example, of many, of how exploration begets innovation that benefits society in surprising ways.

As Greely deployed balloons to collect scientific data, others used them to push the boundaries of aviation. This had started as early as 1897, when S. A. Andrée, a Swedish explorer, used a balloon to try to reach the North Pole. "The history of geographical discovery is at the same time a history of great peril and suffering," Andrée said in a gloomy speech at the Sixth International Geographical Congress in London, adding that in the Arctic, "the cold only kills," and that North Pole expeditions had all ended in failure.

So Andrée proposed a new way to reach the Pole. "I refer to the balloon," Andrée said with a flourish.

Greely was in the audience. He bluntly told Andrée that the plan was too risky and "foolhardy."

Suddenly the two explorers had a public showdown. "When something happened to your ships, how did you get back?" Andrée asked Greely.

Without waiting for an answer, the Swede continued, "I risk three lives in what you call a 'foolhardy' attempt, and you risked how many? A shipload."

Andrée had a point, but after only two days in the balloon, he crashed into an ice pack and was never seen alive again.

But even if Greely was skeptical of Andrée's chances, he knew that aviation had real potential. In 1899, Greely prodded Congress to allocate $50,000 to the army for a "flying machine." As Walker explains, "The other service branches, including the navy, refused to handle it. They thought the project was doomed and did not want the ridicule that would follow."

Greely happened to know an inventor named Samuel Langley, who was secretly working on something called the "aerodrome." Langley used part of the $50,000 to improve the plane's engine; ultimately, it wasn't successful, but by some accounts it influenced and inspired the Wright brothers. Orville Wright later described Langley as a "helping hand at a critical time and we shall always be grateful."

And soon Greely met with Orville and Wilbur Wright. "[Greely] was so impressed with the possibilities of this machine that he asked for a ride and was given one, lying prone over the left wing," writes Walker.

So Adolphus Greely, the Civil War hero who was once left for dead in the Arctic, became one of the very first humans to fly.

More important, he immediately ordered two planes for the Signal Corps, which introduced aviation to the military. Walker argues that "Greely is credited with promoting the development of the airplane" and an MIT aeronautics course calls Greely the "grandfather of military aviation."

Andrée's balloon, the *Eagle*, was the pride of Sweden. Unfortunately, the *Eagle* lost hydrogen too quickly and crashed after only two days of flight.

The thrust of exploration had shifted from the snow to the sky.

As the 1920s loomed, The Explorers Club's Famous Firsts shifted from the snow to the sky. Charles Lindbergh, a (problematic) Club member, became the first to soar across the Atlantic. Amelia Earhart soon followed.

Explorers began using planes not just for stunts or breaking records, but to actually *explore*. The US Navy had taken the baton from Greely's Signal Corps, using planes in 1925 to survey and map the Far North. The leader of this expedition was a handsome, gung ho, always crisply dressed pilot named Commander Richard E. Byrd.

First Byrd mapped much of Greenland. Then he had an even grander ambition—and his idea soon made its way to the White House.

Huddled inside the Oval Office, Calvin Coolidge stared at the maps. His secretary of the navy had lugged in a stack of maps and unrolled them on the desk, giving him a quick tutorial of Arctic exploration.

"You can see there is a lot of unexplored white space on the map," the secretary told Coolidge. The secretary pointed to the North Pole, and he pitched the idea of Byrd reaching it by plane. That had never been done. "Don't you think we ought to let Byrd go?"

The president considered the idea. His response was a simple "Why not?"

So that was that. Soon Byrd led an expedition that steamed to the Arctic, along with a special plane that used skis as its landing gear. As Lowell Thomas and Lowell Thomas Jr. write in The Explorers Club book *Famous First Flights,* hundreds of candidates applied to join Byrd on his quest, including doctors and lawyers and college students and "even husbands who frankly admitted they wanted to get away from their wives."

But Byrd wasn't the only explorer with the idea of flying to the North Pole.

Enter a man who had a bit of experience with races to the Poles: Roald Amundsen. He had already claimed the undisputed prize of First to the South Pole. And now, fifteen years later, with nothing left to prove, at precisely the same time as Byrd, Amundsen brought together a crew of Norwegians and Italians to try to reach the North Pole in a blimp-like dirigible.

The race was on.

Amundsen tried to downplay the rivalry, even suggesting that he wasn't particularly interested in the North Pole. "Our main purpose will be to find land, if it exists in the polar region," Amundsen said before the mission. "We have one main purpose—to get across. Flying over the Pole itself, that will be

Commander Richard E. Byrd. He once described the Antarctic as "perhaps the dreariest of places," explaining that "Our base, Little America, lay in a bowl of ice, near the edge of the Ross Ice Barrier. The temperature fell as low as 72 degrees below zero. One could actually hear one's breath freeze."

incidental." This statement, quite frankly, is almost certainly a lie. And it's reminiscent of Amundsen's audacious misdirection, back in 1909, of claiming to head north when he really went south.

The timing of Byrd's and Amundsen's missions was so simultaneous, the two actually met face-to-face.

"Glad you're here safely," Amundsen said to Byrd when he arrived. "Welcome to Spitsbergen."

Amundsen was more than simply polite—he gave Byrd essential help in reaching the Pole. The Norwegians helped Byrd locate a good runway for his plane, they supplied him with woodworkers to make improvements to his skis, and they even built him an emergency lightweight sledge in case his plane crashed. (Amundsen soberly remembered the last time he raced someone to a Pole; he was determined not to leave another rival dead.)

Byrd was shocked by this camaraderie. "You're being very generous for a rival," Byrd told the Norwegian.

"But we are not rivals," Amundsen said. "We are collaborators in a joint assault on the polar regions."

So on May 9, 1926, Byrd and his copilot, Floyd Bennett—thanks in part to Amundsen's generosity—pointed their plane north and headed for the Pole.

Navigation was not easy. "Byrd now concentrated on navigating a straight course toward a rather obscure distant point in the Polar Sea which had never been spotted from the air, and only once by human beings," writes Lowell Thomas. "Byrd now had to do it without the aid of landmarks, for there were none in that unexplored realm at the top of the world."

Byrd scanned the endless sea of ice. Even after decades of exploration, much of the North was still unknown and it was hard to tell what was solid ground. "One of the mysteries of exploration was still unsolved—how about land in the Arctic?" writes Lowell Thomas. "Suddenly, rising out of the sea, a line of snowcapped mountains came into view. But as Byrd turned to motion to Bennett, the 'mountain peaks' proved to be an Arctic mirage, merely white clouds across the sky. So what might have been a newly discovered Byrdland, simply wasn't there."

For good luck, Byrd had pocketed a coin that Robert Peary had taken to the North Pole nearly two decades before. And he would need more than good luck to please the toughest audience of all—his children.

His kids had asked before he left, "Daddy, will you see Santa Claus?"

Byrd gently dodged the question, but assured them that "I'll tell you all about his place at the North Pole."

But a search for Santa would have to wait. As the plane rumbled north, Byrd's engine began to leak and the motor threatened to blow. Oil squirted from the engines and splattered against the plane, freezing instantly. If they kept flying, the engine could go kaput and kill them. But if they tried to land on ice that wasn't solid, then they'd plunge to their death. With the Pole less than an hour away, Byrd decided to keep going.

As every second ticked off the clock, they were both closer to the Pole and closer to the engine combusting. Byrd stayed focused and used a sun compass to keep heading north. They had already poured extra fuel into the engine and tossed the empty cans overboard—that's how it was done back then—and now the fuel was running out.

Finally, at 9:00 a.m., Byrd's sun compass told him that they were at the North Pole. But there was no way to know for sure. "As many have discovered since that day," Lowell Thomas explains, "the North Pole is nothing but a geographical spot in that sea of moving pack ice." There would be no landing of the plane. There would be no heroic raising of the flag. The best Byrd could do was film a quick movie from the cockpit, and then unceremoniously drop a US flag on what he hoped was the North Pole.

Commissioned by the *New York Times*, this painting by Anton Widlicka depicts Byrd's Antarctic camp he called Little America. It also depicts (through the towers on the left) what was then the longest radio transmission in history—from the Antarctic to New York. The painting now hangs on the "four and a half floor" landing at The Explorers Club.

Byrd and Bennett barely made it back to their base. Amundsen led the Norwegians in "Viking cheers" for Byrd's accomplishment. And only three days later, Amundsen himself floated over the North Pole in his dirigible.

So who won the race?

At first glance, the obvious answer is Byrd. But years later, research cast doubt on the accuracy of Byrd's flyover. The experts found that Amundsen came closer. And the mystery is even deeper. Decades after Henson, Peary, Egingwah, Ooqueah, Ootah, and Seeglo approached the Pole, research suggests that they fell a bit short. It's also unclear whether Frederick Cook reached the Pole. This means it's possible that the first person to truly reach the North Pole is none other than Roald Amundsen—the same man who first reached the South Pole.

But the real lesson of Byrd and Amundsen's race is not about the North Pole or South Pole or who had the most accurate reading of a sun compass. The real takeaway is a shift in emphasis. Aircraft had arrived. Flight was the future. And the thrust of exploration was no longer about north or south, east or west.

Explorers now had a new frontier: up.

Byrd with his rescue dog, Igloo, who accompanied him on many expeditions. He signed the photo, "To the Explorers Club with all the best wishes in the world to my fellow members."

The Explorers Club Annual Dinner

Every year, The Explorers Club holds a black-tie gala called ECAD, or The Explorers Club Annual Dinner. This tradition started in 1914, a time when the Club was still obsessed with the Arctic. The cover image for the 1914 ECAD program showed men shivering in the snow; the tagline was "Recollections of Good (C)old Times."

It's a formal affair. Club members wear tuxedos and gowns—far more tuxes than gowns in the early days—which is a touch ironic, given that most exploration occurs in the field, where the attire is more Arctic jacket than dinner jacket. The one time when explorers all meet in person is the one time when they look nothing like their normal selves.

Another tradition is the serving of unfamiliar food from far-flung places, designed for members to bring back cuisine from the places they had visited. These dishes have ranged from whole alligators to sautéed python to—allegedly—a preserved woolly mammoth in 1951. (Yale researchers debunked the latter, proving the meat came from sea turtles.)

But the food is never the point. "The food was appetizing and beverages were varied and plentiful, but these good things play a minor part in the evening's enjoyment," explains the 1929 *Explorers Journal*, "for every man is meeting chums whom he rarely sees otherwise, and real talk and unrestrained laughter are echoed from all four walls."

Invitations and menus from past ECADs, featuring dishes like flying foxes, bird's nest soup, and reindeer meatballs.

EXOTIC HORS D'OEUVRES

Caribou
(roast and ragout)
Arctic Char
(frozen whole, smoked and steaks)
Reindeer Eyeballs
(raw and pickled)
Arctic Lake Trout
Ptarmigan
Arctic White Fish
Canadian Seaweed
King Crab
Whale Liver Pâte
Seal Meat, Eskimo Style
Muktuk
Fiddleheads
Equus Alaskensis

DINNER MENU

TURTLE SOUP AMONTILLADO
•
ROAST PRIME RIBS OF BEEF AU JUS
•
RISSOLE POTATOES
•
BRUSSELS SPROUTS AU BEURRE
•
SALADE CHIFFONADE
•
BAKED ALASKA
•
CHERRIES FLAMBÉ
•
VANILLA ICE CREAM
•
COFFEE
•

65th ANNUAL DINNER COMMITTEE

RUSSELL H. GURNEE, CHAIRMAN

ALLYN BAUM
E. LOVELL BECKER, M.D.
DR. LEON R. CAHEN
JAMES A. HOUSTON
PAUL H. JEHEBER
HERMAN W. KITCHEN
ROBERT H. MALOTT
ROBERT S. MATHEWS
GEORGE F. MILLER
JAMES SANDS
RICHARD T. SILVER, M.D.
JOHN SPENCE
NORMAN A. STAPLES
RICHARD STEEL
DR. CHARLES L. STOLOFF
HOBART M. VAN DEUSEN
GEN. F. T. VOORHEES
COLEMAN S. WILLIAMS

HORS D'OEUVRES PREPARED BY ERIC HOFNANN, CHEF.
COURTESY OF THE DEPARTMENT OF NORTHERN AND INDIAN AFFAIRS, GOVERNMENT OF CANADA.

HOUSTON

Tenzing Norgay and Edmund Hillary.

FIRST TO SUMMIT EVEREST

For the first half of the twentieth century, much of exploration focused on soaring through the sky—but this is not the only way up.

Humans have longed to reach the highest peak of the highest mountain for all of recorded history, and on May 28, 1953, Tenzing Norgay and Edmund Hillary realized something very simple: it's hard to sleep on the top of the world. They pitched a tent on the side of the cliff. They jammed oxygen tanks into the ground and used them to anchor the tent's ropes and keep it from toppling. The ground wasn't level. They had to awkwardly split the tent over two ledges. "Tenzing lay on the bottom ledge, almost overhanging the slope," Hillary later remembered, "while I stretched out on the top ledge with my legs across Tenzing in the bottom corner of the tent."

Beneath them was a 27,000-foot drop. The air was so thin that they needed oxygen tanks even to sleep; Hillary figured that if they breathed one liter per minute, maybe they could eke out four hours of shut-eye. The next morning, with the temperature at 17 degrees, Hillary's boots were so frozen he couldn't put them on. He warmed them with a Primus stove; Norgay cooked them a meal of chicken noodle soup.

Hillary was a tall New Zealander; he started his career as a bee farmer. Norgay was a Nepali-Indian Sherpa, then pushing forty, who had been climbing Everest for twenty years. They were far from alone on the mountain, a fact usually omitted from this story. When they looked below they could see the tiny dots of their companions, part of the larger Everest expedition—more than four hundred people in total—that included Sherpas, porters, a team of British climbers, and the British commander John Hunt.

"It's not the mountain we conquer,
but ourselves."
—SIR EDMUND HILLARY

This photo (like most from the era) only features Hillary and Norgay, but the larger Everest expedition included a team of over four hundred.

Norgay and Hillary couldn't reach the top alone. Just as Henson and Peary used a staggered relay system to approach the North Pole, one team of climbers would advance to lug supplies up the mountain, then another team would climb to relieve them, rinse and repeat.

Now, near the very top, Hillary—like Shackleton before him—used an ice axe to cut tiny steps into the mountain. They wheezed into their oxygen tanks. They could see Tibet in the distance. Finally, just before noon, they reached the summit, a goal that had by then killed at least three hundred people, including George Mallory, the British mountaineer who once said he wanted to climb Everest "because it's there."

Hillary reached out to shake Norgay's hand. Instead Norgay gave him a fierce hug. This moment instantly turned the two of them into celebrities, and soon they would dine with the prime minister of India, be feted around

In honor of Tenzing Norgay, every four years the Club gives out the Tenzing Norgay Award for achievements in extraordinary mountaineering.

the globe, and meet with the Dalai Lama and seemingly every head of state. But in many ways that wasn't the point. And perhaps more important than the duo summiting Everest was the realization that they were a team, partners, collaborators. They were "Hillary and Norgay" or "Norgay and Hillary," not just Hillary and a helper. This marked something of a shift in exploration—a new appreciation and (belated) recognition of Sherpas.

J. R. Harris in 2018 on the Alta Via 1, an eleven-day trek through the Italian Dolomites.

THE SOCIETY OF FORGOTTEN EXPLORERS

While it's right to celebrate the summiting of Everest, it's just as important—perhaps more so—to address the question of *who* in exploration we're celebrating and including.

It's true that in 1937, The Explorers Club awarded Matthew Henson a "Life Membership."

But it's also true that for decades, African American members were not permitted. Perhaps just as damning, even when Black explorers were *technically* allowed to join, in practice this was rare and challenging.

Consider the case of J. R. Harris, who, at age thirteen, caught the bug for exploration at a summer camp in the Catskills. He learned to use a compass and read a map, and suddenly this city kid wanted to spend as much time as he could in nature. He started backpacking. Decades before smartphones or GPS, Harris would head off the grid and spend time by himself and time with indigenous communities. He roamed across Alaska, Iceland, and the Yukon. Why the Yukon? He saw a show on the Discovery Channel about the caribou migration, and simply thought, "Oh man, I need to go up there."

"I was born curious," says Harris, citing the one trait that unites every explorer. "And I'm still curious about everything." Harris says that he's "different from the typical explorer in that most of my expeditions are solo, and on a smaller scale. I'm basically a curious guy with a valid credit card."

Harris is also different from the typical explorer—or at least the famous explorers of yore—in that he is Black. Obviously, this shouldn't matter. Exploration has no color. But it mattered when Harris applied for membership to The Explorers Club in 1993, and his sponsor gave him a surprising piece of advice: *Don't send them a photo.*

The Explorers Club Research Collections

Flags that have been to the moon. Books from the fifteenth century. Teddy Roosevelt's membership application. You'll find all of these items and more in the Club's Research Collections, comprised of a library of roughly 14,000 books, 5,000 maps, 500 films and videos, 10,000 photographs, 550 linear feet of manuscripts, and an art and artifact collection of 1,000 objects.

Looking for the sixteenth-century edition of Richard Hakluyt's *Principal Navigations*, considered by many to be the most important collection of English travel writing ever published? It's one of the library's 1,400 rare books. Curious to see the maps of Napoleon?

Check out the rare first edition of *Description de L'Égypte*, twenty-three volumes that helped launch the modern study of Egyptology.

These days the books are historical treasures, mementos from a storied past. But that wasn't always the case. "It seems that some of our members are not yet aware that they may borrow books from the Library for home reading—subject to a few reasonable regulations," *The Explorers Journal* explained in 1929. "Our Library is intended, not as a museum of untouchable curios, but as something for the members to use and enjoy."

So members listened. In 1935, the *Journal* happily noted, "The number of books taken out for home reading was 436. . . . The policy of lending books (except specially valuable volumes) for use outside the library has operated successfully thus far." Although perhaps the program became a bit *too* successful. In 1947, the *Journal* politely reminded members to please return the books to the library.

For the first century of the Club's existence, the Research Collections were organized by a team of volunteers. A full-time archivist was hired in 2003 to bring order to the chaos. Lacey Flint is the archivist as of this printing who also oversees the files of deceased members. Some of these are names you'd recognize—the John Glenns and Charles Lindberghs of the world—but thousands more are not, and each one has a compelling story. So the stories in this book are hardly comprehensive, but instead meant to provide a sense of the Club's reach. For every Richard Byrd there are a hundred worthy names that aren't even mentioned. "There are 3,600 deceased members," says Flint. "At least three-quarters of them could have their own book."

Harris in 1997, on the last day of a twenty-day solo backpacking trip across the Mackenzie Mountains in the Canadian Northwest Territories, one of the most remote regions in the Western Hemisphere. He chartered the plane to take him across a river to the small community of Norman Wells.

As Harris remembers it, the sponsor told him, "If they see what you'll look like, they will not let you in." So Harris followed that advice and didn't include a photo. He was granted membership.

Harris might have been a dues-paying member, but he wasn't treated like one. There were some who were civil, even kind, but others would ask him, "What are you doing here? You can't be a member." People demanded to see his membership card. He tried to be social and he regularly went to the Monday evening lectures (he still does), but "only a couple of people reached out and were friendly." (Harris clarifies that the ones who showed kindness did so "probably at the risk of negative reaction from others," and he appreciated it.)

Things were worse at the black-tie Explorers Club Annual Dinner (ECAD). Harris and his date were seated at a table for ten, and most of the other eight ignored him. Later in the evening, when Harris's date went to the ladies' room, Harris was left standing alone. A member came up to Harris and handed him an empty wineglass. "Go get me another glass of wine," the guy said.

The 1955 Explorers Club Annual Dinner. For the first several decades of The Club's existence, the membership looked a lot like this: white, wealthy, male.

"Do I look like a waiter?" Harris asked. "I'm wearing a tuxedo, just like you."

At this point, another Explorers Club member—an Honorary Member—happened to see what was going on. This member was tall and lean, a New Zealander, with great slabs of a jawline. He saw Harris standing alone and introduced himself. "Hey, how are you doing? I'm Ed Hillary." Hillary was friendly. He wanted to know what Harris did, where he was from, and where he explored. "How long have you been a member?"

"I'm new," said Harris.

"Yeah, I don't see a lot of people talking to you here."

"Yeah. It is what it is."

Hillary told him not to call him Sir Edmund ("I'm Ed"). In the middle of their conversation, another Club member approached and said that Hillary needed to meet someone.

Hillary shot him a look. "Tell him I'll be there in a minute."

The guy left, and Hillary and Harris continued talking.

A few minutes later the guy returned. And he said to Hillary, incredulous, "What are you doing *here*?" The implication was obvious. *Why are you talking to this Black guy?*

Harris, as Chair of the Diversity, Equity, and Inclusion Committee, at the Society of Forgotten Explorers ceremony.

Then Sir Edmund Hillary, as Harris remembers, "got really pissed." Hillary didn't leave with the other guy. Instead, he told him, "Fuck off."

Hillary turned back to Harris. "Listen, J.R., I'm really sorry about all of this. Hang in there. The Club is doing good things."

Harris hung in there. He hung in there for decades. And over time, something very simple happened. The racist old white members? Many of them died. New members joined. Younger members. More diverse members.

Harris finds it ironic that things have come "full circle," and that he now sits on the Club's board of directors, and chairs its Diversity, Equity, and Inclusion (DEI) committee. He helped create the Society of Forgotten Explorers, which puts a spotlight on Black explorers whom history has overlooked.

As for the ugly past? "To be honest, I don't really dwell on that," says Harris. "That's the way it was then. I prefer to focus on what the Club is now."

This is why during the 2022 ECAD weekend, in a special ceremony in the Clark Room, Harris introduced a segment on the "Forgotten Four" that honored the Inuit. "Peary and Henson would never have made it [to the Pole] if it wasn't for them," Harris told the packed crowd.

The Club and World War II

1939. The eve of World War II. And the explorers knew it. "We sit helplessly waiting for the greatest catastrophe of all times to descend upon us," reports *The Explorers Journal*. "We sit as if mesmerized and some of us sympathize with the bird watching the snake coil itself for the fatal strike. There is no neutrality today."

So the Club did not remain neutral. "We should insist that dictators, kings, presidents and governments should not place themselves, nor any of their puppets, above common morality. We should proclaim that one undivided justice is the human ideal. This is the explorer's creed," wrote Herbert Spinden, the Club's president, in 1944.

The Club continued to function during the war. They continued the lectures and the smokers, and they established a Committee on the War Effort, comprised of "members who have worked in various parts of the world and who can advise the Government on those areas." A concrete example is food rations. Club members had ample experience in the field with limited rations—as well as knowledge of how other cultures throughout the world survived (and thrived) on a diet unfamiliar to the US Army—and more than one hundred chimed in with specific suggestions. As the 1942 *Journal* explains, "On the strength of these replies, a very valuable report was prepared which may not only help the dietetic experts of the Quartermaster Corps to design concentrated rations for our troops, but may also help our troops to be made self-sufficient in the field."

And if members at first felt "helpless," they did not remain that way. The Club jumped in to support the Allies. Many fought directly in the war, some went on daring reconnaissance missions to map enemy terrain, and still others returned to active duty years—or even decades—after their tour of service had ended. Fifty-three-year-old Richard Byrd, now a rear admiral, rejoined the navy to survey airfields on the front lines. This is old hat for Club members. Incredibly, one of the survivors of the Greely expedition, David Brainard, later fought in World War I. He also served as a Club president and lived until 1946.

Ootah, Egingwah, Seegloo, and Ooqueah are now honored at the Club's Samuel L'Frack Terrace, alongside names like Ernest Shackleton and Amelia Earhart.

Harris noted that the Inuit saved Matthew Henson's life. When after failure upon failure, Peary thought about giving up on the Pole, the Inuit convinced him to keep going. Seventeen Inuit women uprooted their lives and spent a year helping Peary to sew clothes and teaching survival skills. "Their names rarely appear in published accounts, and when they are mentioned, they are simply 'the women' or 'the wives,'" notes Genevieve LeMoine, curator of the Peary-MacMillan Arctic Museum at Bowdoin College.

After these speeches, outside on The Explorers Club terrace, four names were added to the stone plaques on the floor. "First to the North Pole—Ooqueah. Ootah. Egingwah. Seegloo." Their names are nearby the plaques of Teddy Roosevelt and Ernest Shackleton.

A flame was lit to commemorate the new plaques. And in a longtime tradition, a loud bell rang that could be heard throughout the six flights of the Club—the bell of USS *Cutter*, the ship that rescued Adolphus Greely. That bell, in 1884, was a symbol of a long overdue Arctic rescue. That bell, today, is a symbol of long overdue recognition.

Thor Heyerdahl planning his expedition at The Explorers Club, 1947, along with Seamus Chief of Clan Fearghail, second in command Herman Watzinger, and legendary explorer Peter Freuchen.

KON-TIKI

During World War II and for most of the 1940s, exploration had been knocked from the headlines and public consciousness—the world had more pressing matters. It would take a surprising expedition—involving a Norwegian and a raft—for exploration to recapture the public's imagination.

In 1947, you could find the Club's headquarters on West Seventy-Second Street, only a few blocks from where it is now. Here's how one member described it at the time: "There is nothing more than a brightly polished little brass plate with 'Explorers Club' on it to tell passers-by that there is anything out of the ordinary inside the doors. But, once inside, one might have made a parachute jump into a strange world, thousands of miles from New York's lines of motorcars flanked by sky-scrapers."

This young explorer, from Norway, was only a junior member at the time. When in New York he didn't miss a meeting. He liked that as soon as he stepped inside the Club, he was "swallowed up in an atmosphere of lion-hunting, mountaineering, and polar life." These were his people. Now in its fourth decade, the physical Club itself began to resemble its current form; as the young Norwegian observed, "Idols and model ships, flags, photographs and maps, surround the members of the club when they assemble for a dinner or to hear lecturers from distant countries."

The member's name was Thor Heyerdahl, and for him, like other members in both the 1940s and today, the Club was more than a place for socializing and swapping stories from distant lands. It was a place to do work. To rummage through the hundreds of maps and books and nautical journals. To tap into a collective knowledge that existed nowhere else on the planet.

On a rainy November evening in 1947, Heyerdahl popped into the Club, as he often did, and was surprised by what he saw. "In the middle of the floor lay an inflated rubber raft with boat rations and accessories, while parachutes, rubber overalls, safety jackets, and polar equipment covered walls and tables, together with balloons for water distillation, and other curious inventions," he later wrote. Heyerdahl had stumbled into one of the Club's many demonstrations of cutting-edge tech, or at least "cutting edge" at the time. A colonel in the military (also a Club member) was showing off the latest gizmos that could be deployed in the field, almost like the character Q in a Bond film.

Not every member was impressed. As the colonel demonstrated the rubber boat (an inflatable rescue dinghy), one Danish explorer shook his head and essentially said that it would never work, because he had once tried using a rubber boat in the Arctic, and a fishing hook got caught in the boat, sank it, and nearly killed him. Other members chimed in with their own opinions of the new tech, and a spirited debate ensued (another Club tradition).

The colonel took all of this criticism with good humor. Then he made the Club members a deal. He would let any active members test out the gear for free on their next expedition, as long as they wrote an honest assessment for him when they returned. As it happened, Heyerdahl was plotting a new expedition and this was precisely the kind of equipment he had been searching for.

Nearly a decade earlier, on an eighteen-month trip to the Polynesian islands with his wife, Heyerdahl was astonished to discover what seemed to be traces of the Inca. He turned to his wife and asked, as one does, "Have you noticed that the huge stone figures of Tiki [a Polynesian god] in the jungle are remarkably like the monoliths left by extinct civilizations in South America?"

His wife had not.

Almost no one had. In fact, the idea was radical, even blasphemous. At the time, every historian, anthropologist, and archaeologist thought that the Polynesian islands had been settled by people from Asia, not South America, because, so the thinking went, the Inca did not possess seafaring technology.

At the University of Oslo, Heyerdahl visited libraries and studied books in a wide range of fields, including mathematics, genetics, geography, zoology, philosophy, and ethnology. He uncovered bits of evidence that scholars had overlooked: Polynesian plants that could be traced to South America, Polynesian artifacts that resembled Peruvian artifacts, and, most compellingly, the mysterious god "Tiki" that the Inca once worshipped.

Heyerdahl spent years trying to convince the academics. But the scholars always had the same retort. When Heyerdahl pitched his ideas to one scholar, for example, the old man told him, "You're wrong, absolutely wrong."

The *Kon-Tiki*. The wind has made it hard to see, but
The Explorers Club flag is the second from top.

Heyerdahl carried Flag 123, which is now retired and hangs in The Explorers Club.

Rope from the *Kon-Tiki* raft. Heyerdahl was determined to use only materials that would have been available to the ancient Polynesians, like balsa and this rope. The rope is now in the Club's archives.

Heyerdahl asked him why.

"The answer's simple enough. They couldn't get there. They had no boats!"

"They had rafts," Heyerdahl protested, unwilling to let it go. "You know, balsa-wood rafts."

"Well, you can try a trip from Peru to the Pacific islands on a raft."

Now *that* was an interesting idea.

Which is now what brought Heyerdahl to The Explorers Club. He had taken his theory as far as he could in the library. Now he would go to the field. Years later, the NASA astronaut (and Club regular) Mike Massimino would think of exploration as coming in two different modes: "Galileo mode" and "Shackleton mode." Galileo mode is working in the library and labs. Shackleton mode is braving the hazards of the field.

Heyerdahl would enter Shackleton mode.

He would try to do something never attempted in modern times, and possibly never in history—he would build a raft using only the materials and technology available to the ancient Inca, and then he would sail that raft across the ocean.

He would call the raft *Kon-Tiki*.

So Heyerdahl, nearly broke, spent his nights in Brooklyn at the "Norwegian Sailors' Home" while he planned his mission at The Explorers Club. Given the importance of finding patrons for exploration, he tapped into the Club's network and made connections to government officials. He unrolled the maps and studied a large globe.

Soon Heyerdahl flew to Peru, where he searched for balsa trees that would approximate the kind of wood that the Inca would have used. This was its own mini adventure, as even in 1947 much of the Peruvian forest had been chopped down. The only balsa trees left were deep in a jungle. Using a combination of cargo plane, jeep, dumb luck, and assistance from the Peruvian military, Heyerdahl found his coveted logs.

The Peruvian government pitched in to help. Their incentive? If Heyerdahl pulled off his madman stunt, then it would bring pride and prestige to the nation. Suddenly the history books would need to be rewritten, casting Peru as a key international player.

So in the naval dockyard, a team of twenty Peruvian seamen helped Heyerdahl build his raft. They used only materials the Inca would have used. "Not a single spike, nail, or wire rope was used in the whole construction," Heyerdahl explained. They gathered nine gigantic logs, more than 30 feet in length, and lashed them together with 300 feet of rope. They built a small cabin that could fit six men.

Finally the raft was finished. A team from Peru's navy came to inspect this bizarre vessel, which was somehow supposed to travel 4,000 miles with no modern assistance. Some said the balsa would absorb water and then sink. Others said it would crack and snap. The Peruvian navy made bets on how many days it would take for them to die. One naval officer went even further, telling Heyerdahl that if he makes it across the ocean alive, he will buy him and the crew as much whiskey as they can drink for the rest of their lives.

The *Kon-Tiki* set sail on April 27, 1947. The humble raft raised its flags—the flags of Norway, France, the United States, and finally, the flag of The Explorers Club. After filling out an application, Heyerdahl had been permitted to check out Flag 123. He also brought four months' worth of food (including experimental military rations) and 275 gallons of water.

There was no rescue vehicle to shadow them. There was no plan B. They did bring an early ham radio that could let them reach civilization, but if Heyerdahl's hunch was wrong, they would almost certainly die.

So much depended on the balsa wood itself. If it became waterlogged, the raft would sink. Early in the trip, Heyerdahl stuck the tip of his finger into the damp wood of a crossbeam—the finger pressed so far in that water oozed out. Heyerdahl tore a chunk of that wood and tossed it into the ocean. It sank.

But to Heyerdahl's delight, as the days and weeks ticked by, the wood remained dry enough to float and bob along the ocean. The sailing was easy. The navigation was simple. Heyerdahl's entire theory was based on the trade winds, which he knew cold from studying all of those charts at The Explorers Club. The winds would blow them exactly where they needed to go.

Yet there are other ways to die in the ocean.

On May 24, around noon, Heyerdahl lay down on the raft, shirtless, and relaxed after a refreshing dip in the water. He felt the warm sun on his skin.

Suddenly he heard a member cry out: "SHARK!"

That itself didn't frighten Heyerdahl. They had seen sharks before and they knew how to handle them, but this was something else entirely—a whale shark.

It was 50 feet long. The jaw itself was the size of a man. "Walt Disney himself, with all his powers of imagination, could not have created a more hair-raising sea monster," wrote Heyerdahl. The beast swam around the *Kon-Tiki* slowly, menacingly. Heyerdahl knew that if it attacked, the raft would shatter.

Cover of the French edition of *Kon-Tiki and I* (1949), written by crew member Erik Hesselberg.

Heyerdahl grabbed a harpoon. So did the rest of the crew. They all stood at the sides of the raft, holding their harpoons, ready to strike. Heyerdahl knew these harpoons were like "toothpicks" to the whale shark, but what other choice did they have?

The whale shark continued to circle the raft. Once, twice, then a third time. It circled for another ten minutes. The men readied their harpoons. It circled for a full hour—it felt like a full day—filling the crew with dread.

One of the crew, Erik Hesselberg (the only professional sailor on the raft), could take the tension no longer. Hesselberg held the harpoon above his head. The whale shark saw him. Then the beast headed straight toward Hesselberg. The creature swam underneath the raft, just under Hesselberg, who, with all of his strength, stabbed the harpoon downward.

Hesselberg made contact. He struck the beast "deep into the whale shark's gristly head."

The Explorers Club

This is to certify that

THOR HEYERDAHL

is qualified and has been elected a

Member

of The Explorers Club

Given under our hand and seal

the EIGHTH day of JUNE 1942

President

Secretary

Heyerdahl made the cut—his certificate of membership to The Explorers Club.

"The *Kon-Tiki* expedition opened my eyes to what the ocean really is. It is a conveyor and not an isolator."
—Thor Heyerdahl

The whale shark swam away, and they never saw it again.

The men exhaled.

Not only did Heyerdahl and crew survive encounter after encounter with sharks, but they became so competent in this deadly game that they began killing sharks with their bare hands.

"Sharks soon became an almost daily occurrence," Heyerdahl explained. Lest you think this is a tall tale, photos and even videos show Heyerdahl manhandling sharks and then hauling their bodies on the raft. "One strong jerk and the shark is on deck," Heyerdahl explains calmly. They tried eating shark but didn't love it; it tasted like haddock.

At night, the men stared at the stars and basked in the silence. "The world was simple—stars in the darkness," Heyerdahl reflected. "Whether it was 1947 B.C. or A.D. suddenly became of no significance. . . . We were swallowed up in the absolute common measure of history—endless unbroken darkness under a swarm of stars."

Throughout the journey, using an early ham radio that was powered by a hand-cranked generator, Heyerdahl gave occasional updates to newspapers, and these dispatches captivated the world. As Club archivist Lacey Flint says, the dramatic radio updates from *Kon-Tiki* helped "bring exploration back into the spotlight."

And Heyerdahl made history on August 7, 1947. One hundred and one days into the journey, exactly as he had predicted, the *Kon-Tiki* reached the Polynesian islands.

"Hurrah!" Heyerdahl shouted as the raft crashed into a reef, nearly killing the entire crew. All six made it safely to shore, along with their journals and photos and essential supplies. Heyerdahl had done it. This was a stunning vindication of exploration as "adventure with purpose"—not just "adventuring for adrenaline."

He soon visited the White House and shook the hand of President Truman. He wrote a book that became a bestseller, and even made a documentary that won an Oscar. And in a solemn ceremony at The Explorers Club, Heyerdahl returned Flag 123, which, over the next fifty years, would travel to Mongolia, Cuba, and then back to the Polynesian islands.

Thor Heyerdahl, once the wide-eyed junior Club member, was now one of the most celebrated explorers on the planet.

But that's not the end of Heyerdahl's story. There was a hitch.

Decades later, another Club member—using Heyerdahl's own playbook—would show that his core theory was entirely wrong.

Illustration of the *Trieste*, which looks straight out of a Jules Verne novel.

FIRST TO THE DEEPEST POINT IN THE OCEAN

In 1904, the very same year that The Explorers Club was founded in New York City to share tales of the Arctic, an explorer across the Atlantic had a very different mission on his mind. While Greely and company cast their eyes north, Auguste Piccard, a gifted Swiss physicist, was interested in going up and down. Piccard was a young student at Zurich's Polytechnic School, and he also served as a balloon pilot in the Swiss army reserve. Piccard had a wild idea. If a balloon could help him fly in the sky, then maybe it could help him descend deep into the ocean.

Piccard sketched the idea of an "underwater free balloon" that he called the "bathyscaphe," from the Greek words for "deep" and "ship." Essentially, the bathyscaphe was made of two parts: a blimp-shaped metal shell filled with gasoline (which is lighter than water) and beneath that, a cabin for a two-person crew. It looked straight out of a Jules Verne novel. The pilot could raise or lower the bathyscaphe by discharging solid weights, or pellets, which changed its buoyancy.

It was brilliant. It was also decades ahead of its time. Piccard had the seeds of this unorthodox idea in 1904, but his prototype would not be tested until 1948. It first achieved a manned depth of 90 feet, not exactly the stuff of legends. So Piccard made improvements (in collaboration with the French navy). As he was then in his sixties, Piccard enlisted the help of his son, Jacques, who began to pilot the bathyscaphe. Both Piccards made more upgrades and finally, in the 1950s, they had a new and improved vessel: the *Trieste*.

The *Trieste* might be at the forefront of scientific innovation, but it was almost comically impractical to use. It had no real way to propel itself out into

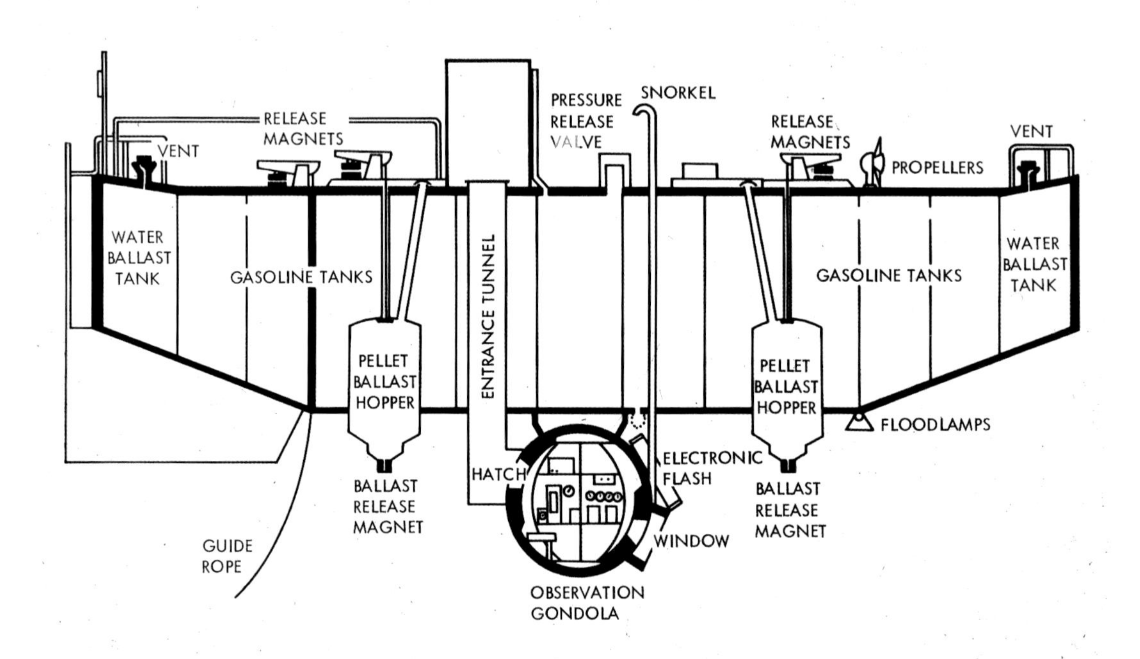

An illustration of the *Trieste*'s systems. As Walsh describes it, "The float had ballast tanks to provide positive buoyancy while on the surface. When vented, they filled with seawater so that the slightly heavy bathyscaphe would submerge. . . . Once the dive began, the descent is slowed or stopped by releasing solid weights. For this purpose, ballast containers (shot tubs) are fitted to the float. They contain several tons of very small steel pellets, or 'shot.'"

the ocean, so it needed to be tugged by other ships. It had no obvious commercial application. In short, it was expensive and a tough sell to investors.

But Piccard found one eager buyer: the US Navy.

Auguste Piccard no longer owned the *Trieste,* but he soon dispatched Jacques—the one person (besides himself) who knew its secrets—to work with the navy as a consultant. The Piccards were nearly all set: the US Navy would provide resources—the ships they needed to tug the *Trieste* into position for a dive, and the infrastructure in place in case anything went wrong. The Piccards just needed a pilot.

Enter a young navy lieutenant named Don Walsh.

The Piccards got lucky. It's hard to imagine a better fit for this mission than Walsh. As a kid growing up during the Great Depression, Walsh lived in the Bay Area—raised by a single working mom—and they shared a home on a hill with two other divorced mothers and their kids. From this perch, Walsh had an imperial view of San Francisco Bay, and he watched, spellbound, as the Golden Gate Bridge was being constructed.

As the bridge materialized from both sides of the Bay, he thought that it looked like "two great animals approaching each other." He watched the many ships coming and going. He tried to imagine their destinations. He wondered what else was out there. "This imprinted on me a desire to become a sailor of some sort," says Walsh now. During World War II (Walsh was too young to serve) he wanted to be a pilot, and he later briefly flew a J-2 Piper Cub with his local Civil Air Patrol, but ultimately he flunked the vision test.

The navy it would be.

Walsh served on his first submarine in 1956. "It's like your first girlfriend or your first kiss," says Walsh. "You always remember your first submarine." A few years later, when only twenty-eight years old, he found himself steering a strange new vessel called the *Trieste.*

Walsh, Jacques Piccard, and a team of fourteen took the *Trieste* to a naval ship repair station in Guam, which was near the Mariana Trench and the Challenger Deep, the deepest point of the ocean. It's nearly 7 miles deep. As James Cameron later put it, it's so deep that you could stack Mount Everest at the bottom with four Empire State Buildings on top and "not even break the surface."

The interior of the cabin itself, 38 cubic feet, was just roomy enough for two people to sit in chairs and monitor the walls of equipment. Or as Walsh describes the space: "If you're a megaoligarch, you probably have a refrigerator at home that's bigger than thirty-eight cubic feet. And if you're inside the bathyscaphe, it wasn't much warmer than the household refrigerator."

Walsh and Piccard did not rush things. They performed test after test. For several months in 1959, as Walsh remembers it, they worked "from dawn to dusk, seven days a week" to ensure the *Trieste* was up to scratch. They had no blueprint to follow. As Walsh says, this was like how the Wright brothers began, when there were only two flying airplanes in the world, "and they took turns flying them."

This meant that if a piece of equipment broke, which happened frequently, the team had to invent a replacement. "We were inventors by necessity," says Walsh. "It's the burden and fun of pioneering in a new field."

Like a runner training for a marathon with progressively longer routes, Piccard and Walsh descended to just a few hundred feet, then eventually 5,450 feet, and then 23,000.

Now they were ready for Challenger Deep. Virtually nothing was known about the deepest point on the planet—nothing about the creatures living there, the water pressure, the ecosystem. The only provisions they brought onboard were a stack of chocolate bars. (In a patriotic flourish, Walsh brought Hershey's and Piccard, the Swiss, brought Nestlé.)

Oceanographers knew that the Mariana Trench—1,580 miles long, and in the shape of a crescent—was roughly 200 miles southwest of Guam. But the precise location of Challenger Deep was trickier to locate. The problem was that the floor was so deep (7 miles!) that it was out of range of the navy ship's depth-sounder. The solution? Bombs.

Small blocks of TNT were dropped into the sea. "Using a stopwatch, we would start it when the charge went off and stop it when we heard the return echo on the ship's fathometer hydrophone," explains Walsh, clarifying that other members of the naval team did the bombing. This gave them an "acoustic survey" to locate the Challenger Deep. "We did not care about exact depth measurement, only that fourteen seconds was deeper than twelve seconds, and so on."

Soon the bombs gave the answer: they had found the right location. And at 0830 on January 19, 1960, the *Trieste* sank beneath the surface.

In the first few hundred feet of the descent, Walsh and Piccard could still see the bluish water of the Pacific. By 600 feet, the water turned to a dark gray. And soon Walsh could see only darkness. When you are deep enough in the ocean, it looks like outer space.

They sank farther into the depths. At 4,000 feet, there were signs of trouble: some water drops began to weep into the hull. This wasn't alarming, as weeping had occurred during the dives. "The remedy was simple," Walsh explains with his typical matter-of-fact logic. "If the number of drops increased with depth, the dive was over and then we would surface."

Don Walsh and Jacques Piccard at the bottom of the sea, each holding their nation's flag.

They plunged farther into the darkness: 10,000 feet. 15,000 feet.

At 31,000 feet, Walsh and Piccard heard a loud snap. It turns out that a window had cracked.

This, of course, could mean death. But it's that very logic that convinced them not to worry too much about it—if the window had truly broken, then they would already be dead. ("It was not a pressure boundary," says Walsh, "and therefore not a mission critical.")

So they kept descending.

And all of these years later, Walsh tells the story as if there really wasn't much drama at all. That's how exploration often works in real life as opposed to the movies. "We had been doing increasingly deeper test dives for several months," says Walsh. All of the manipulations to operate the *Trieste* were the same, he says, whether you're dunking 70 feet in a Guam harbor or plunging deeper than any human in history. "Really, it was just another day at the office."

At 34,000 feet, Walsh flipped on the fathometer, which is used to measure depth; it let them gauge the distance to the ocean floor and had a range of 300 feet. They flipped on the *Trieste*'s outside lights that, hopefully, would reveal a glow when the light reflected off the floor.

Walsh, Piccard, and the crew after making history.

Then 35,000 feet. Nothing from the fathometer, nothing from the lights.

They sensed they were close, so they slowed their descent even more.

Nearly 36,000 feet. Walsh could see that the bottom was near. They moved even slower.

Suddenly Piccard noticed something. "Do you see that fish on the bottom?"

Walsh looked out the viewport and then he saw it—what seemed to be a white flatfish, about a foot long, that looked a bit like a halibut. (This later sparked a debate in the scientific community: Could a vertebrate live that deep in the sea?)

Then, at roughly 36,000 feet beneath the surface, the *Trieste* finally landed with a gentle thud. Walsh and Piccard had just traveled deeper into the earth than any humans in all of history.

The two men shook hands. And as matter-of-fact as Walsh can be, he knew in that moment that this was no ordinary day at the office. They had brought a camera into the tiny cabin (courtesy of *Life* magazine); aiming it at themselves, they snapped a photo holding the flags of both the United States and Switzerland. Walsh considers it one of the world's first selfies.

And what does the bottom of the world look like? At the time Walsh still wasn't sure. The *Trieste*'s lights did give a hint of visibility, but the landing of the vessel stirred up so much sediment that when he looked out the window, all he could see was a "bowl of milk."

Once the Trieste surfaced, Walsh and Piccard climbed to the top of the vessel in triumph. They posed for a photo that would make the cover of *Life,* and the magazine declared the mission "one of the most significant explorations of the 20th century."

For most explorers, this would be a career capstone. But for Walsh, incredibly, his journey had just begun, and it would continue for the next sixty-plus years. Walsh was eighty-nine years old when interviewed for this book. He spoke with the verve and sharpness of a young college professor. Walsh became an oceanographer, he commanded submarines, he dove to the *Titanic,* and he has made forty expeditions to the Antarctic and three trips to the North Pole. Because Walsh has done so much work in the Antarctic, part of the region (the Walsh Spur ridge) is named after him.

Walsh joined The Explorers Club in 1961. He served on the Club's board, he was an honorary president for fifteen years, and he was named an "Honorary Member," joining an exclusive list of explorers that has included Matthew Henson, Tenzing Norgay, Edmund Hillary, Chuck Yeager (of *The Right Stuff* fame), and the Apollo astronauts. Honorary Membership "is an interesting category," says Walsh with a hint of a smile. "The bylaws only permit twenty living Honorary Members at one time, so somebody has to die to create an opening." (It's almost like the Supreme Court of The Explorers Club.) Walsh is one of the longest-tenured members in the Club's history, having been active for more than half of its existence.

As a kid growing up in the Great Depression, he had watched the construction of the Golden Gate Bridge and dreamed of following those ships to unknown destinations. That's a dream he keeps pursuing, even now. He's making plans to visit the Antarctic, Chile, Argentina, and Spain. Because apparently if you're a living legend at The Explorers Club, ninety is the new thirty.

And as for Jacques Piccard and his father, Auguste? That family's story is far from over. Not only is a Piccard the inspiration for Jean-Luc Picard of *Star Trek*'s *Enterprise,* but Jacques's son, Bertrand, who is also a member of The Explorers Club, is working to revolutionize air travel as we know it.

To be continued . . .

Buzz Aldrin on the moon.

FIRST TO THE MOON: APOLLO NIGHT AT THE EXPLORERS CLUB

Throughout its history, The Explorers Club's elders have passed what they have learned to the younger generations. This role of mentorship is one reason why, in 2019, on the fiftieth anniversary of the Apollo 11 mission, the astronauts gathered with their colleagues for a historic night at the Club.

The majority of the surviving Apollo astronauts—Michael Collins, Charlie Duke, Rusty Schweickart, Walt Cunningham, Harrison Schmitt, Fred Haise, Al Worden, and Buzz Aldrin—sat down to swap memories, reminisce, and share bits of wisdom with the younger explorers. The mood was relaxed. (In a quiet whisper, Buzz Aldrin complimented Michael Collins on his socks.)

Richard Garriott, son of the astronaut Owen Garriott, facilitated this conversation between old friends. The Club members inched forward in their seats, all too aware that this was a once-in-a-lifetime opportunity.

In honor of the eighteen planned Apollo missions, here are eighteen insights—some silly, some surprising, some profound—that the legendary astronauts shared at The Explorers Club that historic evening.

1. THEY'RE GRATEFUL FOR THE "LADIES OF DOVER, DELAWARE."

Today there's a growing appreciation for NASA's women mathematicians (many of whom were Black) who were long overlooked. There are many stories like this. As Michael Collins told the Club, he often thinks of the women who were instrumental in creating the suits astronauts wore in outer space.

A core part of the astronauts' pressure suits, explained Collins, is the rubber bladder. Seamstresses were hired to make the pressure suits because they were so tailored to the intricacies of the human body. "Their job was intricate, and a very ancient technique of cutting strips of rubber that would make this extremely mobile, complex object," said Collins. "If one of them messed up just a tiny bit, Neil would have gotten out and started to say, 'One small step . . .' and then he'd say 'Oops!' And air would be leaking out of his bladder."

Collins noted that this is just one small example, and that there are countless jobs like this that went unheralded, "but I always think of the little Ladies of Dover, Delaware, with their glue pots."

2. FAILURES BEGET PROGRESS.

On January 27, 1967, the astronauts Roger Chaffee, Ed White, and Gus Grissom were training for Apollo 1. They ran simulations in the command and service module (CSM). Then a cabin fire erupted. Within minutes they were dead.

This was a grim reminder that the risks of exploration were still real and the stakes were mortal.

"A lot of things weren't working in those days," said Walt Cunningham, who was on the backup crew of Apollo 1 and knew the deceased astronauts well. Cunningham, like all of NASA, was devastated by the loss, but it didn't make him want to quit. He wanted to get better.

As Cunningham explained, "That initiated changes in the Apollo program . . . everybody started operating differently." In the wake of the fire, said Cunningham, NASA made more than a thousand changes to the spacecraft, so by the time he flew the CSM on Apollo 7, "to this day, Apollo 7 is still considered the longest, most ambitious, most successful new test flight of any new flying machine, ever. And a lot of that came about because our friends, Griss and White and Chaffee, sacrificed their lives."

3. THE FIRST WORDS SPOKEN ON THE MOON ARE NOT WHAT YOU THINK.

As every third grader knows, when Armstrong's boot struck the moon he declared it to be "one small step for man, one giant leap for mankind."

But these were not the first words spoken.

When the lunar module gently touched down on the lunar surface, it was Buzz Aldrin's job to monitor the instruments and verbally acknowledge

Michael Collins practices in the command module simulator
on June 19, 1969, at the Kennedy Space Center.

Buzz Aldrin descends from the LM [lunar module], aka the *Eagle*, and prepares to walk on the moon. As he revealed to the Club, this was more complicated than it looks.

contact. So when the dashboard panel "Contact" illuminated—meaning the LM's sensors were on the ground—Aldrin excitedly said, "Contact light!"

As Aldrin told the Club, only half kidding, "Mine were the first words on the moon. Contact light. Engine stop."

4. THE "SMALL STEP" ISN'T AS SMALL AS YOU'D GUESS FROM THE TV FOOTAGE.

Aldrin wanted to clear up a common misconception. "The bottom of the [LM's] ladder is not the lunar surface," he explained. It's a large pad with the landing gear. "Now when you come down the ladder and you get to the last rung, and you jump down from there, you're not on the moon yet. You're on the landing pad."

And that last rung posed a challenge. "Now, Neil had a good idea. He said, 'I think that because we may get tired out there, we ought to see if we can jump back up to that bottom rung on the ladder.' Good thought, Neil!"

The Club chuckled; Aldrin shared the part that's usually omitted from the Apollo coverage.

"So we did that. . . . And I got down to the bottom . . . and then jumped up. . . . And I missed. And I had to do it again. 'C'mon, Buzz!' "

5. LONELINESS WAS A MYTH. BUT CONCERN FOR THE "WHITE MICE" WAS REAL.

When Armstrong and Aldrin descended to the moon, Michael Collins remained all by himself in lunar orbit in the CSM, which is why he was often described as the "loneliest man in history."

Nope.

"I was not lonely. I had a happy little home in the command module," said Collins.

His real concern was the white mice.

At the time, NASA feared the moon-trotting astronauts might come back to Earth with lethal pathogens. So they would be quarantined. To help assess the risk of any pathogens, NASA sent a batch of white mice along with the astronauts. Collins obsessed over the mice. "If one of those poor little things didn't do too well, we were in deep trouble," said Collins with a chuckle. "So every time I was asked, 'Weren't you the most lonely person,' I would think, 'Oh God, those poor little white mice, I hope they're doing all right.' "

6. "IT WAS A VERY SIMPLE THING."

The astronauts are humble. During the Apollo 15 expedition, for example, Al Worden was the first person to do a spacewalk in deep space; his job was to retrieve film magazines from the mapping cameras. Worden described the technical tasks he had to perform to the Club and then said matter-of-factly, "It was a very simple thing."

This kind of modesty made an impression on the younger members, such as Lisandro Martinez, an Argentinian polar researcher who was then new to the Club. "They explored with so much humility," Martinez later said, adding that after this night, "I understood the mission of the Club."

7. WE MIGHT REMEMBER "ONE SMALL STEP," BUT THE REAL PROJECT WAS A "DAISY CHAIN."

"The public today doesn't realize the steps it took to get there," said Walt Cunningham, noting that as the decades have passed, we tend to forget about all of the Mercury and Gemini and Apollo missions that led to the culmination of Apollo 11. Each step was critical. And progress can look slow at the start.

Michael Collins thought of the flights as a "long and fragile daisy chain of events, and if any link in the chain breaks, that's the end of it."

The most fragile link in this daisy chain, according to Collins, was not actually landing on the moon, but getting off it.

And we'll let Buzz Aldrin tell this story . . .

8. APOLLO 11 CAME PRECARIOUSLY CLOSE TO DISASTER.

"We came pretty close to not being able to come home," said Aldrin.

After he and Armstrong had planted the flag and moonwalked, what the jubilant planet didn't realize at the time—NASA kept this a secret—is that just before Aldrin went to sleep that first night, he noticed a "little black object that didn't belong there."

It was a piece of a circuit breaker. Something had broken. It turns out that when Aldrin reentered the LM after the moon walk, his backpack had knocked into the circuit breaker. And it wasn't just any circuit breaker—it was the breaker for the engine that would propel them off the lunar surface. This engine was critical. If it failed, Aldrin and Armstrong would starve to death on the moon, flipping this moment of triumph into perhaps the most scarring tragedy in the history of exploration.

"We didn't know what the hell we can possibly do," Aldrin explained.

When they went to sleep, they didn't have a solution. Mission Control would work on it through the night. When they woke up, Mission Control still didn't have a solution.

But they did have one last idea. In a burst of desperate inspiration, Aldrin used a pen to push in the circuit breaker.

"Hey, we got circuit! Hey, we got power!" Aldrin realized, euphoric, and thanks to his quick thinking, the world never had to hear the phrase "The *Eagle* is grounded."

9. LIFTOFF IS SNEAKY QUIET.

"In every movie that you've ever seen about space, if there's a rocket engine going, it's like . . ." Rusty Schweickart waved his arms frantically and made a series of loud noises, indicating how noisy and turbulent it's usually portrayed.

"That's not true at all," said Schweickart, the LM pilot on Apollo 9. The very beginning is loud. But then "ten seconds after liftoff it's almost totally quiet."

10. ROBOTS CAN'T REPLACE HUMANS.

"It's always the things that you never plan for that crop up on a flight," said Al Worden, who then shared his own example. On Apollo 15, when they filled the water tank before the flight, "the guy who filled it did not tighten the cap enough."

This meant that in the zero gravity of flight, water oozed through the film cap. It formed a little ball on top of the tube. And that ball kept getting bigger. "In space, it didn't have any place to go," said Worden. "This could be a really serious thing. If it ever broke loose and started floating around . . . it could start shorting out electronics, and you've got a big problem."

The only way to deal with the growing water blob, they eventually realized, was to wrap it in a towel, which absorbed the water. This is the kind of improvisation that's crucial to exploration. "Robots will never, never take the place of people in space," said Worden. "That's because they can only do what they're programmed to do. People can at least think a little outside the box."

"Earthrise." Taken aboard Apollo 8 by Bill Anders, on Christmas Eve, this iconic photo shows Earth peeking out from beyond the lunar surface. Astronauts Frank Borman and Jim Lovell were aboard; they were the first crewed spacecraft to circumnavigate the moon. Wilderness photographer Galen Rowell later called it "the most influential environmental photograph ever taken."

11. THE "OVERVIEW EFFECT" IS REAL. . . .

When John Glenn first went into orbit, he looked out the window and said, his voice full of awe, "Oh, that view is tremendous."

Seeing Earth from space has since been called the "Overview Effect," and the Apollo astronauts found that the reality matched the hype. "There's that jewel of Earth that's suspended in the blackness of space," said Charlie Duke. "It was breathtaking."

12. . . . AND THE OVERVIEW EFFECT HAS CONSEQUENCES.

Rusty Schweickart went even further than Duke. "I just looked in awe at this incredibly beautiful planet. And all of these questions came floating in," he said, and the questions came in the dead silence of space. "How did I get here? Why am I here? . . . What do I mean when I say, Am I *me*? Or am I *us*?"

It took Schweickart several years to process these questions. But eventually he came to realize that "we have a responsibility to preserve life, and to continue this unbelievable process of evolution that we are a part of."

Schweickart felt that this was the real message. That he was "a sensing element for humanity, as we begin moving out from Mother Earth into the cosmos." He thinks of this moment as "Cosmic Birth," the moment of birth out of planet Earth. "If you think about human birth, it's only *after* birth that we love our mother," said Schweickart. "Before that we're just totally dependent on her. But after birth, we recognize that not only do we love our mother, but we also have responsibility for our mother."

13. WE STILL NEED TO TAKE RISKS.

Walt Cunningham has found that as our society has evolved, there's a heavy focus on mitigating risk. "And that's a good thing," he said. "But at the same time . . . we were fighting like hell to have that particular opportunity, and that was risky, because it was the first."

As Charlie Duke said, "If you're going to accomplish something, you have to take risks. Spaceflight is not risk-free. And I have seen a change, I think, in some of the organizations . . . they don't want to take any risks. They don't want to fly. . . . And that's sad."

Duke said that after the cabin fire that tragically killed the crew of Apollo 1, many felt like the program was dead in the water. "But we weren't giving up," said Duke. "[We said], *We're going to do this!* The attitude was, Let's fix this! We gotta go! We gotta launch! And I see that missing a little bit right now."

14. THE TRIUMPH WAS GLOBAL.

The space race might have been the US versus the USSR, but something interesting happened in the aftermath.

Also in attendance that night was Club member Kathryn Sullivan, who in 1978 was selected as one of the first six women astronauts. Sullivan noted that whenever she travels internationally and speaks to people about the moon landing, they almost feel like they're a part of it.

"I think everyone I've met regardless of their nationality talks about when *we* went to the moon. Mankind," said Sullivan. "Tell me something else that had that kind of aspirational, unifying effect across cultures, religions, and combat boundaries and diplomatic hassles. That really stuck with me. . . . It's a *world* accomplishment."

15. TO BECOME AN ASTRONAUT, FOLLOW YOUR PASSIONS.

"Do whatever turns you on," said Al Worden, when asked to give advice for aspiring astronauts. "I think it's very important that young people follow their educational interests in things they really love to do." Worden's logic? If you lean into subjects and topics that genuinely interest you, the odds are you'll do better.

(He then adds, in a bit of real talk, "You've got to be really outstanding to be an astronaut.")

16. THEY'RE BULLISH ON THE FUTURE OF SPACE EXPLORATION.

The last time a human stepped foot on the moon was 1972. Over fifty years and counting. "The [NASA] program has evolved much slower than anyone would have acknowledged back in the day," said Rusty Schweickart, who cofounded the Association of Space Explorers. But now he's optimistic about the future.

Schweickart praised the innovation occurring in the private sector, calling it the "real juice" of space exploration—specifically crediting the reusability of first-stage rockets, which dramatically slashes the cost of launches. He then acknowledged the elephant in the room. "I'm not sure we would've ever gotten there if it wasn't for some semi-wacko named Elon Musk."

Laughter throughout the Club. (In the Club, as in the broader world, Musk is a polarizing figure.)

"The day will come when we're going to be living and working in space," said Worden. "We're going to need plumbers, we're going to need electricians, we're going to need all kinds of service people. . . . I think there's going to be room for everybody in space."

17. THEY'RE PROUD OF THE SCIENCE.

Since the inception of the Club—or perhaps for all history—there has been a tug-of-war in exploration between the glory of "being first" and the substantive benefits of science. Think back to Greely. The mission was to gather scientific data as part of the International Polar Year, but there was also the not-so-hidden objective of getting as close to the Pole as possible.

This was also true for the Apollo program. In a sense, the race between the US and the USSR to "get to the moon first" was little different from Amundsen and Scott's chase to the South Pole—it was about pride and glory and honor and even a bit of ego. This goes with the territory. But even though it rarely fetches headlines, the astronauts remain proud of their scientific legacy.

Consider the rocks.

After Armstrong descended the ladder, before he planted the flag or posed for the camera, he reached for the ground and scooped up a "contingency sample" of lunar rocks and soil. That's how important this was to NASA—it was the very first assignment.

When Lisandro Martinez said that on this night he sensed "the mission of the Club," this is what he meant. To use exploration to further human knowledge. To answer questions.

To inspire.

Which brings us to their final lesson . . .

18. THE SYMBOL ENDURES.

It's not lost on these legends that ultimately, in the end, what they did was inspire. They inspired explorers and they inspired the world.

They know the moon landing was more than just an expedition. More than expanding the map and chasing dragons. More, even, than unleashing scientific breakthroughs. This was a symbol that will last for generations and centuries and millennia.

We'll let Aldrin and Armstrong have the final word.

On July 23, 1969, the three Apollo 11 astronauts journeyed home from the moon. And from the capsule of Apollo 11, Aldrin addressed the people of planet Earth: "We've come to the conclusion that this has been far more than three men on a voyage to the moon. More, still, than the efforts of a government and industry team. More, even, than the efforts of one nation. We feel that this stands as a symbol of the insatiable curiosity of all mankind to explore the unknown."

Then Armstrong articulated what all of the Apollo astronauts have said for years: They had help. So much help. Armstrong knew there were four hundred thousand women and men who made the impossible possible. The engineers, the designers, the testers, the iron welders, the Ladies of Dover, Delaware—even the technicians in a Guam tracking station who helped ensure they would come home safely. He thanked them. "To those people, tonight, we give a special thank you. . . . Good night from Apollo 11."

The Apollo astronauts celebrating at The Explorers Club.

The Explorers Club flag that accompanied Armstrong, Aldrin, and Collins to the moon. It now hangs proudly at the Club.

Common Traits of Explorers

CURIOSITY

The biggie. "Almost universally, explorers suffer from an overabundance of curiosity," says former Club president Richard Wiese. "You'll find that as a recurring theme. People are driven to see what's over that hillside."

VITALITY

"It's too simple to say 'energetic,' but there's a certain amount of kinetic energy for all of the organizing you have to do, and going to a new place, and getting out of your comfort zone," says Ted Janulis. "There's a vitality that comes with explorers. . . . It's getting out there and doing something."

STUBBORNNESS

"They back up their curiosity with determination and courage," says the oceanographer Dawn Wright. "And sometimes they're stubborn. They say, 'I'm going to make this work. I'm going to find a way to make this work regardless of what you tell me.'"

STORYTELLERS

"Explorers are all storytellers," says Wiese. "It's something so universal. Whether your image is an Aboriginal person in Australia, or a Shaman in South America . . . there was always that one person who stood over that fire and says, 'You'll never guess what happened to me. You'll never guess what I saw.'"

OPEN-MINDEDNESS

"Being open-minded not only to new ideas and new cultures and new people, but also to be open to the uncertainties that are involved," says the conservationist Natalie Knowles. She suspects it's more than even being open, but even *looking* for uncertainties, and being comfortable with running out of gas on the Amazon River. "Enjoying that process of going with the flow and seeing where that takes you."

COMPULSION

"It's a disease, almost a psychological condition," says Trevor Wallace, only half-kidding. "It's an earnest will to share what you've found through the journeys that you take."

QUESTIONING THE BOUNDARIES

Explorers see the world differently. "They don't see the boundaries, they see the possibilities," says filmmaker (and Club member) Jimmy Chin, who took the photo on the opposite page. "They don't see the limitations; they see the potential in life."

UNDERSTANDING OF IMPACT

"I think that before we explore, we have to think about what kind of impact our activities will have," maintains conservationist Callie Veelenturf. Impact on the local communities, impact on the environment, and even impact on the planet. Given our environmental crisis, says Veelenturf, "the money that exists for exploration should be utilized for a tangible purpose. To do good. To make a change. To collect some data that will inform a policy."

BEING A HUMAN

Milbry Polk says that at some level the desire to explore is simply human. It's in all of us. "Everybody is an explorer, not just a few elite people," says Polk. "It's from our ancestors. If you're curious, then that's the first step of being an explorer."

While membership was not yet open to women in 1932, Amelia Earhart was the guest of honor and anchored Ladies' Night at The Explorers Club.

“WHY ARE THERE NO GIRLS?”

At the end of Apollo Night at The Explorers Club, for one of the final questions, Richard Garriott brought his young children to the stage. (Incidentally, both of them are explorers—two of the youngest people to reach the North Pole.)

Garriott’s six-year-old daughter, Kinga, wearing a blue NASA flight suit, had a very simple question for the Apollo astronauts: “Why are there no girls?”

The room broke into thunderous applause.

Walt Cunningham tried to answer the girl’s question. He focused on the fact that NASA wanted to start with test pilots, because test pilots would be best suited to handle the rigors of space, and that test pilots were used to “sticking your neck out there.” Left unspoken was the reality that in the 1960s all of the test pilots were men.

On the surface, in a literal sense, Cunningham’s answer was true, and it’s important to acknowledge the stark facts. But it left the room unsatisfied.

Then Rusty Schweickart gave a simpler answer: “It’s because the world was not quite as smart as we are now.”

The room erupted in applause again.

Much like the Constitution of the United States, the founding documents of The Explorers Club contain language and logic that undercut its grander purpose. Or to be more candid, the documents were sexist. The 1905 bylaws state that “persons eligible for active membership shall be men who have engaged in exploration, or who have added to the geographic knowledge of the world.”

As the Club’s longtime archivist Lacey Flint puts it, “The interesting thing about history is that it’s not always easy, and it depends on who’s telling the story.” For nearly a century that history was told by men, and that history is packed with contradictions. Early on, the Club realized that it could benefit from the contributions of women explorers, even as it denied women membership. By 1912, women explorers, such as the prolific travel writer Ethel Brilliana Tweedie, began speaking at the Club. These lectures were so popular that the Club instituted a regular series of Ladies' Nights, featuring explorers like Mabel Cook Cole, an anthropologist who studied folktales.

The Club would lurch backward before moving forward. In 1925, five years after the Nineteenth Amendment granted women the right to vote, the Club's board minutes stated that "ladies shall be invited to the Club on not more than two special occasions during each year."

This baffling decision made no sense to women like Harriet Chalmers Adams, an explorer who once crossed Haiti on horseback, wrote dozens of articles for the National Geographic Society, and hurled herself into the trenches of World War I to serve as a war correspondent. Frustrated with The Explorers Club's Neanderthal policies, she cofounded the Society of Women Geographers, an organization that exists to this day.

The policy certainly made no sense to Amelia Earhart. After her historic solo flight across the Atlantic, she gave a lecture at the Club to the awe and appreciation of its members. By now the Club realized it had to do something. The 1932 board minutes officially acknowledged her "splendid accomplishment and . . . acts of calm courage," and created an "honorary role of women." As Flint puts it, this meant that women could now "be a part of the Club, sort of, but not an official member."

Incredibly, the exclusion of women lasted for another five decades. And in 1981, that policy made no sense to a well-known member of the Club. "Women had played a significant but unheralded role in the history of exploration," wrote Carl Sagan, stating what should be obvious to all.

Women had been adventuring, exploring, and contributing to human knowledge—they just didn't need the fame or glory. And they did it all without recognition or support from the Club. Sagan reminded his colleagues of just a few examples: "There are several women astronauts. The earliest footprints—3.6 million years old—made by a member of the human family have been found in a volcanic ash flow in Tanzania by Mary Leakey. Trailblazing studies of the behavior of primates in the wild have been performed by dozens of young women, each spending years with a different primate species. Jane Goodall's studies of the chimpanzee are the best known of the investigations which illuminate human origins.

Margaret Mead (top left), Harriet Chalmers Adams (top right),
Ethel Tweedie (bottom left), and Josephine Peary with Inuit (bottom right).
All contributed to exploration, even if they received little to no credit at the time.

Ace pilot Bessie Coleman, a pioneer of early aviation, who was affectionately called "Queen Bess" and "Brave Bessie." The first Black woman and first Native American to become a pilot, she was known for her daring stunts and aviation acrobatics in numerous air shows. She gave speeches around the country that promoted both civil rights and aviation. In 1926, Coleman was tragically killed in a plane crash at the age of thirty-four.

"The undersea depth record is held by Sylvia Earle," Sagan continued in his letter. "The solar wind was first measured *in situ* by Marcia Neugebauer, using the Mariner 2 spacecraft. The first active volcanos beyond the earth were discovered on the Jovian moon Io by Linda Morabito, using the Voyager 1 spacecraft. These examples of modern exploration and discovery could be multiplied a hundredfold. They are of true historical significance. If membership in The Explorers Club is restricted to men, the loss will be ours; we will only be depriving ourselves."

The Club listened (finally); the policy was changed. New members included exploration icons such as oceanographer Sylvia Earle, archaeologist Anna Roosevelt, and astronaut Kathryn Sullivan. "Women have always been explorers. It's in our DNA. That's what makes us human," says Milbry Polk, an explorer who, at the age of twenty-three, crossed Egypt on a camel to retrace the route of Alexander the Great. She wondered why she didn't encounter more women explorers, and she was puzzled as to why they were so rarely featured in the history books.

So she decided to write her own. After decades of meticulous research—Polk's personal library includes 1,200 books on women explorers—she wrote *Women of Discovery,* which celebrates the contributions of women like Gudrid Thorbjarnardóttir, who, in roughly AD 1000, traveled from Iceland to Rome, making her perhaps the first person to bring news of the "new world" to Europe. (This was five hundred years before Columbus.)

Women were admitted to the Club in 1981, but reservations would linger for years. Consider the senior leadership. As recently as 2000, the Club had never elected a female president. A British conservationist named Faanya Rose, who had climbed in the Nepalese Everest region multiple times, dared to challenge the status quo. She wrote notes to all of the women in the Club and included the tagline "I will be your voice." She also wrote a letter to an elder Norwegian explorer. As Rose now remembers it, he said to her, "I like what you say. It would be my privilege to sponsor you to the board." The explorer was *Kon-Tiki*'s Thor Heyerdahl, then eighty-five years old, who helped secure Rose's election as president of The Explorers Club.

Rose now says she has no criticism of her predecessors, as "we all stand on the shoulders of those who came before." And in her personal experience, even in the "old days," the actual environment wasn't that retrograde. "The reputation that we were a group of grumpy old men members . . . that was more of a reputation than a reality," says Rose. "I didn't feel any resistance to my becoming president."

But she does feel that her election helped make the Club more inclusive, and that she helped "change the atmosphere of the Club." And during her tenure, the Club began to focus more on conservation, arguably its most crucial work today.

And the numbers are beginning to catch up. In terms of the Club's membership rolls, "men had a seventy-five to eighty-year head start," notes Flint, but says that in the last few years, "the young members coming into the Club are actually more women than men."

During the Club's celebration of Apollo 11, Kathryn Sullivan, one of the Club's first female members (and who helped deploy the Hubble Space Telescope), was asked to give advice to young women who wanted to become astronauts. "Pay attention to people that impress and inspire you," said Sullivan. "They don't have to look like you. They don't have to be female. They don't have to be your race."

Astronauts Kathy Sullivan and Sally Ride (both Club members), in space on October 13, 1984—aboard the Space Shuttle Challenger on mission STS-41G, the first flight to include two women.

She encourages the asking of questions—something good explorers always do. "Can I be courageous? Can I dare? Can I build something? Can I explore something no one's ever done before? *People* do that," Sullivan said. "People of all sorts of stripes and flavors. Think about that. Take notes from anyone you meet, and anyone you read about." (This could even be in the pages of a book about The Explorers Club, for example.)

Sullivan gives a few final bits of advice to young women: "Aim high. Dream big. Work hard. You will meet people who think it is their prerogative to edit the list of things that you are allowed to be interested in. No one's allowed to edit the list of things that you are interested in. If you're interested, you're interested. . . . If you're interested in something, explore it."

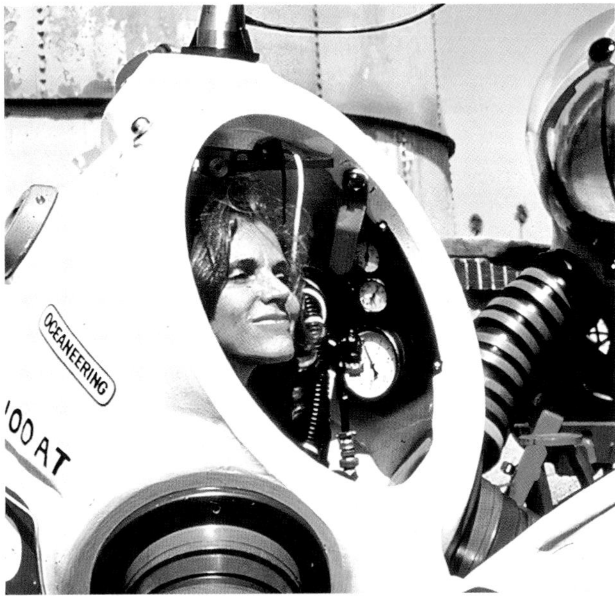

Mountaineer Lhakpa Sherpa (who has climbed Everest ten times; top left), oceanographer Sylia Earle (top right), anthropologist Jane Goodall (bottom left), and conservationist and former Club president Faanya Rose (bottom right).

Dr. Edith Widder diving in the deep diving suit,
named "Wasp," off the coast of Santa Barbara in 1984.

SEEING THE (UNDERWATER) LIGHT

Kathryn Sullivan's advice of "if you're interested in something, explore it" channels the experience of another iconic Club member.

"The adults on the beach warned me, 'You're going to get hurt, little girl. Stop! That tail is poisonous.' But I knew they were wrong. I always knew the horseshoe crabs on the shoreline weren't dangerous; I thought they were the coolest creatures ever," explained Sylvia Earle in *The Explorers Journal*.

As a young girl, Sylvia had questions about the world and about the ocean. "From my early childhood days on a ten-acre farm in New Jersey, where I explored the nearby woods, to my teenaged years in Florida, where I roamed the beaches and befriended horseshoe crabs, my parents encouraged me to be curious, to venture out on my own, and to treat others with dignity and respect," says Earle. "When I told them I wanted to be a biologist, they warned me that most girls did not do that, and that it might be tough to make a living, but they told me to follow my heart. They said, 'whatever it is, we are behind you.'"

And for this the ocean is thankful. Sylvia Earle, of course, is the oceanographer now known as "Her Deepness," and *Time* magazine's first "Hero for the Planet." She holds the record for the deepest walk on the seafloor, she was the first woman to serve as chief scientist at the National Oceanographic and Atmospheric Administration, and she once even fought off an angry shark. (Your move, Thor Heyerdahl.)

Earle has deservedly been decorated with every type of public honor, such as National Geographic's Explorer in Residence. But then there are the private awards such as this rare, hallowed ceremony at The Explorers Club.

The candles were lit. The fireplace roared. Club members, clad in black tie, held candles as they marched with Sylvia Earle up the stairway and into the Clark Room. Then a loud bell tolled—the very bell from the ship that rescued Adolphus Greely.

The members began a chant. "Earle! Earle! Earle! Earle!"

Faanya Rose gave a speech to honor Earle, happily noting a shift in the Club's history. She acknowledged that the Club was founded by a "group of gentlemen," but "little did they imagine that women would take the Club by storm, or rather on a wave, in the eighties when Sylvia came on the scene." She joked that Earle's career was like a Tootsie Pop because it "goes on and on."

Rose, like all members in attendance, held a glass of brandy. After her speech, in a dramatic flourish, she tossed the brandy into the fireplace, or the "Great Fire of Exploration." Each member in turn gave a speech, then tossed their brandy into the flames.

"We are at the sweet spot of human history," Earle later said. "More has been learned about the ocean in the last decade than throughout all of human history. For the first time, we have access to information about our ocean as never before. Now we can actually do something. What will we do with this new knowledge? As a new generation that knows more than anyone has ever known before, what will you do with your future?"

Some Club members have an answer. One of them is an oceanographer named Edith Widder.

As a kid, Edith Widder liked to climb trees. One Sunday afternoon, after church, she was still wearing a "stupid frilly dress" that she hated. Her parents told her she could go out and play if she promised to stay clean.

She agreed to the promise. And she didn't break it. When she climbed her favorite tree and jumped down, at the last second, she remembered her promise and leaped in a way that protected her dress but not her back. She felt a stab of pain.

At first she shrugged it off, but the lower back pain never really went away. During her freshman year at Tufts it became so bad that she couldn't sit or stand. Finally, she saw a doctor and they said the only thing they could do, as a last resort, was to attempt a dangerous spinal fusion.

The surgery itself went according to plan, but in the recovery room, as Widder says, "it all went to shit," and blood hemorrhaging nearly killed her.

Then it did kill her.

Widder's heart stopped beating. She stopped breathing. The doctors flipped her on her side, pumped the blood out of her lungs, and tried to get her breathing again. Her heart flickered to life, then stopped beating again. In total she had three resuscitations.

While technically dead, Widder had what she describes as a "classic out-of-body experience" of seeing herself from above. And she then felt a sense of peace that lasted for days. Visitors brought her flowers. Her friend commented on the beautiful yellow roses, and Widder realized something shocking: she was blind.

Somehow, while recuperating from her surgery, Widder had managed to function without realizing she couldn't see. Blood had hemorrhaged into her eyes, and all she could see was a "swirling darkness with glimpses of light."

This strange visual cortex lasted for months. Eventually Widder's eyesight returned, but the memory of these surreal streaks of light stayed with her.

Flash forward many years. Now Widder, who had wanted to study marine biology, began to study bioluminescence—the creation of light by living organisms. "I was super intrigued by anything that has to do with light," says Widder. "How we see light. How animals produce light."

And she would later study bioluminescence in the depths of the sea. In 1982, for her first dive, Widder plunged 800 feet in the Santa Barbara Channel. This was at night. She switched off the headlights of her diving suit, the Wasp, and was instantly surrounded by an underwater fireworks display. "This was just utterly, completely breathtaking," she says. Only unlike normal fireworks, here you are in the middle of the action. You're part of the brilliant display, because any movement you make can trigger these rippling explosions of light.

The fireworks were mostly blue, green, and aqua, just "the most brilliant aquamarine palette you can imagine." If she moved her arm she'd see pops of blue. Activating the thrusters of her suit caused "these vortices of neon-blue light," almost like how when you throw a log on the campfire, embers would spark and swirl. And these embers were icy blue.

Widder was blown away. And not just from the dazzling pyrotechnics—her scientific curiosity was piqued. From her past research, Widder knew how much energy it takes to produce light. How was this happening? "This has to be one of the most important processes in the ocean," she said to herself in 1984. "Why the hell aren't more people studying it?" She had so many questions. What was causing this? What creatures gave off the light? And how does this fit into the planet's ecosystem?

Widder was so overwhelmed by the brilliant displays of bioluminescence, it changed the course of her career.

So she devoted her career to answering these questions, and now she has a hypothesis.

"It's coming from the marine snow," says Widder. "Bacteria grow on marine snow. That's kind of a longish story, but it's very important because it has to do with the carbon pump."

Marine snow is organic matter. It's basically the mix of fecal pellets and dying plankton that are sinking down through the water column. This is the primary source of food for deep-sea creatures that don't come to the ocean's surface.

The understanding of bioluminescence is part of how Widder became the first person in history to capture footage of the legendary giant squid, *Architeuthis*. And more important, bioluminescence somehow fits into the puzzle of the earth's carbon pump and carbon flux (the two are related)—the carbon that's exchanged between the oceans and the land and the atmosphere. "Carbon flux is a big part of the story of life," says Widder. "And we've disrupted it tremendously with the burning of fossil fuels, and putting CO_2 into the air and the ocean, where it's converted to carbonic acid and is making the oceans more acidic." We've disrupted the chemistry of the ocean. We've disrupted the entire ecosystem with a host of actions—overfishing, mining, drilling for oil, filling the oceans with plastics—"and all of these things are interfering with these basic cycles of life, which we don't even understand yet."

Widder notes a striking irony, and here she speaks directly to the themes of this book: "We have this history of exploration followed by exploitation." Pick almost any example: Robert Peary makes his "conquest" of the North Pole and exploits the Inuit; Columbus explores the "new world" and exploits indigenous people. This is a complicated history that modern explorers are all too aware of. In the case of bioluminescence and the carbon cycle, however, the usual story is flipped. "We've done it in reverse for the ocean," says Widder. "We've been exploiting the ocean before we've explored it.

"We have to understand how the world works," she continues. "We're talking about the largest habitat on the planet. Clearly bioluminescence plays a major, major role in the life processes and how carbon cycles through the system, and how animals interact and communicate. And we know almost nothing about it."

Bioluminescence has led to tech and medical breakthroughs. When scientists examined the bioluminescence on a jellyfish, for example, they discovered green fluorescent protein. This breakthrough, which Widder says "has been equated to the invention of the microscope in terms of the impact

Widder's diving suit, Wasp, was developed by the off-shore oil industry for diving on rigs down to 2,000 feet deep. In 1984, Widder was part of a team of scientists testing it as a tool for exploring the largest, least explored ecosystem on the planet—the midwater.

From an evolutionary perspective, says Widder, bioluminescence is used for three things that creatures need to survive: to search for food, to look for a mate, and to defend against predators. For finding food, some fish use bioluminescence as a sort of flashlight to help them see in the dark. To discover a mate, bioluminescence can be used to advertise and scan for specific light patterns—sort of like an underwater dating app. For defense, bioluminescence can be a kind of camouflage, to match the sunlight from above. Widder suspects that bioluminescence has evolved as many as fifty separate times, "which is a clear indication of the survival value of the trait."

it has had on the understanding of cell biology," earned the 2008 Nobel Prize in Chemistry.

"This is where we need to be putting our resources and talent," says Widder. She's excited by new underwater technologies that can help us answer these questions—new deep-diving submersibles, new camera systems, new sampling systems. "But we need new explorers," she says. "And we need them more than any time in human history."

Money Matters: How Explorers Find Capital

The way Richard Garriott sees it, there are three types of people who walk into the doors of The Explorers Club: (1) the young explorers who are eager to get out there; (2) the old explorers who love sharing stories; and (3) the capital.

Capital is so important that it deserves its own category. And it's an overlooked part of exploration. Who's getting funded? What projects get greenlit?

Broadly speaking, there are five types of funding capital for expeditions.

1–GOVERNMENT AND MILITARY SPENDING

An obvious example is NASA. And the military spends R&D funding on tech, and that tech can power exploration.

2–MEDIA FUNDING

Media companies need content. They're willing to pay for it. This is true today and it will be true tomorrow. It was also true in the earliest days of the Club, when Shackleton partially funded the *Endurance* by agreeing to sell the story to a newspaper.

3–SPONSORSHIP

Modern explorers are becoming more savvy at finding innovative ways to incorporate brands, partnerships, and corporate sponsors. This can be necessary. One member describes himself as a "working-class explorer," and says that if he doesn't happen to get a coveted grant, "then I've got to find another option, or I won't be able to pay for the oil to heat my house this winter."

4–PRIVATE EQUITY

Private equity has funded exploration for centuries. For example, the Peary Arctic Club was formed as a fundraising vehicle to get Robert Peary to the North Pole.

5–GRANTS

Since the 1960s, the Club itself has issued grants, directly empowering and fueling exploration.

Dr. Dawn Wright preparing for the dive.

DIVING AND MAPPING

Perhaps there are still dragons to chase. And the world still needs mapmakers. Just ask Dawn Wright, an oceanographer who, in 1991, climbed into a submersible called *Alvin*—a vessel first commissioned in 1965—and descended to the ocean floor. She watched the water change colors as she sank. It started out blue, then it turned gray, and finally it became pitch-black—now it felt like she was looking into outer space. This is the same eerie sensation Don Walsh experienced decades before.

But she felt a sense of calm. Peace. And suddenly, like Edith Widder before her, she saw flashes of light in the darkness; these were bioluminescent bluish-green siphonophores, aka worms. The worms were bumping into one another and twirling around like a fireworks show right outside the window.

Wright sat in a fetal position in *Alvin*'s tiny cabin, scrunched up, fascinated by these flickering colors outside the viewport. She is the first African American woman to dive to the ocean floor. While in the *Alvin*, she studied the floor's cracks and fissures, carefully measuring their size and location. Some were only 1 meter wide; one was the size of multiple football fields. These cracks give us precious clues about the nature of earthquakes and volcanoes and the chance of future disruption. "This ties into the bigger picture of understanding the earth, so we can predict what it might do," says Wright.

So those tiny cracks in the seafloor? They matter. "Me looking at the distribution of cracks in the seafloor, it might seem like a completely esoteric or ridiculous thing to do, but it's a tiny part of the bigger picture. We're all providing pieces to this puzzle that we're trying to put together," says Wright. "To me, that's science. Everybody makes their own little contribution to the larger whole. Everybody has their own little Lego brick. One brick seems like nothing. But when you snap all of these bricks together, you can build an R2-D2."

Wright also did something else while exploring the bottom of the ocean, something that would make John Glenn smile: she worked on making a map. She used a combination of photography, video, and sonar to develop a map of this strange new underwater terrain. And then she would spend the next few decades creating and improving our maps—both the ocean and the land. And she creates maps that live and breathe and even speak to us.

"Maps are a window to reality," says Wright, who is the chief scientist of Esri. Her team uses a technology called GIS, or a geographic information system, to design maps that are interactive and three-dimensional. These maps help explain the world.

For context, consider The Explorers Club's storied "map room," which sits on the building's top floor—the home of the maps of Gertrude Bell. Even the walls of this room are covered in maps; one wall displays a map of Greenland, showing that icy world where Greely was stranded all those years ago. (To peel back the curtain, much of this very book was written in the map room. It's also a favorite workspace for the filmmaker Jimmy Chin, who viewed it as his "little hideaway.") Wright says of two-dimensional maps like this, "They're beautiful, and you can discern many things on the map by looking at it, and that can be powerful in and of itself. But that's it. That's basically all you can do."

Now consider the GIS maps that can analyze a trove of data, expand in three dimensions, create virtual worlds, and even spit out predictions. They can answer questions like *Where is the next major fire going to be? Where is the next outbreak of a pandemic?* The GIS maps not only help us navigate the world of today, but also chart the world of tomorrow.

Marie Tharp, the Woman who Mapped the Ocean

Dawn Wright loves maps, and she points to one map in particular that inspired her exploration: a 1977 map of the ocean floor, from geologist and cartographer legend Marie Tharp.

"That is *the* map," says Wright. "For many of us entering oceanography, especially marine geology, that map is so impactful," she goes on to explain. "It's so *beautiful*, for one thing," and it "brings the seafloor geology to life."

Wright fell in love with this map, so she decided to learn more about Tharp (also a Club member). And she discovered that, perhaps not surprisingly, Tharp was only credited as the second author of the map (Bruce Heezen was the first), but "she did all the work." This happens quite a bit in science, says Wright—the real "doer" gets relegated to second fiddle. Regardless, Wright credits Tharp not only with mapping the ocean floor, but inspiring a generation of oceanographers.

Margaret Amsler in 2007, dive-tending off Laggard Island, in the vicinity of Palmer Station.

THE THRILL OF THE KRILL

Like Dawn Wright and Sylvia Earle, Margaret O'Leary Amsler dives deep underwater to make scientific discoveries. She just does it in colder places.

Take, for example, that time in 1987, when Amsler stood on the edge of an ice floe. She was cold and her suit had a leak. The wind howled and the temperature dropped.

At the time, most Antarctic explorers still wore crushed neoprene dry suits that offered little protection against the wind.

Then Amsler realized something alarming: *I can't bend my legs.* The dry suit had frozen and now it functioned more like a hard cast, which would make it tough for her to climb back into the Zodiac boat and return to the research vessel.

And that raised another problem: the research vessel itself, a new steel-based ship called the *Polar Duke,* struggled to navigate through the perilous sea of icebergs. Earlier in the trip, the ship temporarily lost both engines. And the wind blew a huge iceberg in the *Duke*'s direction. With the engines off-line, the ship was powerless to escape the maw of the iceberg if it drifted too close. They were at the mercy of the wind.

But the engines roared back in time, the *Duke* reached the ice floe, and now Amsler had a chance to do what she came here to do. She is a marine biologist who spends much of her professional life in Antarctica, often diving beneath the ice to solve scientific riddles. Now she was haunted by a question: *How do krill survive the winter?*

People rarely think about that 2-inch speck of oceanic life, but the krill has a hidden superpower. "Its sneaky power is that it's superabundant," says Amsler.

"It has to be superabundant because everything in Antarctica feeds on it." The krill powers the entire ecosystem of Antarctica, and that, in turn, is linked to the global food chain.

Amsler, along with many international biologists, is a big reason—arguably the biggest reason—we know what we know about the krill. "Krill have a pretty complicated life history," she explains. Reproduction happens during the summer, when there's an abundance of light, which triggers photosynthesis for the microscopic phytoplankton that the krill eat for dinner. (Krill, like humans, are friskier in the summer.) After reproduction, the embryos shed from the female, the eggs hatch while sinking in the water, and it takes nine months for them to develop into proper "teenager" krill. So, if the krill feed and mate in the summer and if it takes nine months to develop, how are they surviving a winter that has no sunlight and therefore no food?

There had never been a way to answer this question. The krill lived under the ice, so it would be impossible to tow a net behind a boat—the usual way of collecting krill—without shearing the cable and losing your net. In Amsler's early years of krill exploration, the wooden research vehicles lacked a hull that could safely navigate these icebergs, meaning you couldn't get close enough for a dive.

Then came the *Duke*. With a new steel construction, the *Duke* brought Amsler within striking distance of the krill. Then she used a Zodiac to bring herself to the edge of the iceberg. In one attempt her suit froze and she couldn't move her legs, but she would keep trying.

Using a tether, Amsler dove into the freezing water and swam beneath the ice floe. Then she descended farther, until she could look up and see the ice above her, from the perspective of the krill.

Amsler was surprised to see the iceberg wasn't a solid ceiling, but instead had jumbles of caverns, tunnels, and even what looked like cathedrals. Light filtered through the frozen terrain. It was surreal. It was beautiful. And on the undersurface of the ice, Amsler spotted the mysterious young krill. "They would stick with the ice throughout the winter, because there were microscopic plant particles in the ice," she explains.

So Amsler and her colleagues dove again beneath the ice and brought aquarium nets, and they would "swat them like they're butterflies" to collect the krill for research. She measured their feeding rate and growth rate. Most important, she discovered that the young krill "rely on the annual formation of sea ice for their survival and growth through the winter." Now that the Antarctic is getting warmer, the ice is more likely to melt. Will the krill soon face an existential crisis?

During a submersible exploration of the Antarctic Peninsula, Amsler found herself surrounded by a dense swarm of krill. "As a krill biologist at heart, this was an epic, nirvana moment for me."

"That's the kind of thing that never would have been verified without the change in technology—from a lovely wooden vessel to something more high-tech and modern, and capable of penetrating the ice," says Amsler.

Amsler is being modest. It's true that this kind of scientific discovery—an understanding of what makes other species tick—is not possible without advancements in technology. But it's also true that these gulps of knowledge are not possible without the fieldwork of explorers like Amsler. It's not possible without the women and men who are willing to risk getting smashed by icebergs, or losing control of their legs, or freezing to death in a leaking suit.

Exploration is often in the field. And the field still matters.

Apollo 11 takes flight.

Apollo's Engines: Lost and Found

Let's quickly wind back the clock to 1969. As Apollo 11 surged into the atmosphere, at an altitude of 38 miles, the F1 engines split from the rocket and splashed down into the Atlantic. No one knew where they were. And for more than forty years, they had been abandoned and forgotten.

Until a secret expedition by Club member David Concannon, who began the project in 2010 and then later worked with a surprising ally—Jeff Bezos. "They are dissolving away in the saltwater," Bezos once said of the engines. "We should go get them and put them in a museum." So Concannon and Bezos (and a sprawling team) worked to do just that.

In some ways this was even trickier than finding the *Titanic*. "We're not looking for something 882 feet long. We're looking for something the size of a car," says Concannon. "It's finding the eye of the needle in the haystack."

It took a team of 105 people almost three years, but Concannon and Bezos found the prized engines. Bezos would later serve as Honorary Chair of The Explorers Club.

David Concannon, Jeff Bezos, and the team that found the Apollo 11 engines.

Explorer James Cameron and the *Deepsea Challenger*.

EXPLORATION AND SIDE HUSTLES: FROM OSCARS TO OCEANS

There's a sneaky truth about exploration. It's rarely discussed. It's not glamorous or sexy or even all that adventurous. The truth is this: most explorers have a day job or a side hustle.

Just ask James Cameron. At the 2013 Explorers Club Annual Dinner, he confessed that to a large degree, the reason he makes movies is to subsidize his scientific exploration. "I say only half jokingly, I make a movie like *Titanic* or *Avatar* once a decade so I can pay for the other stuff," he told the Club. "Exploration isn't cheap."

In some ways he didn't have a choice. Cameron has felt the pull of exploration since he was a little kid, a self-described "science geek," who looked up to his heroes—the astronauts, Jacques Cousteau, Don Walsh, and Jacques Piccard. Young Jim was enthralled by Walsh's trip to the bottom of the ocean. As a kid, he'd enclose himself in a large cardboard box and imagine it was a submarine.

That childhood curiosity never left him, and you can make the case that his contributions to deep-sea exploration rival his accomplishments in film. Think back to the movie *Titanic*. All of those present-day underwater scenes of exploring the wrecked ship? Cameron spent more than a hundred hours piloting small, remotely operated vehicles of his own design to create an archaeological survey of the interior—research that has led to a definitive understanding of the forensics of the Titanic's sinking. He has dived the wreck thirty-three times—more than anyone in the world. As he once put it, "I knew that if I made the film, I'd get to dive down for real."

In 2012, Cameron set out to do something that had not been done in half a century. "There are human footprints on the moon. And rovers are

Cameron plotting and planning the *Deepsea Challenger* expedition.

exploring the surface of Mars. We can Google a satellite picture of any place on the earth's surface. So we often think that our planet has been completely explored," Cameron has said. "But the depths of the oceans remain a mystery. And the extreme depths have barely been glimpsed."

It had been fifty-two years since Walsh and Piccard reached the bottom of Challenger Deep. And while they had proved that the descent was possible, no one had returned to study the bottom of the seafloor, to search for life, or to conduct any scientific experiments. The way Cameron saw it, "a combined area greater than North America" remained completely unexplored.

So Cameron funded, co-designed, and engineered a vessel called the *Deepsea Challenger*—a spiritual successor to the *Trieste*. The fundamental technology is similar to that of Auguste Piccard's invention. It's still a bathyscaphe. But the lime-green vessel had a vertical structure (like a torpedo) instead of horizontal (like a blimp); it had thrusters; it only had room for one pilot; and it was loaded with all kinds of gizmos to explore the bottom of the ocean: 3D cameras (which Cameron helped to invent), a payload bay for instruments, and a mechanical arm that could fetch rocks and samples.

Cameron and his team had to build everything from scratch. They worked in secret in suburban Sydney, Australia, hiding in plain sight between a plumbing supply store and a plywood shop. It took more than three years. When this "vertical torpedo" was finished, the team ran it through test after test after test—just like Walsh and Piccard in 1960. (This multiyear effort is one of the main reasons that Cameron makes so few movies.)

They first dove to 30 feet, then 3,000, then 10,000. At a crucial test dive of 27,000 feet, Cameron realized that he was now as deep as Ed Harris's character in *The Abyss*. And just like in *The Abyss,* things went wrong. "Oh shit," Cameron said as the systems malfunctioned. He had trouble slowing down. The water pressure squeezed the machine. It then occurred to Cameron that he was in a "dead metal coffin."

Cameron made it back to the surface. The engineers fixed the systems, but there was no way to know for sure. On March 26, 2012, in the darkness of night and in the middle of a storm, Cameron was ready to pick up where Don Walsh had left off. He took with him Explorers Club Flag 161—a flag that had once been to the top of Everest. And then there was one more thing he needed to do. Just before Cameron entered the tiny chamber, he looked into the eyes of his childhood hero.

"All right, Jim," said Don Walsh, shaking Cameron's hand.

"I'll see you in the sunshine," Cameron said.

The descent began.

Deepsea Challenger was hoisted into the water, and then Cameron plunged into the darkness. Soon he felt at peace. He put on a black beanie and stretched his legs as best he could—not much, since he was scrunched into an almost fetal position. "You feel yourself getting farther and farther from the world you came from," he later said. In a strange sense, he felt that going deeper into the ocean was like going deeper into subconsciousness.

10,000 feet.

20,000 feet.

(Unlike in 1960, this time the window didn't crack.)

And at 36,000 feet, for the first time since Dwight Eisenhower was the president, humans had again reached the bottom of the ocean.

Cameron let out a deep sigh. He grabbed the radio. "Surface, this is *Deepsea Challenger*. I am on the bottom."

Seven miles above him, mission control cheered and clapped.

Cameron's Deepsea Challenge Expedition was science-focused. He made a series of progressively deeper dives to explore the deep trench systems in the western Pacific. At the Challenger Deep, he trawled the bright green vessel over the terrain, looking for creatures but spotting nothing. "There's no sign of critters," he said over the radio. On a technical and superficial level, he found the terrain to be "flat and featureless." But on a deeper level he felt a certain purity at the bottom of the ocean, as it's possible to sense "the vastness of all we don't know." Maybe he felt like that kid who stuffed himself into a cardboard box and pretended to explore the ocean.

When he returned to the surface, he did not do so empty-handed. Cameron discovered sixty-eight new species on the expedition, he mapped more of the ocean floor, and he pushed back the dragons. He also became the first person in history to descend to the Challenger Deep, the deepest place on the planet, as a solo pilot.

Months later, at the 2013 ECAD, Cameron accepted the Club's highest honor—The Explorers Medal. He looked around at the packed crowd. He thought about the people in the room. John Glenn. Scott Carpenter. Kathryn Sullivan. "For those of you who know me, humility doesn't come naturally," he said onstage. "But it's easy to be humbled in this room. . . . It still brings a lump to my throat."

Cameron articulated something felt by most members of The Explorers Club. "Something that all explorers seek," said Cameron, is "that place that other people have experienced but you haven't yet, or maybe no one has been there and seen it, and you can bear witness."

For those who aren't paying attention, it might look as if Cameron is a filmmaker who explores as a hobby. This gets it backward. As Cameron said at the ECAD, he has spent far more time leading expeditions than he has making films, so "this raises the question . . . What's the hobby and what's the primary vocation?"

Cameron spent years preparing for the expedition, hands-on, co-designing the vessel.

Two deep sea legends: James Cameron and Don Walsh.

Auguste Piccard, who flew in a hydrogen balloon to become the first human to enter the stratosphere. The brilliant physicist is also the inspiration for the character Professor Calculus in the comic series *The Adventures of Tintin*.

FROM APOLLO ROCKETS TO SOLAR WINGS

Let's return to 1904, that fateful year when The Explorers Club was founded and Auguste Piccard, the brilliant Swiss scientist, first dreamed of the bathyscaphe. The *Trieste* was not Piccard's only creation. One of the most prolific inventors in history, Piccard discovered the isotope uranium 235, he designed the world's most precise scale, and he used his aerial balloons to validate a little-known concept called the theory of relativity from one of his colleagues, Albert Einstein. The two were friends and communicated regularly.

With the *Trieste,* Piccard hoped to dive deep into the ocean. But he also thought about the sky. He wanted to go higher than anyone had ever been. Piccard designed an airtight pressurized cabin that could handle the rigors of the stratosphere, and he did more than simply sketch the blueprints. He flew the balloon himself. On May 27, 1931, Piccard piloted a balloon 51,775 feet into the air, reaching the stratosphere. He was the first to do so. NASA has credited Piccard with effectively building the world's first spacecraft.

Then Piccard's son, Jacques, joined Don Walsh to explore the bottom of the ocean, and later dedicated himself to ecology and conservation. Jacques often thought of his dive to Challenger Deep. And he thought about how he had found evidence of life on the bottom of the ocean—doubted by many—and this helped scuttle governments' plans to dump toxic waste in ocean trenches.

Exploration had led to conservation, and the idea stuck with Jacques. He eventually designed his own submarine, called the *Ben Franklin,* that would survey the Gulf Stream currents and observe underwater life. Piccard would drift underwater in the *Ben Franklin* for a full month; NASA studied his trip to help prepare astronauts for long-term confinement.

Auguste Piccard didn't just design aircrafts and vessels—
he personally piloted them to new heights and depths.

Jacques Piccard was friendly with NASA. By then he had moved his family to Cape Kennedy, Florida, and he knew many of the astronauts. Sometimes he'd invite the astronauts to his young son's birthday party.

The son's name was Bertrand. He grew up hearing stories of his grandfather's balloon rides to the stratosphere, of his father's trip to the bottom of the sea, and even tales of his "Uncle Don's" piloting of the *Trieste*. Bertrand would welcome Apollo astronauts into his room and show them the rocket posters on his wall, and they'd explain how the stuff works.

Bertrand remembers when everything clicked. In July 1969, he watched his father bravely climb into the *Ben Franklin* and leave to study the Gulf Stream. That very same week, at Cape Kennedy, he witnessed the launch of Apollo 11.

The eleven-year-old said to himself: *I would like this type of life. I want to explore. I want to do impossible things. I want to do things that no one has done before.* And Bertrand's father, Jacques, had impressed on him that scientific exploration—real exploration—needs to serve the quality of life for mankind, and is not just about attaining some record.

In the first chapter of Bertrand's career, his "day job" was practicing medicine as a doctor (also useful). He somehow found time to become a pioneer of hang gliding. Then he became a balloonist who won races across the Atlantic. This sparked the audacious idea of circumnavigating the globe in a balloon. There was something deeply romantic about the concept—flying all the way around Earth without an engine, being pushed solely by the wind.

This was the dream envisioned by Jules Verne. And now Piccard was doing it. "It was the first time in my life where I felt I could do something that no one had done," says Piccard. The quest would take him a decade, and it involved a race against billionaires like Richard Branson—Piccard was the underdog. "I failed twice, but all the others failed also," he says.

Even in failure, Piccard felt there was something symbolic, even philosophical, about flying a balloon. "You are pushed by the wind, at the speed of the wind, and the direction of the wind," Piccard explains. Sometimes it's 20 miles per hour. Sometimes it's 150 miles per hour. If you want to go left or right, you need to change your altitude and find another wind that has a better direction. "For me, it became a philosophical approach," says Piccard. "You drop the ballast to change altitude and find a better wind. And in life, you drop the ballast of your certitude, your habits, your beliefs, your paradigms, your dogmas, and you change altitudes psychologically, in order to find other influences, or other visions of the world, or solutions or answers that give another direction to your life." He adds that in a balloon, "you need to play with the forces of nature. And nature is always the strongest."

Piccard had failed twice in his attempt to circumnavigate the globe in a balloon. He succeeded on his third try, along with copilot Brian Jones. In March 1999, he traveled 45,000 kilometers in twenty nonstop days. The scariest part? When Piccard took off in Switzerland, he left with 3.7 tons of liquid propane. When he landed in Africa, he only had 80 pounds, or roughly 1 percent of his original stock. "That was tight," Piccard says. This underscored to him the priority of efficient fuel. "It was wrong to say 'the sky is the limit.' The limit is the fuel."

Piccard had just completed the longest flight in the history of aviation, and he was nearly out of fuel. That fuel was a hard constraint. This nudged him to think of something even bigger, even grander. How could he improve upon this flight? "If I want to do better, I need to get rid of the fuel. And getting rid of the fuel meant that I needed to invent a system that would fly only on solar energy."

Incredibly, his grandfather, Auguste, had the same idea in 1942, publishing an article that called for solar energy and heat pumps. Now Piccard would fulfill his grandfather's vision through Solar Impulse, his new company:

Dr. Bertrand Piccard, following in his father and grandfather's footsteps.

"I wanted an airplane that could get enough energy from the sun to run electric motors, but at the same time, charge the batteries in order to fly at night."

All of the experts in aviation told Piccard the same thing: *Impossible.* It's true that solar airplanes had flown before but only during the daytime, and none could store energy. This was considered a nonstarter. "They were so stubborn," he says. They were trapped in the old way of thinking. *If an airplane is big, it must be heavy. If an airplane is light, it must be small.* Piccard's plane needed to be big (to have enough surface area for the solar panels) and light (so it would require less solar electricity).

"The aviation industry refused to build it," says Piccard, who turned to a shipyard to build the plane's carbon fiber pieces. Years later, Piccard was told by the CEO of Airbus that his engineers had told him, "Don't help Piccard. He will never build this airplane." And when the airplane was built, the engineers said, "He will never fly." When he actually flew, the engineers said, "He will crash."

And at times it seemed like the doomsayers might be right. The engineering challenge was formidable. "It needed to have a wingspan bigger than a jumbo jet, but the weight like a family car," says Piccard. One day they made a load test for the wing. It broke. And it took two years to rebuild it.

Then another year. And another. Piccard and his partner, André Borschberg, had to overcome a gauntlet of engineering, manufacturing, and bureaucratic

Bertrand Piccard and copilot Brian Jones were the first people to circumnavigate the globe in a balloon.

obstacles, and it eventually took him thirteen years to build *Solar Impulse*. But he knew that working through challenges goes with the territory. After all, it took his father and grandfather more than a decade to create and perfect the *Trieste*. Exploration doesn't happen at the snap of your fingers.

Meanwhile, the world began to take note. As Piccard completed test flights and nailed his project's milestones, environmentalists and politicians began to understand the historic implications of this quest. Al Gore, Richard Branson, and Elie Wiesel rallied to the cause and became patrons of the project, along with Club members James Cameron and Buzz Aldrin. "If the around-the-world balloon flight was the last adventure of the twentieth century, Solar Impulse is undeniably the first to represent the challenges of the twenty-first," said another Club member, Prince Albert of Monaco.

Just as his father and "Uncle Don" took the *Trieste* first to 70 feet underwater, then 500, then 1,000, and so on, Bertrand Piccard put the *Solar Impulse* through its paces. In July 2010, the plane became the first to fly all day and night only on solar power. He flew from Switzerland to Morocco in 2012.

And finally, in 2016, Piccard was ready for his trip around the world. Once again the Piccards made history. His grandfather was the first to reach the stratosphere. His father joined Don Walsh as the first to reach the bottom of the ocean. And now he was the first to circumnavigate the globe in a plane that was powered by the sun.

As Piccard soared above the Atlantic, he flew over an oil tanker. And he saw that the tanker left a trail of oil in its wake. "I was there in my solar-powered airplane and I thought, 'There are really two worlds. The old world that's polluting and destroying the planet. And the new world that is now able to use these clean technologies.'"

The journey happened to coincide with the 2016 Paris Climate Accords. On Earth Day, April 22, while flying *Solar Impulse* over the Pacific, Piccard was connected via live satellite to the secretary-general of the United Nations, just as the heads of state were celebrating the accords. His message to the United Nations was that with clean technologies and renewable energy, "everything is possible."

Piccard's vision for solar power now extends well beyond airplanes. The *Solar Impulse* birthed the Solar Impulse Foundation. The goal is to explore solutions that can protect the environment in an economically profitable way. The team was happy to discover one creative idea. Then a second. Then a third. "Now we have identified 1,350 of them," says Piccard with a smile. "By the time the book is published, maybe it will be two thousand."

Solar Impulse on its legendary flight.

He shares one example: "a process that takes all the household waste of a city, and you can turn that into construction stones." Here's another example: a system that recovers the heat from a factory chimney and then, while letting the smoke escape, funnels that heat back into the factory, which massively reduces the energy consumption.

Piccard's exploration, like that of his father and grandfather before him, has expanded the very idea of what is possible. So it's no surprise that he and his copilot, André Borschberg, were awarded The Explorers Medal and joined the Club's ranks. "The Explorers Club was part of my life since I was born," says Piccard.

And he's far from finished. Piccard could have retired after that historic balloon flight, but instead he pushed himself toward an even bigger breakthrough in solar energy. And now he is exploring how to transform the world with clean energy. He can't imagine stopping. "Exploration is a mindset," says Piccard. "Once you're an explorer you never stop exploring. There's always something else that drives your curiosity."

This third-generation Club member has thought deeply about how exploration has evolved, and where it is headed. The map has been filled in. Even

Bertrand Piccard (right) with his partner and copilot, André Borschberg.

the moon has been reached. So what is left to explore? The way Piccard sees it, perhaps the most important discoveries of all.

"I think it's very, very important to make the next step," he says. "Which is to push the young people to explore new ways of thinking and new ways of doing. In order to become the pioneers of a better quality of life." Exploring leads to innovation, and innovation unlocks the answers to questions we haven't even thought to ask. This is why the Club, in a sense, is still in its early chapters. "We need to be explorers," says Piccard. "We need to be pioneers. We need to go into the fields that have never been explored before."

Solar Impulse: A proof of concept, a proof of hope,
a proof of a sustainable future.

3—CURIOSITY IN ACTION

THE NEW GOLDEN AGE OF EXPLORATION

Years ago, John Glenn had described exploration as "pushing dragons back," but then he added something else. In that same speech, he noted that exploration can also be defined as "curiosity in action."

All of us are curious. Explorers simply act on that curiosity. This means that you don't need to climb a mountain, dive to the ocean floor, or trek to the Poles to be an explorer. In this new golden age, around the globe, people are contributing to exploration through a wide range of action: conservation, storytelling, linguistics, archaeology, cultural preservation, astronomy, planetary defense, the journey to Mars, and on and on and on.

Modern-day explorers are beacons for what is possible. They advance human knowledge. They focus on progress. They inspire.

A stream inside the Dracula Reserve, currently at risk of destruction from illegal mining.

THE TWO CALLIES: A TALE OF NATURE'S ANGUISH

In 1931, an explorer named Earl Hanson traveled to South America. He was on a quest to survey the earth's magnetism, and he carried with him Explorers Club Flag 44. Hanson returned the flag safely to the Club in 1933, where it remained for decades. In 1992, the flag was carried by Ken Clayton, a scuba diver, to search for a German submarine that was mysteriously lost during World War II.

And in 2021, the same flag was carried by Callie Broaddus in Ecuador, on a trek through the tropical Andes cloud forest. Many parts of this lush terrain had never been studied by scientists. Broaddus and her crew had discovered what could be twenty-one new (or new-to-science) species of orchids, reptiles, and amphibians.

Then they discovered something chilling.

Roughly halfway through their trek, one of the crew, an Ecuadorian named Marco Monteros, had left on a side mission to find more orchids. Monteros found a new trail he didn't recognize. He followed it and discovered something so alarming that he knew Broaddus needed to see it at once.

It was getting dark. Monteros returned to Broaddus and the group, and now they all followed this strange new trail that seemed eerily out of place. The steps were muddy with steep drops on both sides. As with the rest of this trek through the Andes, when you step your foot ahead in the mud, it immediately slides back to where it was before, like a muddy treadmill.

Soon Broaddus and her crew arrived at the bottom of the trail. It opened into a canyon. One side looked the way it should: lush, verdant, and packed with the dense foliage that makes the Ecuadorian rainforest so beautiful.

Callie Broaddus and team on the Dracula Transect Expedition, carrying Flag 44.

The Dracula Expansion Expedition team with Flag 211 on a previously unstudied 1,050-acre plot of cloud forest Reserva. Broaddus's co-leader was Javier Robayo, also now a member of The Explorers Club.

The other side was butchered.

For a stretch of 400 meters, it looked like someone had stripped the canyon of all its vegetation and wildlife; in fact, that's exactly what had been done.

Miners had illegally pillaged the canyon in search of gold and pyrite. This land, part of the Dracula Reserve ecological corridor, bordered a protected stretch of forest—safeguarding forests like this is Broaddus's mission in life. "The really tragic thing is that there was pyrite over everything," says Broaddus. The miners had found pyrite, or "fool's gold," and the presence of pyrite usually means that gold is nearby. That meant the miners would be back to drill.

Callie Broaddus's twenty-five-day expedition had started many years ago, in a sense, and it had been started by her sister. When Finley Broaddus was seventeen years old, she was diagnosed with an aggressive, fatal cancer. Finley cared deeply about climate change, and she was frustrated that society didn't do more to act. "She had a hard time doing anything about it from her hospital bed," says Callie.

So when friends of Finley tried to send her flowers or teddy bears, Finley said, actually, if you want to help, there's something you can do instead. Finley wanted to launch an organization that could help fight climate change. She had a goal of raising $18,000 by her eighteenth birthday.

By the time Finley passed away, at age eighteen, the fund had reached nearly $100,000. "Aside from the obvious trauma of losing a sister in such a tragic way, she had an enormous impact in the way that I saw the world," says Callie.

Callie Broaddus (then twenty-four years old, living in DC, and designing kids' books for the National Geographic Society) felt obligated to do something that would honor her sister, and she also wanted to leverage the power of youth to drive change. "I kept thinking about the fact that she was only eighteen when she died, and had done so much," says Callie. She realized that "young people have enormous financial power that wasn't being tapped."

Broaddus teamed up with Bella Lack, a British teen wildlife advocate, and with support from thousands of international kids and youth, they created the world's first entirely youth-funded nature reserve—Dracula Youth Reserve. They work with local partners to engage and empower young people in the whole conservation process—from scientific exploration to education and storytelling. "We're losing species before we know they exist," says Broaddus, with real passion in her voice. "Species extinction is one thousand times its natural rate." She thinks of biodiversity as a fabric in nature, and the more threads you have in that fabric, the stronger the global ecosystem. When we pull out threads the fabric weakens. Soon it will rip and tear. When the biodiversity fabric is weakened, fewer species can survive and the soil is destabilized and "little by little, we begin to whittle down the richness of life."

Ultimately, says Broaddus, "We are not going to survive, long term, on a planet that doesn't have a biodiverse ecosystem. We won't make it."

But that logic is all abstract. Theoretical. On that Ecuadorian expedition in 2021, Broaddus saw the looming threat with her own eyes. The miners were real. So after the expedition team discovered the evidence of illegal mining, they located the miners' camp. They decided to confront them the next morning.

In the predawn glow, Broaddus could see the miners had two large domed tents, big enough to fit cots. She saw a row of machetes. She knew the miners might have guns, ostensibly for hunting.

"What you've done is illegal," Broaddus's co-leader on the expedition, Javier Robayo, told the miners, undeterred by the machetes or the possible guns. Then she and the Ecuadorans gave the miners a crystal-clear message: *We'll be watching you.*

And they stuck to their word. They set up a camp on the border of the property, close enough to keep eyes on the illegal mining activity. They also flew a drone over the area. "We started constant monitoring of the mining activity," says Broaddus.

The timing of their expedition was crucial. They had caught the miners in phase 1 of their mining, an initial survey of its potential. And there was indeed gold in them hills. If Broaddus's team hadn't discovered the miners, phase 2 would have meant drilling and the inevitable destruction of the surrounding vegetation. The canyon would become a pit.

As of this writing, Broaddus and her partners have successfully kept the miners at bay, but she knows they will be difficult to fend off forever—they have deep pockets and a lust for gold. The expedition taught her that the risk of biodiversity extinction is not just theoretical, it's not just a potential scenario, that "the bogeyman is real."

Callie Veelenturf, our second Callie, is one of the millions inspired by Jane Goodall. Even as a four-year-old, Veelenturf had a similar clarity of purpose. When people asked what she wanted to do when she grows up she'd reply, "I want to save the animals."

When she was seventeen, she applied to the Brown Environmental Leadership Lab. During a snorkeling trip to Hawaii (exploration has its

An endangered green sea turtle nesting on Isla del Rey in the Pearl Islands Archipelago, Panama, 2020. Veelenturf conducted the first scientific sea turtle conservation study in the Pearl Islands.

perks), when separated from the rest of the group, she saw a long shadow on the reef in front of her.

When she looked up, she realized that the shadow was a green sea turtle. It was 4 feet long with a massive green shell. The turtle was perfectly still. Veelenturf was so close she could almost touch it. They were both floating on their stomachs, with their heads underwater. With its head cocked, the turtle stared at Veelenturf with one eye. They made deep eye contact. It felt to Veelenturf like they were staring into each other's souls. The moment lasted only a few seconds but it felt like hours. Veelenturf felt a profound desire to learn everything she could about sea turtles, use her time on the planet to protect them and their ocean habitats, and become a marine biologist.

In the same way that Goodall traveled to Gombe to learn everything she could about the chimps, Veelenturf devoted her life to the sea turtles. And they need the help. In 1980, on the stretch of the Pacific from Mexico to Chile, there were once thirty-five thousand leatherback sea turtles. Now there are likely fewer than one thousand. "This species has been around since the

Jane Goodall

"I fell in love with Africa at the age of eight, after reading about how Doctor Dolittle rescued animals from the circus and took them back to Africa," Jane Goodall told *The Explorers Journal,* in an interview with longtime editor Angela Schuster. "I was determined to go to Africa and live with wild animals and write books about them even then."

This she would do. In 1960, Goodall flew to Gombe Stream National Park in Tanzania and began studying chimpanzees. Her work was groundbreaking and revolutionary, but it was initially dismissed by the "experts." When she enrolled in Cambridge's PhD program in 1961, the professors told her that she had done everything wrong.

"First, they said, giving the chimps names rather than numbers was not 'good science,'" Goodall said. "Second, I was not to talk about them having personalities, or minds capable of problem solving, or emotions such as contentment, sadness, frustration, anger, despair, or even fear. For only we humans had these characteristics. Fortunately, I had a wonderful teacher when I was a child who taught me that, in this respect, those professors were absolutely wrong."

The identity of this teacher? "That teacher was my dog, Rusty," Goodall continued. "Anyone who has shared their life in a meaningful way with an animal—be it a dog, cat, rabbit, guinea pig, horse, pig, or bird—knows perfectly well that we humans are not the only beings who have personalities, intellect, and emotions. We are not the only sapient, sentient beings on the planet. We are not, as was taught back in the early sixties, different in kind from other animals. We are, in fact, part of and not separate from the animal kingdom."

And the rest is history. The iconic Goodall has saved one species (chimpanzees) and inspired another (humans).

time of the dinosaurs," explains Veelenturf. They survived the Cretaceous-Paleogene mass-extinction event, but they might not survive humans.

She traveled to Bioko Island, in West Africa, to monitor the sea turtles more closely. She spent five months living in a tent and eating powdered baby food for breakfast. Dinner was a pot of spam and rice, split between sixteen scientists. It was so humid that when you hung your clothes to dry, they remained wet and grew mold. The environment was so punishing that out of a team of sixteen researchers, only ten finished the program; others were evacuated by helicopter or contracted MRSA.

Every day, Veelenturf scoured the beach and carefully inspected the turtles' nests of eggs, collecting data on their hatching success. She began to see patterns. And after a grant from the National Geographic Society, she flew to the Pearl Islands, off the coast of Panama, to conduct a study of sea turtle nesting. Why were the eggs failing to hatch? Through meticulous tracking, she discovered that at one beach, 65 percent of the nests were harvested by humans. And she learned that local communities were illegally drinking the turtles' blood, eating the meat, and using the shells for cockfighting.

She kept digging. She knew that the biggest threat to sea turtles in Ecuador is fishery "bycatch," the creatures that are accidentally caught in fishing gear. This kills forty thousand sea turtles each year. So Veelenturf helped develop a clever solution. She knew it was a nonstarter to tell the fishermen to stop fishing. But she also knew they weren't *trying* to kill the sea turtles; these were accidental deaths caused by the gear.

Veelenturf collaborated with the fishermen. What if they placed LED lights on the fishing lines? "If you place LED lights every twenty meters, that allows sea turtles to see [the lines]," explains Veelenturf, but the target fish aren't able to see that spectrum of light, so they'll still be caught by the fishermen.

Shouldn't sea turtles have the right to live? Shouldn't nature have rights? Veelenturf soon learned that while Ecuador and Bolivia have recognized the Rights of Nature in their constitutions, it's almost entirely absent throughout the world. She arranged a meeting with a senator from Panama, where many of the sea turtles are dying. She met with Panama's first lady. She made her case for the Rights of Nature. Then in collaboration with Panamanian lawyers and the Earth Law Center, she spent two years drafting a law, revising the law, and trying to get it passed. On February 24, 2022, the president of Panama signed Veelenturf's bill into law. "The nature in Panama has the right to exist, persist, regenerate her vital cycles, and to have representation in court," says Veelenturf, who sees this law as a prototype for the rest of the planet, and is now working to spread this framework around the globe.

A wild Andean cock-of-the-rock. "This bird is uncommon," says Broaddus, "with population declining due to habitat loss across its range."

Callie Veelenturf, like Callie Broaddus and hundreds of other Club members, is trying to protect the planet and its creatures from future anguish. The work of the two Callies, while less cinematic and harrowing than the story of the two Greelys, has some surprising similarities. Just in the nick of time, by rallying public support, Henrietta saved the lives of Adolphus Greely and crew. And in the twenty-first century? Both Callies feel that time is running out. But today's mission is not to save the lives of starving men in the Arctic—it's literally to save nature itself.

The work continues. As the Club's UN representative, Callie Veelenturf presented the case of Rights of Nature to the United Nations. Some have called her "the next Jane Goodall." Veelenturf quickly brushes aside that comparison to her hero, but she's amused that they share the same birthday. "I get goose bumps and teary-eyed when I think about her," Veelenturf says. "She's like a beacon of hope and morality." Specifically, Veelenturf appreciates how Goodall "uses science and storytelling and her love of nature to inspire people."

The storytelling part of the science is crucial, and this is something that Jane Goodall has said for years. She even sees it as a mission for explorers. When asked what more explorers should be doing, Goodall was clear and specific in her answer: "Write articles and books and make documentaries about their experiences to share with the general public. Tell stories that will help people to understand the importance of saving the environment, and help them to understand the true nature of animals."

Callie Veelenturf measures pH, conductivity, and temperature near a leatherback sea turtle's nest in Equatorial Guinea.

Asha Stuart in a Himba village in Kaokoland, Namibia. Kaokoland is home to the largest population of semi-nomadic Himba people. Stuart shares images with Himba women as part of an expedition on climate migration and its impact on their people.

EXPLORING BY STORYTELLING

When Jane Goodall encourages explorers to write books and make documentaries, she's touching on something important: explorers are storytellers. This was true since the early days of the Club, which has long welcomed journalists, photographers, and filmmakers into its ranks. And the logic is simple. A core reason for exploration is to expand human knowledge. If you go somewhere and discover something amazing but you never tell a soul, then you fail to enrich our understanding of the world.

"When you come back, it's not just about you," says Rebecca Martin, who works on the Club's grant programs. "It's about the place. It's about the people. And why do they matter? Why are they important to the world? It's through storytelling that you can convey this."

Thanks to the acclaimed photojournalist (and longtime Club member) Carol Beckwith, for example, we now have a deeper understanding of the indigenous cultures of Africa. Her photographs evoke empathy in a way that technical field reports simply can't. Or take John Houston, an Arctic filmmaker who uses storytelling to help the world understand Inuit culture.

Or consider Jimmy Chin, codirector of the Oscar-winning *Free Solo, The Rescue,** and *Return to Space.* There's a reason he chooses this medium. "Stories are one of the most powerful ways to communicate ideas, and express an examination of the human condition," says Chin.

---

*In *The Rescue*, Chin shares the incredible story of how divers risked their lives to save a boys soccer team trapped in a flooded Thailand cave; the cave divers, of course, were Club members.

These ideas aren't always simple. They aren't always something that you can quantify or cleanly document in a literal sense. "There are a lot of human experiences that are ineffable," says Chin. "And stories help translate these ineffable experiences," which helps "broaden people's sense of the human experience. That's the power of stories. They create empathy. They broaden people's view of the world, and that can be life-changing."

One of the Club's newest storytellers, for example, explores cultural undercurrents to promote a deeper understanding of the world.

India. 2012. On a trip to the Arabian Sea, en route to the temple-filled town of Gokarna, Asha Stuart stepped off the bus. She walked through a bazaar packed with trinkets and cigarette stands. Then she bumped into someone fascinating: a man who looked like her. An Indian man who was Black.

They didn't share a verbal language so they couldn't communicate, but Stuart sensed they shared something deeper. "We were both thinking, 'I think you're Black,'" Stuart says now, remembering the scene.

Intrigued by this moment, she pored through the research and she studied the history. She learned that this region of India was partially populated by people of African descent who were brought here via slavery. The man she bumped into was a Siddi.

Stuart now had a mystery she needed to solve. How come most people had never heard of the Siddi? How have the Siddi been able to preserve their African culture? So for her first expedition with National Geographic, she spent time with the Siddi and filmed a documentary to share their story. She stayed at a nun's house and woke up at 4:30 a.m. every day to join them for breakfast.

"I was interested in understanding what it's like to be Black somewhere else, outside of America," says Stuart. How did they experience racism? How were they treated by the "mainstream" culture? How could they be so resilient?

Her short film, *Lost Tribe of Africa,* tells the story of how the Siddi (which means "enlightened one") still live mostly hidden in the forest. "Although we're thousands of miles away from Africa, her spirit never left us," says one Siddi in the documentary. "The African soul is woven in our identity."

When the Siddi venture into cities like Bangalore, they are mocked and reviled. Strangers point at them and say, "Look at his skin, it's so dirty!" or "Look at that black ugly man!" The Siddi are in the lowest rung of India's caste system, dismissed as "untouchables." There are those in the higher castes who believe that if you so much as touch a Siddi, you will be cursed. So Siddi can only work as laborers. They aren't allowed to eat with actual dishes, but instead must use banana leaves. They're forced to eat outside. As Stuart's narrator says, "We are treated worse than their animals."

The documentary captures not only the wrenching plight of the Siddi but also their resolve and resiliency. They teach children their dances and music, which Stuart describes as "strong drum rhythm that can be found in East Africa." They find strength in cultural festivals. "Through our Siddi traditions we can free ourselves," says the narrator. "We can be free from discrimination, free from the caste system, free from hate, free to be Siddi."

Stuart would go on to tell more stories from overlooked or marginalized communities. "Their voices don't have the platform," she says, "and they don't get heard." This is why, in 2021, she set up camp in the 110-degree heat of Namibia, to learn how climate change is affecting the Himba people.

Many Himba live in Kaokoland, a rural and deserted part of northern Namibia. But droughts have killed their livestock and stolen their water. When Himba women learned that Stuart had arrived to tell their story, they traveled for miles to share their truths: about women who died in childbirth because they had no water to drink; about depression and suicide; about children who were so desperate for water that they reached too far into the well and their hands were cut off.

Stuart has found that because of climate change and climate migration, traditional cultures like the Himba are at risk. The Himba must relocate to the city, where they, like the Siddi, face bigotry and discrimination. Because of the way the Himba dress—with traditional clothing and mud dreadlocks—they struggle to find even the lowest-paying jobs. No one wants them to drive taxis. No one wants them to wait tables. Now they might be forced to surrender their customs and assimilate into the larger culture. With a tradition that stretches back centuries, says Stuart, the Himba have survived colonialism, natural disasters, and political upheaval, but now "climate change is the biggest threat to their existence."

And these are the cultural undercurrents that Stuart explores. "When you think about exploration, a lot of times people think about polar bears or wildlife," she says. "But from a human-to-human aspect, there are so many things in human culture that everyone can learn from."

This can bring empathy, change, and a deeper understanding of the world. After all, as an anthropologist, Stuart has at her core the unshakable belief of "knowing we're all the same." Even if we talk or dress or look different, "the human emotions are the same."

Mario Rigby sailing across a channel in Mozambique.

EXPLORING THE ROOTS

No more sleeping with the hippos, Mario Rigby told himself, exhausted. Rigby was kayaking alone across the length of Lake Malawi, the second-deepest lake in Africa.

This part of the lake was swampy, teeming with hippos and crocodiles. Hippos are fast and deadly. But the night before, Rigby, desperate for sleep, had docked his kayak, pitched a tent, and slept so close to the hippos that he could hear them gurgling. His survival was a minor miracle.

Now a storm was coming. And Rigby, unwilling to roll the dice again with the hippos, decided to approach the nearest village he could find. He was used to visiting random villages. Rigby was on an epic two-year journey to cross the entirety of Africa, all 7,456 miles, from Cape Town to Cairo, on foot or by kayak.

Rigby left the water and headed to a village. He was immediately surrounded by hundreds of people who were curious about this stranger. The one villager who spoke English, serving as a translator, was clearly drunk.

The tipsy translator said something to the man who must be the chief, and the chief said something back. Slurring his words, the translator told Rigby, "You can stay here, it's totally chill." But Rigby was skeptical. The energy didn't feel chill. The vibe felt hostile. Yet he had no choice because the hippos were looming and the storm looked ominous.

So Rigby set up his tent. He had mastered the ability to snooze in dangerous situations: earlier in the trek, while in a conflict zone, he fell asleep in a military truck while getting shot at by rebel forces. Now, grateful for the distance between himself and the hippos, he laid his head down and dozed off into a blissful dream . . .

. . . then woke up to see flashlights and two AK-47s pointing at him, poking through the tent. They belonged to Malawi police officers.

"My friend, you are being arrested. You are not allowed to be here," said one of the officers.

Rigby knew this was nonsense. "Of course I'm allowed to be here," he told the cop. What had he done wrong? What local custom had he misunderstood?

The officer made up a contrived violation, telling Rigby that he wasn't wearing a life vest on his kayak.

"Here's my life vest," Rigby told the cop, pointing to the vest; he knew the charges were bogus. He explained to the cop that he was simply kayaking across Lake Malawi. How was this a crime?

The cops ignored him. They restrained him with shackled handcuffs. Then they forced Rigby to somehow un-pitch his tent while being handcuffed.

What had he done wrong? Then the answer became clear. The cop pulled up the sleeve of his uniform, and he showed Rigby something on his own body that explained everything.

The idea to cross Africa was inspired, in part, by a TV show that Rigby (who was raised in Germany) had adored as a kid: *The Black Panther.* In this overlooked cartoon that aired years before the Chadwick Boseman block-buster, T'Challa goes on a walkabout before he becomes king. "He decided to learn about the cultures of African people," explains Rigby. "He wanted to learn about the environment before he became a leader. This was actually quite normal in African culture. You go through rites of passage. We com-pletely miss this in the West."

As a teenager, Rigby couldn't shake that idea. He thought about it for a decade. Then, in 2015, he had a wild bit of inspiration: What if he created his own rite of passage? "I wanted to create an impact on the world," he says, "but I can't create an impact if I don't know what the world is about."

On the second day of Rigby's walkabout, while leaving Cape Town, his wal-let was stolen by a gang of kids. He had little money left. This compelled him to be more social and knock on strangers' doors, politely asking for food and shelter. "It really forced me to be patient, and to learn, and to have their trust and vice versa." This served him well. Villagers were usually welcoming, generous, and happy to share.

Mario Rigby with schoolchildren in Kibera, Kenya. "These kids live in some of the worst conditions in Africa," says Rigby. "However, an NGO organizes a soccer team to help teach them how to get out of poverty."

Mario Rigby after climbing Mount Kenya, the second highest mountain in Africa. (He notes that it's a "much steeper climb than Kilimanjaro.")

Usually. Not tonight. No country or continent is homogeneous, and tonight Rigby experienced something different altogether.

When the cop rolled up the sleeve of his uniform, he gestured at his own skin—his dark skin.

"My friend, look at my skin," said the cop. "Now look at your skin." The cop's point was unmistakable: *We're both Black.* "You, my friend, are African. You are not European," the officer told him.

According to the logic of this Malawi police officer, if you are African, then you're a lower person than the European. As Rigby explains it now, the cop, who had likely never kayaked across the lake or even dreamed of using a kayak, thought that "there's no way that a Black man could be someone that just explores for no reason." If you are African, according to the officer's worldview, the only reason for you to be on the water is if you are a fisherman.

According to the World Bank, Malawi was the poorest country in the world at the time. "They're not teaching them how to swim," says Rigby. "That requires infrastructure and resources."

The police officer's mentality was just a reflection of the legacy of colonialism. "If a white European comes, he's a hero. He can do it all," explains Rigby. "But as a Black African man, you have to put your head down. You can't do anything. He genuinely believed that."

The cop put Rigby on the back of a motorbike and brought him to a jail. They locked him inside with several other inmates.

The jail cell was pitch-black. Rigby could hear coughing and people talking in their native language. The heat was sweltering. The cuffs were so tight that his hands turned purple. There were no toilets, not even a urinal, and "it smelled like piss and shit." The men had to urinate in small water bottles, which was impossible for Rigby because he was handcuffed. The other inmates, in a show of empathy, held the bottle and helped him.

Only one thing saved him from that jail cell. Rigby happened to be friends with an Italian named Francesco who worked for the Discovery Channel; he had joined Rigby in Africa for a few weeks. While Rigby kayaked across the lake, Francesco lagged behind (on foot) by a few days.

Soon Francesco caught up and discovered Rigby was imprisoned. "You have my friend," Francesco told the police. "You have to release him."

That's all it took. They released Rigby on the spot.

They apologized to Francesco, saying it was all a misunderstanding.

"Did you feed him?" Francesco demanded to know.

They said that they had not, but only because they did not know what kind of food Rigby wanted.

It was crystal-clear to Rigby what had happened. They trusted Francesco because he was white. The white man's word had merit. The Black man's word was ignored. Rigby filed a formal complaint with the head of the police, and later he received a letter that apologized on behalf of the Malawi government. In addition to the apology, the government gave Rigby what was essentiality a "get out of jail free" card, a letter to present to the police if he was arrested in the future.

After being released from the jail, Rigby returned to confront the corrupt village chief who had not believed him. The chief had kept his kayak and belongings. The police, now on Rigby's side (thanks to the white Italian who vouched for him), escorted him to the chief and said, "You must make sure that this person has every single one of his belongings."

The villagers came to watch, fascinated. The chief returned Rigby's kayak and tried to shake his hand. Rigby refused. The villagers surrounded Rigby in awe and carried his kayak back to Lake Malawi. They cheered him as he returned to the water.

Mario Rigby meeting with tribal elders, He was continuously astounded by the generosity, wisdom, and authenticity he encountered on his trek through Africa.

Rigby paddled away, and he continued his trek across Africa. The sting of that arrest was offset by the generosity, wisdom, and authenticity he encountered at almost every turn. Africa taught Rigby about sustainability, which is now his passion and the focus of his work. As Rigby walked across Africa, in village after village he discovered sustainability projects that were actually *working*. In Tanzania, he found "more windmills than I have ever seen in my life, trying to leapfrog into the third industrial revolution." He found solar panels in small villages. He was inspired by villagers supporting one another with a microgrid that shares energy among neighbors. "They're moving in the opposite direction of the Western world of borders, individuals, and 'let's not share,'" says Rigby. "In high school [in the United States], we're told not to share, that sharing is cheating, and you'll go to detention. But over there it's a very different kind of economy. Sharing is easier."

The Explorers Club is proud of its Famous Firsts—the members who were first to the Poles, to the summit of Everest, to the bottom of the ocean, to the moon. And these should be celebrated. But there are a few important "firsts" that preceded them, and Rigby rightly points out that exploration hardly began with The Explorers Club, or even with Columbus or Magellan and the sixteenth-century quests for the "new world." Those worlds had already been explored.

"Exploration is something that was always needed, and started from the first humans," says Rigby. "There was a time when scientists said there were only two hundred humans left on the planet. Those two hundred humans decided to do something about it. They left Africa and traversed the entire world. That was needed for survival."

As for the future of exploration? "We need to explore to understand ourselves, so that we can move into a world that's going to be completely different from the one that came before," says Rigby. "We are no longer islands unto our own. We're global communities. Exploration helps bridge that gap."

The EC50

Mario Rigby is part of the inaugural class of The Explorers Club 50 (EC50): "Fifty People Changing the World." In 2021, the Club launched the EC50 to highlight incredible explorers—from diverse backgrounds all around the planet—who tend to be overlooked. The EC50 is now an annual program with a printed publication, and it gives the explorers three years of complimentary membership.

Included among the first inductees were Bolortsetseg Minjin, a paleontologist who helps preserve fossils in Mongolia; Paige West, an anthropologist who works to protect the culture of indigenous people of New Guinea; Craig Mathieson, who trains teenagers how to be explorers at Scotland's Polar Academy; and John Houston, an Inuit art specialist and Arctic filmmaker. They work in different fields—art, space, conservation—but they're all insanely curious, and they likely all would agree with Houston's take on exploration: "If you're not learning and growing, then what are you doing?"

The first issue of *The Explorers Club 50* publication.

Jupiter's volcanic moon, Io, imaged by the *Galileo* spacecraft. Dr. Rosaly Lopes discovered seventy-one previously unknown active volcanoes on Io.

EXPLORING THE SPACE VOLCANOES

The space race inspired a generation of explorers—and not just Americans. On April 12, 1961, the Russian cosmonaut Yuri Gagarin became the first man to travel into space. The capsule launched from what is now Kazakhstan.

Six thousand miles to the south, in Rio de Janeiro, a Brazilian businessman excitedly told his four-year-old daughter that the Russians had gone into space.

"Would you like to go into space, and go to the moon?" the father asked.

"Yes, I would love to go to the moon," the daughter replied.

At the time, the girl didn't really know the meaning of the word "space." She had never heard of Russia. She was four years old. But her father's excitement was contagious, and it stuck with her.

Soon the girl, Rosaly, began to watch the news and follow the space race. She was fascinated by the Apollo missions. Buzz Aldrin, Neil Armstrong, Michael Collins—they became her heroes.

At age six, she decided she wanted to become an astronaut. But even as a kid, she grasped that 1960s NASA wasn't exactly recruiting women from Brazil, particularly if they were nearsighted. Rosaly's older sister had an idea: *Maybe you could become an astronomer?*

Rosaly liked the idea. When her friends played "house," the other girls would say things like "I'm married, and I have three kids" or "I'm married, and I live in a big house with four kids." Seven-year-old Rosaly would proudly say, "I'm not married. I'm an astronomer working for NASA, and I'm very busy."

After the Apollo 13 mission, when Rosaly was thirteen years old, the Brazilian newspapers wrote a glowing story about Frances "Poppy" Northcutt, the first woman to work as an engineer at NASA's Mission Control. It was Northcutt's calculations that brought Apollo 13 back to Earth. Suddenly Rosaly had a role model.

Fast-forward fifty years: After an education at University College London, Rosaly joined NASA's Jet Propulsion Laboratory (JPL). Today she is helping us explore the galaxy in ways that rival even the astronauts.

It starts with volcanoes.

Rosaly Lopes knows more about space volcanoes than anyone else alive. She treks to erupting volcanoes here on Earth ("I need a volcano fix at least once a year"), she crunches data to study the volcanoes of our solar system, and she uses volcanoes to crack the code of extraterrestrial mysteries.

Just as the explorers of yore discovered new lakes and mountains, Lopes is discovering new volcanoes in outer space. Using data from infrared satellite imagery, for example, Lopes and her team discovered active volcanoes on Io, the innermost moon of Jupiter. For perspective, in 1979, *Voyager* traveled to Jupiter and sent back images of Io, delivering surprising evidence of volcanoes. *Voyager* discovered twelve. Lopes discovered seventy-one. Her skill at discovering volcanoes was so masterful, her colleagues at NASA began joking with her: "Oh, big deal, you found another volcano. It's just like collecting stamps." (In 2006, Lopes's discovery of volcanoes landed her in *Guinness World Records*.)

Why are volcanoes so crucial? To understand their secret powers, consider Io. The moon has more than four hundred active volcanoes, so many that "it looks like a pizza," as Lopes says. At first this baffled scientists. *Why does it have active volcanoes?* The moon should have cooled ages ago, and it made no sense that it had molten lava. So they cooked up more theories. And eventually the scientists realized that the gravitational force of Jupiter pulled Io one way, but the gravitational force of the other moons pulled in the opposite direction, creating a tug-of-war. This friction is what keeps Io molten.

"Then we found out with the *Galileo* mission, years later, that the moon next to Io, Europa, actually has an ocean under its icy crust," explains Lopes. And it turns out this is common in the moons of the outer solar system. They have ice on the surface and an ocean underneath. They're called Ocean Worlds. And in the case of Europa, there are signs of volcanism. Volcanoes mean heat. "If you have heat," says Lopes, "and if you have water, those are two of the ingredients you need for life."

Suddenly those volcanoes aren't just stamp collections.

Today, in addition to volcanic research, much of Lopes's work is focused on creating geologic maps of the solar system. Like Dawn Wright, she's continuing

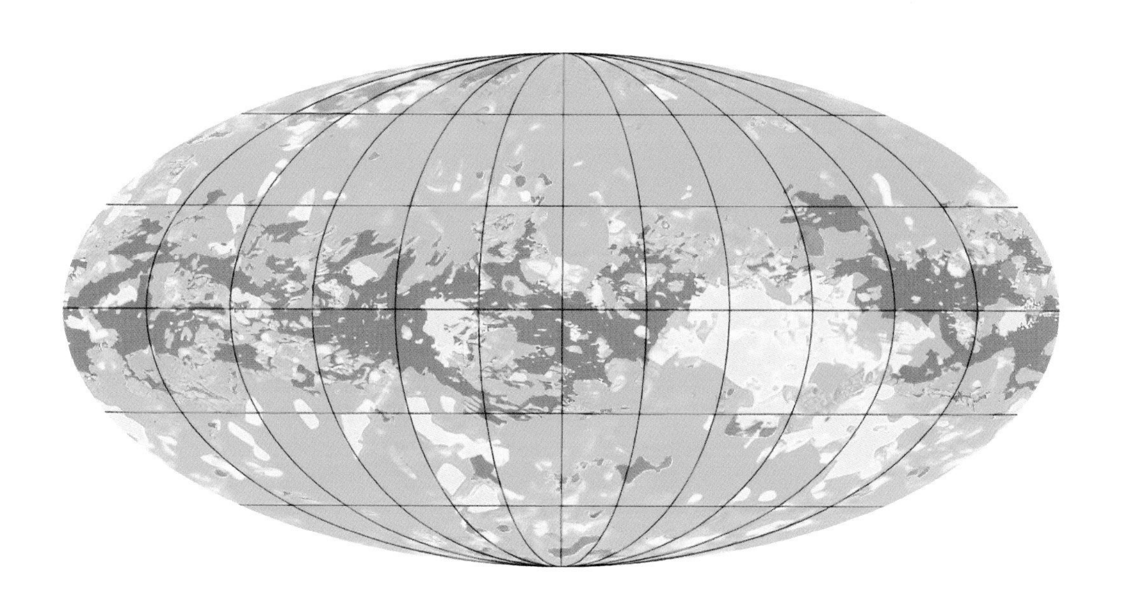

The first geological map of Titan, the largest moon of Saturn, created using data from Lopes's team. Different terrain is represented by different colors. Plains are green, dunes are purple, mountains are yellow, lakes of liquid hydrocarbons are blue, and karst-like terrains, called labyrinths, are pink.

Rosaly Lopes standing by the edge of the Ambrym lava lake with Explorers Club Flag 112. She led an expedition to make infrared measurements of the lava lake to compare with the lava lakes on Jupiter's moon Io.

to map the universe. In 2019, for example, her team used data from radar to create the first geological map of Titan, the largest moon of Saturn, and revealed a stunning world of dunes, lakes, plains, and craters. She literally showed us a new world. "But the lakes are not made of water," Lopes explains. The lakes are made of methane, which exists as a gas on Earth but a liquid on Titan. When NASA unveiled Lopes's map, the image was so arresting that it was used as artwork, shower curtains, and even iPhone cases.

Lopes still thinks back to those dreams she had as a four-year-old girl who wanted to go into outer space, whatever "space" meant. That's one of her first memories. "I'm not able to explore the moon, or potentially Mars one day in person, but I can explore through the eyes of spacecraft," says Lopes. "And it's amazing how much we've done through spacecraft, exploring other planets and asteroids."

This exploration, of course, eventually brought her to a certain Club on Seventieth Street, where she became a member in 2004. She both attends and gives lectures, often bumping into Buzz Aldrin and Jim Lovell and her childhood heroes. Whenever she steps foot in the Club, she sees those signs of the Famous Firsts: first to the North Pole, the South Pole, the summit of Everest, the deepest point of the ocean, the moon. And thanks to Lopes's research understanding volcanoes and the geology of Titan, she's working on reaching her own Famous First.

"We still don't understand how life starts," says Lopes. "But we know some of the conditions have to be water, organic materials, and heat." And NASA found these conditions on Titan, which is why "we think that Titan is one of the best candidates for a place to have life." NASA is planning to launch a new probe to Titan called *Dragonfly*. When it gets there in a decade, it's possible that Lopes will have helped attain "First to Discover Extraterrestrial Life."

The villagers of Kalimungoma prepare the land for the arrival of "the Box."

USHIRIKIANO

When Brandi DeCarli and her business partner, Scott Thompson, met with the villagers of Kalimungoma, in Tanzania, they learned a new word: "Ushirikiano," the spirit of working together.

The word fit the job. They worked with the villagers to set up "the Box," a self-contained agricultural solution that arrives in a shipping container—complete with solar panels and locally sourced seeds. Earlier, to encourage local ownership, DeCarli and Thompson offered the village the opportunity to name the Box, and after much deliberation, they chose "Ushirikiano."

Now, just before the Box arrived, they needed to clear and level a tangled field. DeCarli grabbed a machete and began to hack away. A villager grabbed a machete and joined her, then another, then another. Others took up hoes. Soon a team of villagers hacked away at the brush, working to clear the land and break up the soil. DeCarli kept whacking and sweating.

It was hot and the work was grueling. DeCarli felt fatigued, but then someone shouted something: "USHIRIKIANO!" They all rallied their strength and then someone shouted again, "USHIRIKIANO!" They worked even harder. "USHIRIKIANO!" Soon they finished the field.

On deployment day, as Thompson helped guide the Box into place, songs were sung and dances danced as everyone worked side by side, in the spirit of togetherness, to plant the seeds of a more abundant season ahead.

Since then, DeCarli and Thompson (working with the United Nation's World Food Programme) have installed these Boxes around the world, hoping to create an interconnected ecosystem of "smart farms" to provide food security that's not dependent on giant centralized companies.

They know it's a tall order. But then again, Ushirikiano.

Natalie Knowles and Kayapo Elder Takaknhoti look out over a small pool full of freshwater stingrays off the Xingu River. Takaknhoti grew up without contact to Western society and knows the river and forest intimately. Stingrays were highly sought after by illegal poachers, which decimated fish populations until the Kayapo set up guard-posts.

EXPLORING AS AN EXCHANGE

More than one hundred years ago, Teddy Roosevelt nearly died on a quest to be the "first" to explore the Amazon rainforest's "River of Doubt." But of course he wasn't truly the first. And it was only "new" to him, not the indigenous people who already lived there. "The Teddy Roosevelts, they missed a lot," says Natalie Knowles. She acknowledges that the intentions of Roosevelt and other early explorers were generally good—they were curious and they wanted to learn—but suspects that they almost died because "they missed out; they didn't incorporate or include the people who knew how to live in these environments. The people who knew how to survive and thrive. The people who had already had it mapped."

Knowles is taking a different approach. Since 2015, she has worked with the Kayapo in something of a cultural exchange program. The Kayapo are not easy to find. You fly to São Paulo in Brazil, then head north to Maruba, then it's a bumpy seven-hour drive to the frontier town of Tucuma in a pickup truck, and then eventually—accessible only by boat—you reach the rolling hills of the Kayapo.

The Kayapo are some of the world's best conservationists. They protect more than 10 million hectares from deforestation and degradation, land that includes threatened creatures like black caiman, jaguars, and spider monkeys. Now the Kayapo's job is getting harder. Loggers and tourists threaten this biodiversity, so Knowles works with the International Conservation Fund of Canada to help empower the Kayapo. For example, Knowles deploys "camera traps" to aid in detecting endangered species.

The citizen science youth team from the Xingu River (Bytire) community of Rikaro learning to place camera traps, under the leadership of Elder Takaknhoti and his son, Takaknhore. Cameras provide evidence of a range of endangered, elusive, and endemic species within Kayapo territory, while Takaknhoti's traditional ecological knowledge provides a deep natural and cultural history of the area, which Knowles describes as "far more comprehensive than scientific understanding."

And the Kayapo teach her things in return. For example, she once took a walk with a village elder who casually pulled down a vine and collected herbs that can be used for medicinal purposes. The Kayapo's approach to building was also instructive, not only for Knowles but also for some loggers. The village has a simple design—the houses face inward toward one community center. The architecture is clever. They're made from thin grass poles, with little gaps between the poles that allow the air to circulate. "It's a brilliant design," says Knowles. Once a team of loggers tried to "help" the villagers by building them some modern cement homes with tin roofs. The construction materials made the houses far too hot for the environment; they're now abandoned. Learning to appreciate the locals' wisdom, says Knowles, is "what's so exciting about this shift toward inclusive research and inclusive exploration."

One of Knowles's fellow Club members, David Good, shares a similar story of conservation, community, and cultural exchange. Good has a unique background. His father is an American anthropologist and his mother is a member of the Yanomami, an indigenous people who live on the border of Brazil and Venezuela. Good grew up in New Jersey and only discovered his connection to the Yanomami as an adult. He soon learned that he had much to learn.

Good traveled to the Yanomami to look for his mother, whom he had not seen since he was five years old. He found far more than he had expected. The first thing he noticed was a deep sense of community. The Yanomami word for "stingy" is "shi imi." The Yanomami are the opposite of shi imi.

"Whether it's fishing or hunting or chopping trees, they are doing it as a community," says Good. "If you happen to not collect enough firewood, you go back to the village and you're going to be taken care of." They place a premium on reciprocity and giving.

Whereas much of Western society tries to conquer and tame nature—flattening hills for highways or clearing forests for shopping malls—Good found that "everything [the Yanomami] do is in perfect harmony with the rainforest." The Amazon is their source of food, shelter, and health care. Their homes blend in with the environment. If they hunt a monkey, they use the bones to make a bow and arrow. When they hunt, they never let the population get too low. "Even though my Yanomami family has no idea what year it is and has a counting system of 'one, two, and many,' they are amazing scientists," says Good. Nearly quoting Natalie Knowles word for word, he views the Yanomami as the world's best conservationists.

So he developed the Good Project as a way to empower the Yanomami. "The Yanomami have a right to understand the nature of their external threats," says Good. "This allows them to exchange knowledge and information, and to develop better infrastructure." The focus is on enabling the Yanomami to protect themselves from an invasion of illegal gold miners, to monitor the community's health situation to prevent the spread of diseases like tuberculosis, and (thanks to an Explorers Club grant) to install solar panels.

In the spirit of modern exploration, Good is careful to avoid a top-down model or a "white savior complex" approach, with a heavy-handed solution that ignores local nuance and realities, such as the concrete homes built for the Kayapo. And Good is humble enough to know that we have much to learn from the Yanomami. Consider microbe research. In many Western countries, thanks to processed food, antibiotics, and a stressful lifestyle, "we've lost a lot of microbiomes." The Yanomami haven't. Their rich ecosystem drives higher microbial diversity. "Take a look at the Yanomami. You don't see any

In 2019, Natalie Knowles boats up the Xingu River to the Kamoktidjam village, with supplies for the field season.

inflammatory diseases," says Good. "They don't have increasing rates of cancer." There's less diabetes and obesity and asthma. "Their diversity of microbes is immensely higher than ours."

Scientists are just now beginning to understand the link between microbes and our health. Could the Yanomami help solve this mystery? "Microbes coevolved with humans for thousands and tens of thousands of years," says Good. "Only within a snap of a finger, in the last 150 years of industrialized societies, did we see this stark decrease of microbe diversity. The Yanomami, who are not industrialized, had no such decline." He chuckles as he says this, partly joking but a little bit serious. "They might have the key to saving the world."

Seeking Knowledge Through the Visceral

Many define exploration as "adventure with purpose," and that's Justin Fornal in a nutshell. "The most important part of exploration to me is going somewhere and documenting something that may not have been documented before," says Fornal.

His core passion? Helping to preserve vanishing cultures in crisis zones. Fornal co-created HASAN (History, Arts, and Science Action Network), which collaborates with ostracized minority communities around the globe to help them tell their own story. He works with the Yibir, Tomal, and Migdan people in Somalia as well as the Mandaean, Maʻdān, and Yazadi people in Iraq, as "many communities have never had the privilege to tell their own story."

Fornal describes part of his work as "seeking knowledge through the visceral," and says, "I like to use my body to go as far as I can to find out what people are actually doing." This often involves hands-on historic justice: for example, leading a quest to recover the skull of Nat Turner, a Black enslaved rebellion leader, which had been missing since 1831. Fornal found it and returned it to Turner's descendants.

He's also an endurance athlete (who holds the record for the longest continuous Arctic swim) and cultural detective, who will go undercover to get answers first-hand. On one expedition, he was initiated into a coven of witches in Dar es Salaam, Tanzania, to uncover why people with albinism were being abducted and mutilated for the sake of making amulets.

But he's not always out trekking. Exploration doesn't need to involve distant lands. Fornal hosts the Bronx Game Dinner, a cross-cultural symposium that brings together local hunters, immigrant chefs, diasporic spiritual leaders, and explorers of all stripes. Fornal contrasts himself with a buddy who doesn't like to try any food outside his comfort zone, who thinks, I like hamburgers; why should I try anything else? There's "the hamburger mentality" and then there's what Fornal calls "the explorer's mentality." It's a state of mind. As he describes it, the explorer's mentality is "this hunger, this insatiable curiosity to learn, to taste, to feel things that are different and new."

Dr. Justin Dunnavant, who dives in search of answers.

EXPLORING FOR TRUTH

Like many of the newer Club members, Justin Dunnavant wasn't born into the world of exploration. At first, he thought he'd be a businessman. After skipping two grades and graduating from high school at fifteen, he was ready to conquer the world of finance.

Then came the Mayans. During a study abroad program in Belize, Dunnavant volunteered for an excavation of a Mayan ball court. No experience necessary. "They just needed somebody to pick up a trowel and a shovel to help dig," says Dunnavant. So he dug. And he learned two things: (1) "There's so much history we haven't explored and don't know" and (2) "None of the professors looked like me." Even at Howard, a historically Black college, most of the archaeology professors were white.

That racial disparity gave the field some blind spots. When Dunnavant switched his major to anthropology at age seventeen, for example, he discovered that relatively little was known about the East African slave trade, even though it was much older (starting in AD 700) and more extensive than the West's. This is partly because the source documents were written in languages like Swahili. "A lot of the East African research is in other languages that, frankly, most US scholars and European-based scholars haven't mastered yet," says Dunnavant.

So Dunnavant began to master them. He traveled to Egypt, Dubai, Kenya, and Tanzania and studied Arabic, Amharic, and Swahili, and is now able to travel in six languages. He cofounded the Society of Black Archaeologists with Ayana Omilade Flewellen. Eleven members came to their first in-person meetup, and as Dunnavant says now, "That was the most Black archaeologists

Justin Dunnavant when he's not underwater.

that had ever been in one room together." (For context, there are thousands of archaeologists in the United States.)

Dunnavant learned how to scuba dive and now searches for sunken slave ships, which helps him understand the surprising link between slavery and environmental degradation. "We know that plantation slavery in these Caribbean communities required clear-cutting the forests that were on the islands," he says. "It required burning massive amounts of wood for the rum factories." This led to deforestation and shoreline erosion.

Sometimes Dunnavant dives for coral, a key to his research. St. Croix is losing its coral reef. This is devastating for the local fish and marine life, and that impacts the global food chain. Then there's an even bigger problem: carbon dioxide is absorbed in the ocean through the coral reefs' photosynthesis, "so when the reefs die, we're exacerbating climate change."

Dunnavant conducting underwater archaeology of World War II sites off the coast of Hawaii, with the National Geographic and Ocean Exploration Trust.

And slavery made the problem worse.

"We actually have written accounts of enslaved people being forced to mine coral from the seafloor," says Dunnavant. The enslaved people would ride canoes to a coral-rich site, use long wooden poles to break up the coral, and then free dive to remove coral blocks from the ocean. The coral would be dried, calcified, mixed with lime and mortar, and then turned into blocks that slave owners used to build houses.

Dunnavant dives deep—literally and figuratively—to recover items and artifacts that help us better understand our world. "Every time we locate a piece of history that's tangible, it provides an opportunity to tell a story to a wider audience," he says, yet another example of the crucial role of storytelling in exploration.

Astronaut Dr. Ed Lu.

THE ASTRONAUT DEFENDING US FROM ASTEROIDS

One day when floating in space, Ed Lu had a quiet moment to appreciate the view. He looked down at Earth. Then he looked at the moon. He looked back and forth between the two. Lu was in an extraordinarily unique position to see them both clearly, to put everything into perspective.

The main thing he saw on the moon? Craters. So many craters. The moon's surface was pockmarked with craters, meaning it had been smacked by asteroids again and again throughout its history.

Lu considered some basic facts: Earth is larger than the moon. Therefore it, too, must have been pummeled by asteroids countless times. "This would mean the earth has had all life wiped out, or close to it, many times," Lu says now. "It turns out there are many mass-extinction events, and it happens with regularity." Earth would have plenty of craters, too—more than on the moon—but they're covered by oceans and trees and vegetation. "If you put a crater on the Amazon, in ten years, you can't see it. It just grows over," says Lu. "But on the moon, that's not true."

Lu returned to Earth and then he flew more missions. (Lu's astronaut credentials include a six-month stint on the International Space Station; he also performed the first magic trick in space.) But he couldn't shake that eerie feeling he had when looking at those craters on the moon. And this reminded him that as a little kid, he loved two things: dinosaurs and space. Now the two were linked. From outer space, he had an even deeper understanding of how asteroids had led to the dinosaurs' extinction.

An asteroid wiping out humanity is catnip for Hollywood, but this idea is not a goofy sci-fi plot to Lu. This is hard math.

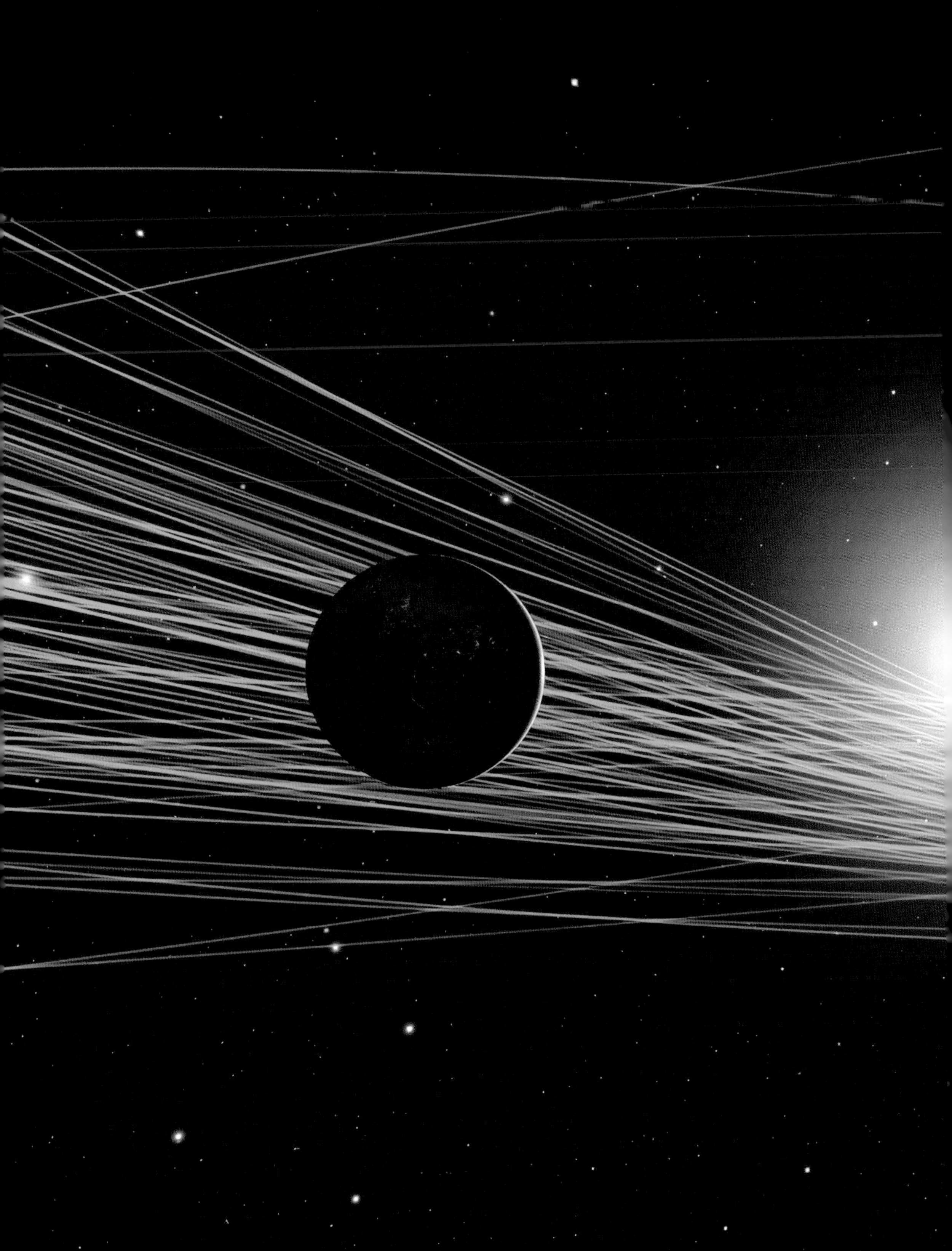

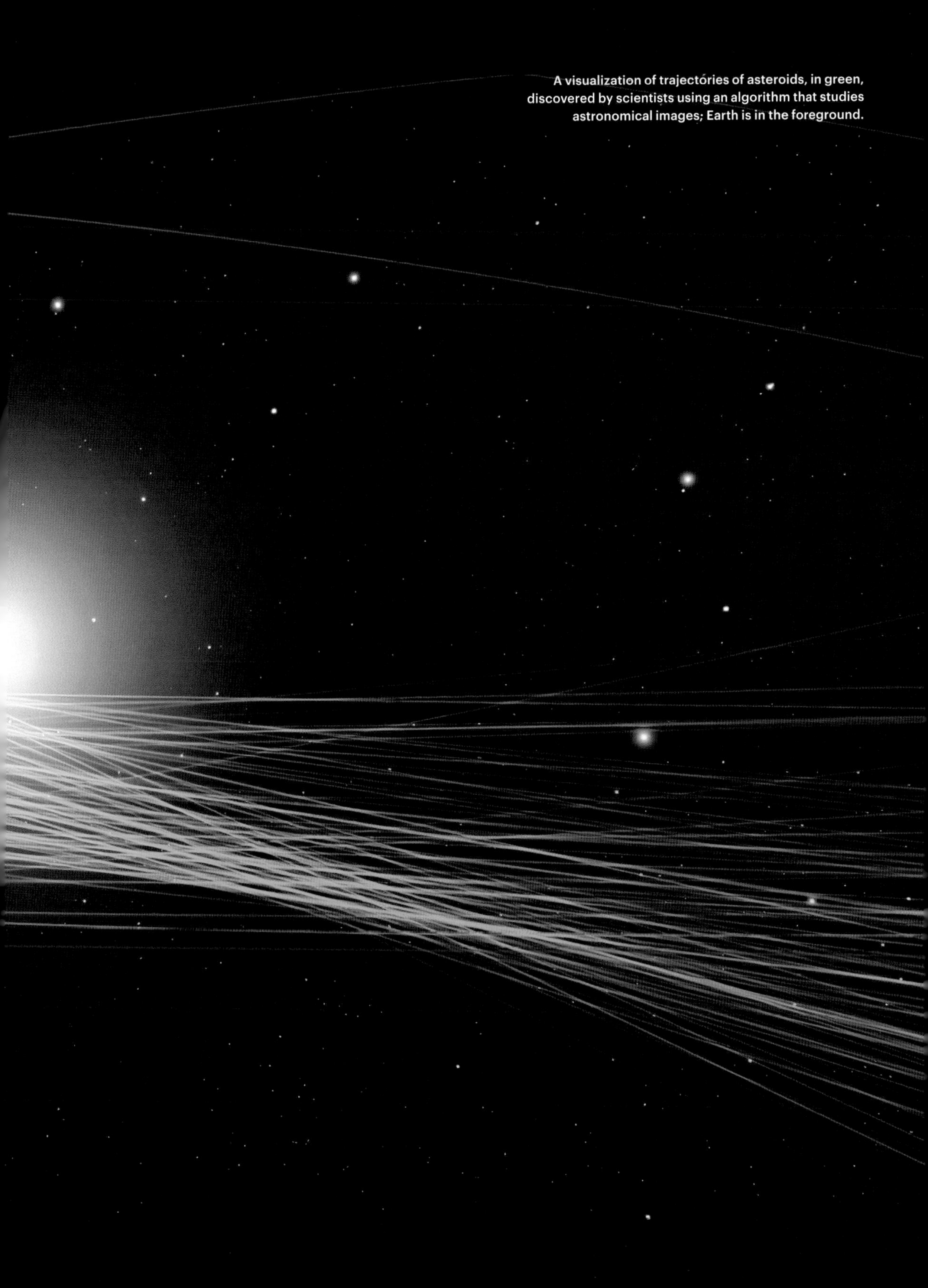
A visualization of trajectories of asteroids, in green, discovered by scientists using an algorithm that studies astronomical images; Earth is in the foreground.

We know that every million years or so, Earth gets struck by something large enough to annihilate human civilization. This sounds like an infinitesimally small chance. But as Lu says, that means that "in the last billion years, it happened a thousand times. It happens a lot."

"Extinction-level" asteroids are not the only ones that can cause problems. Smaller asteroids 50 to 60 meters in length (visualize half a football field) could "take out a city," and they hit Earth every few hundred years. So if you are fortunate enough to live to the age of one hundred, then the chance of a smaller asteroid hitting Earth in your lifetime is 33 percent.

These odds were too high for Ed Lu. So instead of just stewing on the anxiety, he decided to solve the problem.

In 2002, Lu cofounded (along with Apollo astronaut Rusty Schweickart) a program called the B612 Foundation, which has the modest goal of saving Earth from asteroids. The team does two things: (1) works on detecting asteroids that could pose a threat to the planet and (2) creates a means to intercept these asteroids and knock them off course, thereby averting extinction. In other words, Lu and his team are saving all of humanity.

In unwelcome news for Hollywood producers, Lu says that "deflection is easy." "The whole trick is doing this years or even decades before it hits," says Lu. "If you work out the physics, you're basically going to change the velocity of an asteroid by one-millionth of one percent or less. You're not going to make an asteroid make a right-hand turn."

So that's the hard part: detecting the asteroids. This is why the geniuses at B612 are building a four-dimensional "asteroid map" of the solar system, racing to track the locations and trajectories of as many as possible. It's a daunting job. The good news is that more than 90 percent of mega-asteroids large enough to wipe out civilization have been tracked. "None of these will hit the earth in the next one hundred years," he says with confidence. Now the bad news: There are still one million asteroids considered "near Earth" that are large enough to obliterate a city—and the B612 team has only tracked about 1 percent of them.

The stakes literally couldn't be any higher, which is one reason The Explorers Club awarded Lu a Discovery Expedition Grant in 2021. The spirit of exploration is in B612's DNA. "We are driven by a thirst for knowledge," the team's website explains. "Our commitment to discovery is fed by a sense of wonder for the universe, and for our evolving capacity to explore it."

Lu focuses not on the dread of Armageddon, but on the stunning advances in technology that allow this mission in the first place. "It's awesome that we

Ed Lu operating the robotic arm on the International Space Station in 2003.

get to work on this," says Lu. "We live in a society that has the resources and the infrastructure for us to be able to do this. Thousands of years ago, if the planet was hit by an asteroid and wiped out everybody, that's just bad luck. But if it happens twenty years from now, that's not bad luck anymore. We could have done something."

Dr. Gino Caspari and Trevor Wallace's 2017 "Tuva: Horseback Warrior Nomads" expedition. This was the first survey expedition to the Valley of the Tsars, where they explored the origins of an early Iron Age tomb, which ended up being the oldest Scythian tomb found to date.

Club Connections

The question often arises, "What do people actually *do* at The Explorers Club?" Consider the case of Gino Caspari, a Swiss archaeologist. In 2014, Caspari liked to hang out at the Club. He wasn't a member. (At the time, he was getting his master's at Columbia University on a Fulbright scholarship.) But Caspari heard about the Club when he lived in Europe and thought of it as a "magical location," so he attended the Monday night lecture series that were free to the public. He also liked that the beers at the Club were cheap, or at least "cheap for New York."

Caspari frequented the Club so often that, eventually, people began to ask about his research. He was on a decade-long quest to discover the tombs of the ancient Scythians, a nomadic group of horse lords who once roamed the plains of Central Asia. Not much is known about the Scythians. It's a research blind spot. "Archaeology is very much tied to national borders and to language borders," explains Caspari. "Very often a European scholar speaks Russian, but not necessarily Chinese, so they stop at the border." This meant that great chunks of the map were unexplored. "This doesn't make sense," says Caspari with a smile, "as ancient cultures don't adhere to modern state borders."

Soon Caspari became a member, and over cheapish drinks at the weekly Club meetups, he talked shop with other kindred spirits. He soon met a filmmaker named Trevor Wallace. The two hit it off, and Caspari told Wallace about an upcoming trip to Siberia.

"Will you come with me?" Caspari asked.

In 99.9999 percent of the world, the question "Will you come with me to Siberia?" will get an automatic no. The Explorers Club is that .0001 percent exception.

Wallace was in. The two flew to Xinjiang and searched for the tombs that could reveal the secrets of ancient Scythian horse lords. They were thrown in jail by border military guards and talked their way out of prison. Later they discovered the world's oldest Scythian tomb, uncovered a mother lode of eighty skeletons, and investigated the black market of stolen antiquities. Their work continues to this day. So this is what people do at The Explorers Club.

Billy Gauthier standing on a frozen lake, observing the cracks and methane bubbles trapped in the ice. "I've always enjoyed looking at these different lightning-bolt-shaped cracks and cloudy methane bubbles," says Gauthier. "To me it's fascinating that something under your feet can resemble the skies above."

EXPLORERS AS ALLIES

Billy Gauthier is an Inuk sculptor and explorer. Sometimes he creates art, sometimes he works with Adventure Canada (a close partner and sponsor of The Explorers Club) to educate travelers (such as teaching them about traditional Inuit seal hunts), and sometimes he devotes his life—quite literally—to protect nature.

In 2016, for example, he made a powerful argument: *If you don't take this seriously, I will die.* This was not a bluff. Gauthier is from Labrador, Canada, the sprawling land that's home to the Inuit. Nalcor, an energy corporation, was planning to build an 824-megawatt hydroelectric dam by Muskrat Falls.

The problem with this dam? It could poison the community. The dam would send higher levels of methylmercury, a neurotoxin, into the clear waters of Lake Melville. Studies showed that consuming too much methylmercury can lead to a slow deterioration of the human body. The symptoms are numbness and tingling in the fingers, which can be mistaken for signs of diabetes.

This troubled Gauthier. He knew that the local Inuit community, which had once been so healthy, now struggled with diabetes, largely because their diets had changed so drastically, thanks to the influx of American fast food. And Gauthier was tired of seeing his people exploited. This has been happening for centuries. Think back to those overlooked Inuit who accompanied Henson and Peary to the North Pole. "We were almost looked at like the huskies who helped bring them there," says Gauthier.

History had not been kind to the Inuit since the days of Peary. When Americans and Europeans moved into the community, the Inuit "started losing more of their culture," says Gauthier. "And they had more and more

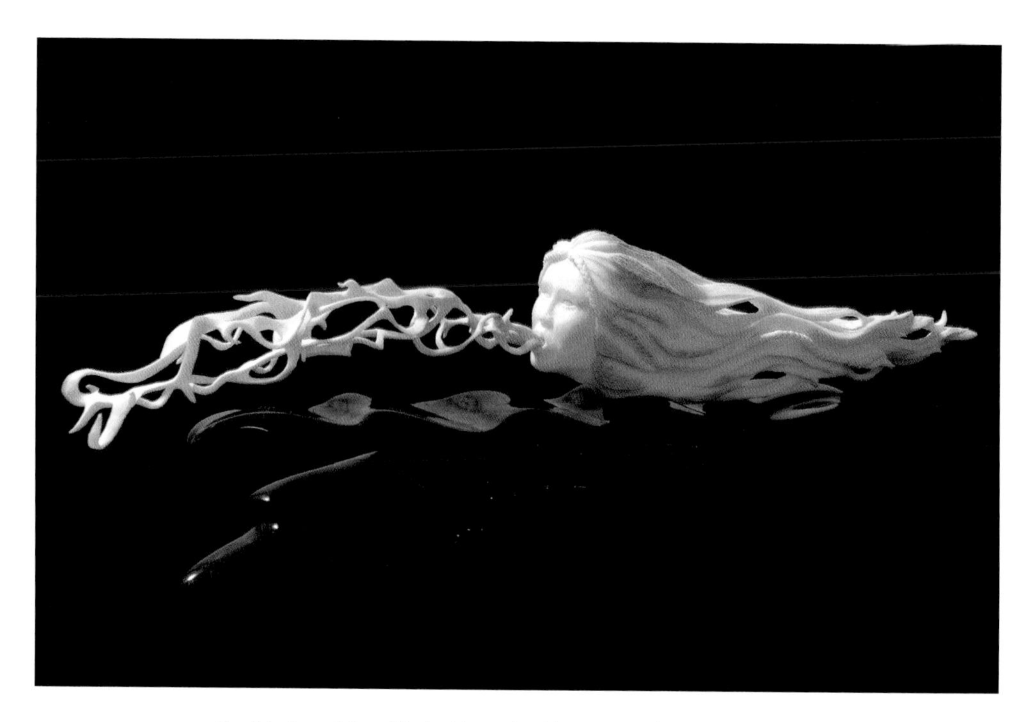

Gauthier's sculpture *Windspirit*, made with moose antler and serpentine. "In the past, Inuit used to believe the winds were caused by massive human-like spirits blowing in the sky," says Gauthier. "Carving the wind out of a single piece of antler was very challenging and extremely rewarding. I need to push the limits of the materials I work with; this is how I learn their true potential, which makes me feel more connected to them. They become a part of me. We can only love the things we know and will only protect the things we love."

problems with alcoholism, obesity, domestic violence, and suicide." And the land itself was pillaged.

Now in 2016 it was happening again, right here in Gauthier's backyard. He knew there was no stopping the construction of the dam. That was a fait accompli. But after researching the science, he knew that a simple action would lower the chances of methylmercury seeping into the Inuit's food: remove all the vegetation near the dam.

At first this sounds like a paradox, but clearing the vegetation would stop the spread of methylmercury to nearby creatures and humans. "If we could convince just one major hydroelectric company to remove the soil, that would be the first time in history that they did it in a way that would minimize the risk of contamination," says Gauthier.

An acclaimed sculptor, Gauthier creates pieces that celebrate Inuit history and culture. He had a platform to bring attention to this issue. He also had plenty of connections: he was on the team of Adventure Canada and served as a cultural ambassador on expedition cruises. Maybe the power and influence of his wealthy collectors could be used to help shine a light on the crisis.

But Gauthier is a realist, and he had a nagging sense that this wouldn't be enough. He needed to take bolder action. That's when he thought about a leader who truly inspired change: Gandhi. The way Gauthier saw it, when Gandhi went on a hunger strike, he told the authorities in India, "My life is in your hands." Gauthier decided to do the same thing. On October 13, 2016, he posted a video of himself eating a local piece of salmon on Facebook, saying it would be the last thing he ate until Nalcor met his demands to clear the vegetation, thereby lowering the risk of poisoning the Inuit.

"Do this, or I am going to die," Gauthier effectively told the company.

He called his mother and told her what he did. She yelled at him and started crying. She knew he was a man of his word and that he wouldn't back down. He also had to tell his fifteen-year-old daughter. She, too, knew that her father was serious.

Telling his family was painful. But to Gauthier, giving up his life was a way of preserving life. "I was willing to give up my life for exactly what gave me life," he says. "There's nothing more worth giving up my life for. Without it there is no me." Everything comes from the land: the food that he eats, the water that he drinks. The land is in him. The land *is* him. So he would die to protect that land.

On the first day he didn't think about food. On the second day he felt hunger. But soon he was surprised to feel something else entirely—clarity. "On the fourth day, I became so much more clearheaded," says Gauthier. He knew that his body was going into ketosis, eating its own fat and tissue, and this can sharpen the mind. He chalks it up to evolution. "For hundreds of thousands of years, people had to think more clearly during those times, to outsmart animals," says Gauthier. (The acuity and benefits of starvation, of course, only last to a certain point. Just ask Adolphus Greely.)

Two others, Jeremias Kohlmeister and Delilah Miriam Saunders, joined him on the hunger strike. Gauthier drank only water but he encouraged the others to drink broth, so that they wouldn't all die at once. (If they died one at a time, Gauthier reasoned, this would extend their window for driving change.) As they starved themselves, Gauthier posted videos on social media and rallied people to his cause. His Facebook post was soon viewed by a staff member at Explorers Club headquarters.

Billy Gauthier—explorer and protector.

Club members jumped into action, setting up a sort of mission control in the Board Room and working on Teddy Roosevelt's Long Table. They tapped into the Club's connections at the United Nations. They started a petition. They reached out to their contacts in the media and outlets began to cover the story, from *Vice* to *The Atlantic* to the *New York Times*. Soon the world began to listen.

Meanwhile, Gauthier continued to refuse food. As the days ticked by and his body grew weaker, a doctor checked up on him. The doctor told Gauthier that, realistically, the authorities could force him to eat. They could hook him up to life support. They could give him an IV if he passed out.

Gauthier looked the doctor in the eye. "I want this to be noted. If I pass out, no matter what happens, even if my mother comes into the room crying, you are not to give me any kind of help." Only one thing would allow the doctor to give him assistance: if Nalcor agreed to his demands.

As Gauthier told the doctor, the hunger strike was part of his indigenous rights. For many generations, Inuit would give up their own food so that others could eat. Old Inuit sacrificed themselves for the young. Now Gauthier was doing the same thing. "I'm willing to give up my food and my life for my people and my land," he told the doctor. "You cannot take that right away from me."

Gauthier kept starving himself. Day 5. Day 7. Day 9. By now Gauthier had the will of the people on his side. Thanks in part to some lightning-quick fundraising, the strikers flew to Ottawa and gave a speech at the capital. They held a rally. They appeared in more news stories. Rallies were held across Canada in support of Gauthier, from St. John's to Toronto.

Finally, thirteen days after his last bite of food, Gauthier received a phone call from Dwight Ball, the premier of Newfoundland and Labrador. Nalcor would agree to his demands.

The land was safe for now. He could eat. Today Billy Gauthier is an official member of The Explorers Club. More than most, he is aware of the complicated history of exploration, a legacy that chronically undervalued the Inuit. But he can separate the dusty past from the glowing future. "The Club brings possibility," says Gauthier. "It brings hope. It brings new ideas to questions you didn't even know you had."

Dr. Laurie Marker with Senay, a female resident cheetah at the Cheetah Conservation Fund (CCF) Centre in Namibia.

THE TRACK OF THE CAT

It started with wine. In 1974, Laurie Marker, a precocious nineteen-year-old, moved to Oregon to open a vineyard. But she needed a day job. On the drive from California, she kept seeing billboards with photos of cheetahs. The billboards had a slogan: FOLLOW THE TRACK OF THE CAT.

Intrigued, Marker followed the billboards to Oregon's wildlife safari and asked if they had any job openings. They did. They liked that she had a background working with animals (in college she had studied to be a veterinarian as well as an enologist), and as Marker says now, "this was rural Oregon, so they were just happy I spoke English."

Her new job was to work in the nursery and treat wounded animals. One day a cheetah came under her care. The first time she saw it, it hissed and spat at her. *Wow, okay, hi,* she thought. And then she looked into those mesmerizing eyes. Suddenly she wanted to know everything about this strange and fascinating creature. (Shades of Callie Veelenturf's simpatico with the sea turtle.)

She asked her colleagues about cheetahs. What's their biology? Why don't they breed well in captivity? Why are they becoming extinct? (In the last century, the number of wild cheetahs plunged from one hundred thousand to seven thousand.)

Nobody had the answers. Marker soon realized that nobody knew *anything* about cheetahs, at least not beyond the obvious. So she dedicated her life to fill in the gaps. "I wanted to collect everything I could and share it with everyone in the world," says Marker. She launched a cheetah breeding program. She traveled to Namibia to study them further. And it was there she discovered that "farmers were killing cheetahs like flies."

Laurie Marker and CCF Senior Ecologist and Forestry Steward Matti Nghikembua check the fence lines at the CCF, which is set on 58,000 hectares in north central Namibia. It's home for many African species in addition to cheetah, such as giraffes, leopards, kudu, Cape vultures, and oryx.

Marker conducts an international Future Farmers of Africa (FFA) training workshop with representatives from cheetah range countries at the CCF. FFA teaches integrated rangeland, livestock, and wildlife management techniques to rural men and women engaged in pastoralism. To date, more than 35,000 people have earned FFA certificates from CCF, making it the most popular training course in the country.

The farmers worried that cheetahs would prey on their livestock, so they trapped them in cages and shot them. *Somebody's got to do something,* Marker said to herself. Maybe the Namibian government, maybe activists, maybe international organizations. Then she realized the truth. There was no "somebody." That somebody would need to be her.

After years of research trips to Namibia, she sold everything she owned and moved there full time in 1991. She would try to save the cheetah. She would go from ranch to ranch, door-to-door, and try to reason with the farmers. Her game plan? She called up the farmers in advance ("If you didn't call ahead, you'd get shot") and asked them a simple favor. If they caught a cheetah in one of their traps, could she come and collect data on the animal before they killed it? Could she put a radio collar on it and release it?

The farmers agreed. So Marker, in the 105-degree heat, sped across the plains of Namibia. She drove an old Land Rover (with no AC) that she held together with duct tape and hay baling wire; her dog rode shotgun and howled in the wind.

Each ranch had a wire gate, sometimes two, and sometimes as many as ten. The ranches were sprawling fields up to 20,000 hectares—nearly the size of Brooklyn. When Marker made it all the way inside and spoke to the farmers, they challenged and tested her. The farmer would point to the wounded cheetah trapped in a cage and laugh about how it bloodied and mangled itself by springing the trap and then trying to run away. "Ha ha ha, isn't that funny!" the farmer would say.

Sometimes they told her gruesome stories about how they killed the cheetah, in an attempt to see if Marker would cry. "They wanted to find out if I was a wuss," she says. But she didn't cry. She kept a straight face, she asked smart questions, and she was genuinely curious about their livestock operations. The farmers were surprised to learn that this young woman had a background in livestock and even served as a national goat judge for many years.

Then Marker got down to business and enlisted the help of the farmer when she anesthetized the cheetah. "Here, take this," she'd say to a farmer and then hand him a stethoscope. "Can you listen to their heartbeat? Isn't that cool?" She had them look inside the cheetah's mouth. She asked for their help holding a vein so she could pull blood. She'd hand a farmer a watch and ask him to help her count the breath rate. "Oh cool, look," she'd say. "That cat has more white on the end of the tail."

She watched the farmers' faces as closely as she watched the cheetahs. "That bought me an hour's worth of time with the farmer," says Marker. "And they looked at the cheetah through my eyes."

Marker explained to the farmers that, amazingly, no one really knows anything about cheetahs. No one had studied their basic biology. No one understands their blood, their breeding patterns. And she did all of this in the heat of the Namibia fields, examining the cheetah on top of its cage or sometimes on the back of her Land Rover. All the while she kept talking to the farmers. Were they killing the cheetahs because the cats had *actually* killed their livestock, or was it a preventive measure?

The farmers began to trust her. And soon the word spread. She built a reputation. Sometimes the farmers were stubborn, but sometimes she would sense a shift, a change in their perspective, and they said they would stop killing cheetahs.

As Marker says now, "That was the start of it."

Her work in Namibia would continue for years and then decades. After a multiyear study that tracked cheetahs' movements, Marker could demonstrate to the farmers—with hard proof—that their livestock was better off (and more profitable) if they let the cheetahs live. Each year she saved more cheetahs' lives.

Marker officially joined the Club in 2006, and soon she found herself mingling with the Buzz Aldrins and Kathryn Sullivans of the world. "I'm not normal, and I don't really have normal conversations with many people," says Marker. "And yet, the people at The Explorers Club, they're not normal either." (Another way Club members aren't "normal": Many recognized the need for conservation decades, or even generations, before the idea became mainstream. More than a century ago, after spending winter after frozen winter on quests to reach the North Pole, Matthew Henson once observed, "The seals are practically gone, and the walrus are being quickly exterminated.")

In one sense, Marker is awed by the members who have been to the moon or the bottom of the ocean. "I'm just a cheetah person," she says with a laugh. But she also thinks that her work is "exploring at a different level." She pauses. "What do we know about our natural world? Not lots. And people don't know that." Marker is now the world's foremost expert on cheetahs. She's the founder and executive director of the Cheetah Conservation Fund, the author of multiple books on cheetahs, and perhaps the person most responsible for saving them from extinction. But in some ways she just did what she set out to do in 1974—she followed the track of the cat.

Marker with Chewbaaka, a cub that came to the CCF as an orphan at ten days of age. (Chewbaaka was named after Marker's favorite *Star Wars* character by a French student conducting research at CCF, hence the French spelling of the furry Wookiee's name.)

Nainoa Thompson, the founder and president of the Polynesian Voyaging Society.

EXPLORING FOR AGENCY

Thor Heyerdahl electrified the world with his voyage of *Kon-Tiki.* The Norwegian proved, beyond any doubt, that it was *possible* for the Polynesians to have sailed from South America. The navigation was simple. You just plopped on a raft and let the wind whisk you to Hawaii. Heyerdahl gave a master class in asking a good question, forming a scientific theory, and then using field research to test that theory. And he did it with gusto; this remains a model for science-driven explorers.

There's only one small problem.

As Doug Herman writes in *Smithsonian,* while Heyerdahl showed that South American roots were theoretically possible, "all other evidence pointed to Southeast Asian origins: oral tradition, archaeological data, linguistic structures and the trail of human-introduced plants. Today we have strong evidence that Polynesians actually reached the Americas, not vice-versa." The consensus from ethnographers, archaeologists, and anthropologists is now clear: the Polynesians almost certainly came from Southeast Asia.

But this now presents an even bigger puzzle than the one Heyerdahl was trying to solve. If the Polynesians came from Southeast Asia, they would have had to sail *into* the wind. This was baffling. How could they have sailed without charts? How could they navigate without a compass?

Enter a Hawaiian named Nainoa Thompson.

In 1976, when he was just twenty-three years old, Thompson joined the crew of *Hōkūleʻa,* a double-hulled canoe that was modeled after the ancient Polynesian vessels. Just as Heyerdahl built a raft using only the balsa wood and materials available to ancient Peruvians, the Hawaiians employed only

The Polynesian Voyaging Society in action.

traditional methods. They lashed together two canoes with a deck straddled in between. This is essentially a catamaran, which suggests that the ancient Polynesians were millennia ahead of their time. "Catamarans are considered a recent innovation inspired by racing sailors seeking speed," explains Sam Low in *Hawaiki Rising,* the definitive account of this story. "But in Polynesia, such craft were invented thousands of years ago—during a time when ponderous single-hull vessels were evolving in the Western world."

The *Hōkūle'a* was a way for Hawaiians to reconnect with their roots. Thompson says that when he grew up in the 1960s, he "found my Hawaiian culture ebbing away." Or as a *Hōkūle'a* crewman says in *Hawaiki Rising,* "We have forgotten our father's footsteps. . . . If we don't care—nobody else cares." The crewman says that when he first saw this double-hulled canoe that symbolized the ancient ways, "it was time to care." As Low puts it, the *Hōkūle'a* stood for "the rebirth of their culture."

The *Hōkūle'a* was first navigated by Mau Piailug, who had been taught the ancient art of navigation by his father, and his father had learned from his grandfather. This chain of oral education stretched back for generations.

To Thompson, who didn't have this training, Piailug was a "miracle man." He was in awe of Piailug's ability to mysteriously read the ocean. It just didn't make sense. How could Piailug possibly guide a canoe across the ocean—at times *into* the winds—without using a compass? Without a map?

The answer, in part, lay in the stars. "I was absolutely fascinated that the stars had a pattern and that you could use them to guide you to Tahiti," Thompson told Low. "All of a sudden, I realized that our ancestry is tied to the heavens and the ocean."

After his first taste of *Hōkūle'a* in 1976, Thompson dedicated his career—his life, really—to learning the art of ancient Polynesian navigation. Through hundreds and even thousands of hours of trial and error, Thompson invented a way to use his hand as a compass. He measured the distance from his fingertips to his knuckles. He measured his fingernails. And by holding his hand to the sky at exactly the right angle, he learned how to measure the stars.

Thompson denied himself the luxury of a magnetic compass, much less GPS or modern tech. But if he could teach himself the art of navigation—and then safely guide the *Hōkūle'a*—that would be a vindication for all Hawaiians.

Think back to the *Kon-Tiki.* Thor Heyerdahl's theory, even if this was not his intent, relegated the ancient Polynesians to passive passengers. They literally just floated where the winds took them. Nainoa Thompson, Mau Piailug, and the other founders of *Hōkūle'a* proposed something completely different:

Nainoa Thompson and Dan Lin holding Explorers Club Flag 124.

The Polynesians could sail against the wind. The Polynesians could sail to any destination they dreamed. The Polynesians, in a word, had agency.

So in 1978, Nainoa Thompson launched the *Hōkūleʻa* on another voyage—from Hawaii to Tahiti, a journey of more than 2,000 miles. They would not have the benefit of Thor Heyerdahl's trade winds.

The ship left Hawaii on March 15, 1978. Thompson studied the stars, he studied the clouds, and he even learned how to navigate from hearing the water slap against the side of the canoe. For thirty-one days they fought through storms, the "doldrums" of no wind whatsoever, and then wind pushing them off course.

Each time Thompson brought them back on track. He constantly scanned the sky, day and night, his skin almost sensing the change in the conditions. He never slept for more than an hour or two at a time, and by the end of the trip his eyes were bloodshot and his body wobbled. "Nainoa was struggling to stay awake," remembers one of his crew. "I said, 'Shit, this guy is going to kill himself.'"

On April 14, Thompson successfully guided the *Hōkūleʻa* into Tahiti, and as Law puts it, "After a hiatus of a thousand years, a Hawaiian navigator had found land in the old way." Thompson had done it. Hawaiians cheered . . . and then they did more than cheer. Thompson and Piailug would take more voyages, they filmed movies with National Geographic, and they helped spur a revival of Polynesian voyaging.

"These voyages, and Piailug's mentorship of Polynesian navigators, stimulated not only the building of canoes, but the revival of Polynesian culture in general," observes Law. "Reinvigorated Hawaiians stood up to demand the return of lands taken from them illegally. In 1993, President Clinton signed the Apology Decree—validating their claims—and today, many Hawaiians are working to regain their sovereignty as a native people."

The work of the Polynesian Voyaging Society continues to this day (and Thompson is still president). More recently, in 2014, Thompson (who later received The Explorers Medal) led a voyage around the world using ancient navigation, traveling 40,000 nautical miles and visiting eighteen nations, encouraging a theme of *mālama honua,* or "care for the planet." Thompson says that the ship returned home to Hawaii with "lessons of hope and action collected from around the world to help us navigate toward a safe, peaceful, and sustainable future for our children."

Club Membership: What "Counts" as Exploration?

Maybe you can jump out of planes while juggling fire. Perhaps you've climbed Kilimanjaro and K2 and Everest ten times. Or maybe you spent the last year in a van, or traversed Siberia on only one ski, or swam across the English Channel while live-tweeting.

These are all impressive feats. They'll no doubt make for fascinating dinner party conversation. They are not, however, credentials for joining The Explorers Club.

"Exploration is really the seeking and discovery of knowledge," says Marc Bryan-Brown, chair of the Club's Membership Committee. "You're looking to answer questions." This wasn't always the case, but the Club now draws a distinction between "adventure" and "exploration." Admittedly, the lines can be fuzzy. And this is not to say that the two are mutually exclusive. "Most of what you'll find in The Explorers Club is 'adventure with purpose,'" says Rebecca Martin, a longtime Club member and consultant serving on the Club's grant programs.

The Explorers Club is not the Tourists Club. If you've had your passport stamped in 130 countries? "Hey, man, good on you," says Bryan-Brown. "That's great. But that's not exploration."

To some extent, the question of what "counts" as exploration is always evolving. As Trevor Wallace, the Club's vice president for research and education, puts it, "The question of 'What is exploration?' is like 'What is art?' Everyone has a different answer." There's one tricky issue that not even all Club members agree on. Does exploration need to involve "fieldwork"? When Bryan-Brown joined the Club in the 1990s, it was "pretty much an absolute" that exploration needs to somehow involve the field—like braving the Arctic or skulking through caves. "This is still pretty true," he says. "We really feel that getting your hands dirty is part of the process."

But that's no longer an ironclad rule. Sometimes there are exceptions. The youngest inaugural poet in US history, Amanda Gorman, captivated the nation with her poem "The Hill We Climb." She also writes poems about exploration. Consider her poem "Earthrise," which reminds us of the perspective of astronaut Bill Anders, who, in 1968, took a photo of the earth from space:

> ***A blue orb hovering over the moon's***
> ***gray horizon,***
> ***with deep oceans and silver skies.***
> ***It was our world's first glance at itself***
> ***Our first chance to see a shared reality,***
> ***A declared stance and a commonality . . .***

Gorman never trekked to Everest or spent a winter in the Arctic, but she somehow captures the spirit of exploration. And she's now a member of The Explorers Club.

Dr. K. David Harrison with Nick Waikai, chief of the Yokoim people, Papua New Guinea.

THE FIRST ENVIRONMENTAL LINGUIST

By committing to decades of practicing ancient navigation skills, Nainoa Thompson helped preserve and restore his Hawaiian culture.

A Club member named K. David Harrison is doing something similar. Not by sailing across the ocean or analyzing the stars, but by learning more languages than you can possibly imagine—even languages that are not documented.

In 1993, Harrison stood in a train station in Moscow and stared at the map. It was a big map. He dreamed about going somewhere in the hinterlands, somewhere isolated, somewhere far away. At the time this wasn't possible, as movement through Russia was heavily restricted. Then the law was changed. Harrison immediately went to the train station, stared at the map once more, and then pointed at the farthest possible destination: Tuva.

A few years out of college, Harrison had been bouncing around Russia, Ukraine, and Poland as a way to immerse himself in the language and cultures. Now he craved someplace even more out of his comfort zone. Since he studied linguistics, he was fascinated by the fact that the Tuvan language had not been scientifically documented.

He took a multiday train ride to Tuva, a small nation inhabited by Yak-herding nomads. He was entranced by this land of wide-open plains, mountains in the distance, with no fences or borders to be seen. In Tuva, land is not privately owned. He loved Tuva so much that when he returned to the United States for graduate school at Yale, he couldn't get Tuva out of his mind.

So he came back to live with the nomads for a full year. There was only one problem. "I realized I didn't have any useful skills in that society," says

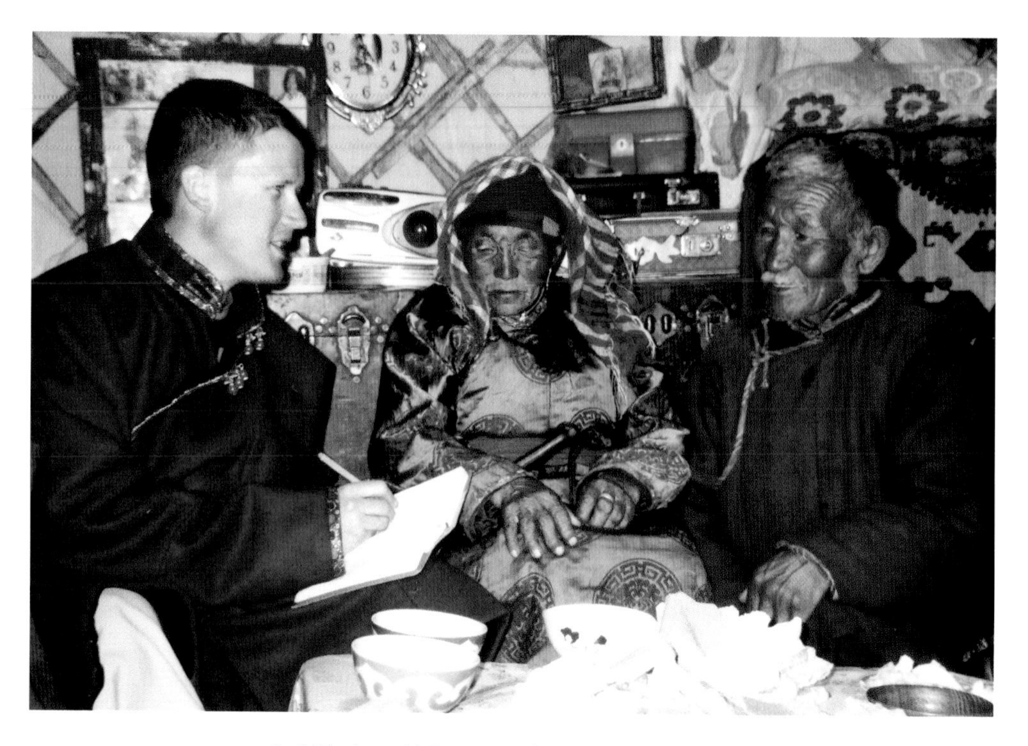

David Harrison with Tuvan consultants in western Mongolia.

Harrison. They found him a role: he was assigned the job of collecting yak manure.

"Yak manure is a very valuable commodity," Harrison explains. He soon mastered the multistage process for collecting it, drying it, stacking it, and eventually bringing it inside the yurt, where you feed it into the stove and then it's fuel to make your tea.

Yak manure taught him lessons about the language. He quickly realized that there's no single word for yak manure; it changes depending on its state. In one page of his notebook he scribbled the title: "100 words for shit."

It soon felt like there were one hundred words for *everything*. The Tuvan language is hyper-dependent on the context and the environment. For example, if you want to say the word "go" correctly, you need to know the nearest river and the direction of the current. You also need to add a key piece of information: Are you going on foot, or are you going on horseback? "That matrix of information helps you select the correct word for 'go,'" says Harrison. At first he didn't know these rules, so he'd just take a stab at guessing, and they would either laugh or correct him. (This was always good-natured.) "But they couldn't explain to me what the underlying system was," says Harrison. "That's the job of the linguist. To collect a lot of speech data and then figure out the underlying rules and principles that govern grammar."

The Tuvans, Harrison learned, were almost always thinking about nature and the environment. No matter what topic he brought up, they would quickly pivot the conversation back to nature. "Even when you greet someone in Tuvan," says Harrison, "the proper greeting is 'Are your sheep fat?' " Or another way to translate this is, "Are your sheep and goats getting fat?" This hyper-specificity when it came to animals and nature was *everywhere;* the Tuvans have twenty-four different names for the colors and patterns of goats.

After many conversations about goats and manure and the current of the rivers, Harrison had his breakthrough insight: *Language is tied to the local landscape and environment.* Suddenly he had a bold new direction for his career, something that had never really existed before: he would become an "environmental linguist." He studies languages in their native habitat. "If you speak a major global language, it's not as connected to local environments," says Harrison. "But if you visit an indigenous community in a single village, their language is more attuned to the local environment."

Harrison documented the Tuvan language for his dissertation at Yale. But that was just one language. And he is just one man. There are at least 7,133 languages on the planet, says Harrison, and thousands are at risk of becoming extinct. So in 2007, Harrison started a partnership with National Geographic, which gave him carte blanche to do any expedition of his choice (good gig if you can get it). He then developed a concept called Language Hot Hotspots, a visualization of where linguistic diversity exists in the world, and where it's threatened. This was his road map. For the next six years, Harrison visited as many of these hotspots as he could, on a race against time to document and preserve these languages.

Why are these languages so important? Just as the Tuvan language was bonded to local geography, countless local languages contain knowledge—even the secrets—of their environment. "This vast knowledge base isn't written down," says Harrison. "It has a huge value to all of humanity, and it's in danger of disappearing."

He gives an example: On an expedition to Futuna, a tiny island in Vanuatu in the South Pacific, Harrison brought along three expert botanists. They greeted the island's village elder. "I'm so glad you came," the elder said. "I just want you to know, we have names for every plant on our island." Then the botanists took out their notebooks, they trekked through the jungles, and they spent two weeks documenting the island's plants. They found *hundreds* of plants they had never seen before. They arranged them all on tarps. "Sure enough, that elder—in combination with other experts in the community—named every single one of those plants," says Harrison. "We basically validated the hypothesis that local people are the scientific experts that should be consulted."

Harrison is also trying to change how explorers collaborate with indigenous cultures. For contrast, consider how a 1921 *Explorers Journal* article describes Colonel Faunthorpe's expedition to India: "Members of the expedition include a native bird collector, a taxidermist . . . a moving-picture operator . . . and about thirty native helpers." They were simply "the help." Nameless and faceless. And even more recently, academic research did something similar. "Linguistics and anthropology used to be fairly extractive sciences," says Harrison. "You go somewhere, you live with a tribe, and then you write a dissertation or a book or something. You basically extract some data from them, and it benefits you."

Now he's trying to change this model. The new framework is the "coproduction of knowledge." Whenever he travels to a new country or location, he ensures that an indigenous expert is a prominent member of the research team—not a fixer who fetches the tents. The local expert is a true collaborator. "That person's name appears as a coauthor on any peer-reviewed paper," says Harrison.

The reason he does this is more than just a question of courtesy, or fairness, or building good relationships. (Although it is certainly all of those things.) The reason, ultimately, is more profound. "Indigenous people are the creators and the stewards of biodiversity," says Harrison, echoing what David Good once said about the Yanomami and microbes. "What they know might save the planet."

Exploration Through Anthropology

By now it should be clear that modern-day exploration has little to do with "adventuring," and as Wade Davis puts it, "anyone who has adventures just hasn't planned their expeditions."

Davis is the author of twenty-three books on exploration. He's an ethnographer and an anthropologist, and he views anthropology as not only a critical part of exploration—but an engine for human progress.

Early twentieth-century anthropologists like Margaret Mead, Ruth Benedict, and Zora Neale Hurston were "real revolutionaries," says Wade, as they "gave us the world that we live in." By spending time in the field and learning about other cultures, anthropologists challenge Victorian-era conventions and suggest new ways of thinking.

The modern era, says Wade, is increasingly a world of "pluralism, multiculturalism, freedom of thought, freedom of religion, and freedom of sexual expression," and this couldn't have happened unless the certainty of old Victorian norms—straight, white, patriarchal—had been "challenged by anthropology."

David Harrison and Gregory Anderson interview Charlie Mangulda, the last speaker of the Amurdag language, in Australia.

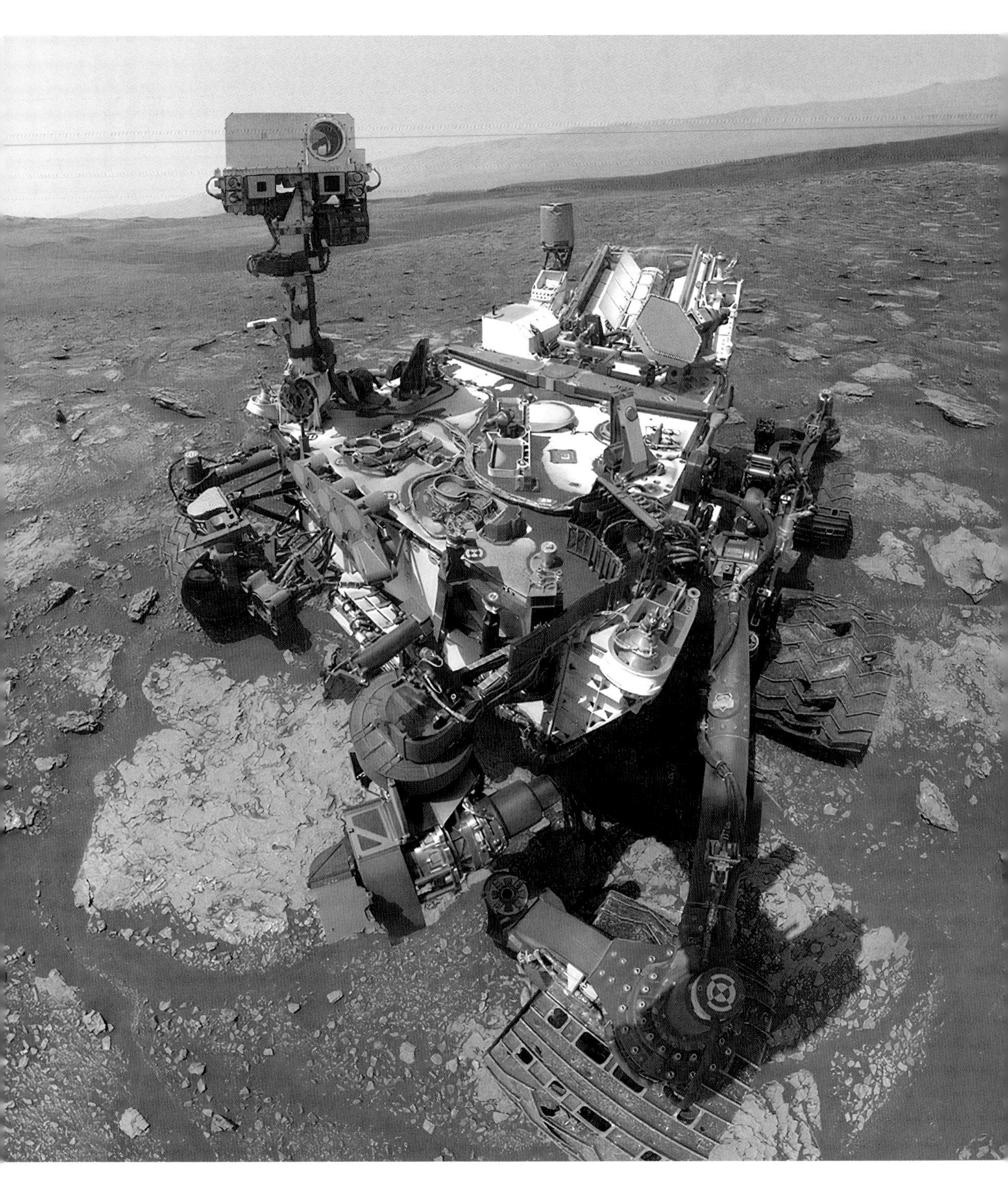

The Martian rover Perseverance.

EXPLORING THE RED PLANET

From an office in New Mexico, a NASA engineer looked at a report. As usual, on schedule, one of the two Mars rovers, the *Curiosity*, sent a batch of data back to Earth. But something looked funky.

The engineer studied it closer. The data, from a parameter called HK29 that measures voltage, looked off. Why is that important? The rover does more than rumble across Martian craters and snap photos—it also shoots lasers. It shoots *a lot* of lasers. Since landing on Mars in 2012, an instrument on *Curiosity* called the "ChemCam" (short for the Chemistry and Camera tool) had zapped its laser more than 880,000 times.

Each burst of the laser requires high voltage. Specifically, the ChemCam shoots a beam for thirty pulses, then it moves, then it shoots another thirty pulses, and so on. The more pulses you shoot, the hotter the machine gets. This is normal. But for some reason, now the "high voltage" readings had careened to dangerous levels that could break the ChemCam.

"This is a two-billion-dollar mission," says the woman in charge of ChemCam, Nina Lanza. Officially, Lanza's title is "principal investigator" of the ChemCam. Unofficially, her Twitter profile says, "I shoot the lasers, pew pew." With her usual humor she adds, "NASA is not cool with you sometimes being like, 'We don't care if it breaks, we'll just use it.' They don't let you do that." Suddenly the mission, or at least a core part of it, was in peril.

We might not (yet) have the ability to send astronauts to Mars-walk across the red rocks, and we're not (yet) able to bring samples back to Earth for inspection, but the laser lets scientists like Lanza literally get a deeper understanding of Mars. The laser cuts into the rocks and reveals their secrets.

Martian real estate.

Using a technology called LIBS (laser-induced breakdown spectroscopy), the laser sponges up data from the interior of rocks (as well as the exterior) and then sends it back home. These lasers have already helped NASA make a trove of discoveries, including: Mars once contained ancient lakes; Mars once had flash flooding; and Mars contains high levels of something called manganese oxides, which could be a hint of atmospheric oxygen.

Translation?

Nina Lanza, just like Rosaly Lopes of NASA's Jet Propulsion Laboratory, is searching for signs of extraterrestrial life.

And the search is heating up.

Lopes focused much of her work on volcanoes; Lanza is focused on rocks—or rock varnish, to be more precise. As Lanza knows from many field expeditions on Earth, rock varnish can form in tough environments that are arid, hot, cold, or have high radiation. Microscopic life can exist under the surface, clinging to rock varnish and hidden to the naked eye. "The surface of Mars is very inhospitable. It's a high-radiation environment. There's no protective magnetic shield on Mars," says Lanza. "But *just* beneath the surface—maybe in a little crack—you're very protected, and you still have access to all of the resources [like water or dewdrops] outside of the rock."

She is now confident that the *conditions* for life are present. The goal of the *Curiosity* rover, which launched in 2011, was to understand the potential habitability on Mars and whether life could exist. "The answer, after ten years, is a resounding yes. Absolutely. Very habitable. Highly habitable." (This does not, however, necessarily mean that Lanza is the biggest fan of colonizing Mars. "Like, that place sucks," says Lanza, laughing. "I love Mars, but it's not a great place to live if you're a person.")

Lanza has been fascinated by Mars ever since the 1996 *Pathfinder* mission, when she saw those early glimpses of the dusty red planet. Something about those images was just *different*. "If you didn't know they were from Mars, you would think they were from a smoggy day in California," says Lanza. They just felt more relatable than the usual photos of darkness in space. "It looked like something you could touch. You go to an alien world and find yourself at home," she adds, speaking with energy and gusto and even joy.

If the goal of *Curiosity* was to seek out the conditions for life, the goal of *Perseverance,* which landed in 2021, goes one step further. *Perseverance* is looking for signs of biosignatures; it's also sampling rocks in Jezero Crater (thought to have once been a lake), and is then collecting and gathering those rocks for an eventual return to Earth. That has never happened before.

The NASA official Mars Sample Return concept, envisioning the equipment which will eventually bring the Martian samples to Earth.

In just a few years, NASA will study these rocks in laboratories. And Lanza predicts that "it's going to change, fundamentally, everything that we know about Mars."

To those not paying attention, "life on Mars" might sound like the most speculative bits of science fiction. Lanza sees it differently. "That's not a crazy thing to even suggest anymore," she says. "Because we know the conditions were ripe on Mars at this time. All the conditions were there. Now *was* it there?"

This is harder to prove.

One way to prove it is with the laser on ChemCam, and this is the laser that had been shut down.

It was too valuable to risk breaking. But it was also too essential to ignore.

Lanza and an international team of engineers sprang into action. They pored through an ocean of their old data and went to the original engineers who designed the circuit board. They worked with their colleagues in France, who happened to discover an old board (similar to ChemCam's) lying on somebody's shelf.

For three months, the teams literally worked around the clock to diagnose the problem. They operated simulated versions of the laser here on Earth. And after months of meticulous trials and measurements, they concluded that they could safely shoot the laser under a certain range of temperatures. The $2 billion mission was saved.

In recognition of this heroic feat of engineering, which was virtually ignored by the press at the time, The Explorers Club awarded Lanza and her team of engineers the Club's Citation of Merit in 2022. Lanza is thrilled for the engineers. "The engineers never get anything," she says. "They're the bedrock of the team. They're keeping the instruments going, but they get no glory, ever. So it's nice to acknowledge them. They don't usually win awards."

And perhaps most important, the ChemCam laser has flared back to life, as did the search for life on Mars. Pew pew.

Dr. Nina Lanza in Haughton crater on Devon Island, Canada, in 2022, during a field research campaign supported by The Explorers Club Discovery Expedition grant. She's sitting next to what she calls "an absolutely massive outcropping of hydrothermal selenite, a type of gypsum (calcium sulfate) that forms large, beautiful crystals as it slowly grows underground in hot waters. I have never seen anything like this anywhere else! Definitely museum-quality samples."

Field research on Earth can help understand Mars. Lanza explains that "sulfate minerals are quite common on Mars, so we took a GRNS (gamma-ray and neutron spectroscopy) measurement on this outcrop to provide a good end-member measurement."

Dr. Sian Proctor—poet, artist, scientist, entrepreneur, explorer.

FOOD, ART, AND THE JOURNEY TO MARS

1969. On board the command module *Columbia,* Neil Armstrong, Buzz Aldrin, and Michael Collins returned from the moon. They didn't do this on their own. In offices scattered across the globe, NASA scientists and technicians worked to track their ship and guide them home.

One of these tracking stations was in Guam. A man named Ed Proctor, one of NASA's overlooked Black technicians, helped crunch the numbers to compute the exact trajectory and speed for landing safely.

The Apollo 11 astronauts knew that without Proctor and the other brilliant teams of engineers and scientists, the *Eagle* never would have landed. They were so grateful for the engineers' work that they made a special trip to all of the tracking stations, including Guam. Neil Armstrong shook Ed Proctor's hand and thanked him.

Proctor kept that note for the rest of his life. He treasured it. And he passed his love of space to his daughter, Sian, born just months after the Apollo 11 mission.

Sian was a feisty, independent kid who loved airplanes and playing outdoors. She was fascinated by astronauts and fighter pilots; she even kept a photo of an F-16 in her locker. Maybe she could be an astronaut? That was her childhood dream. But as with Rosaly Lopes and Dawn Wright and countless other would-be space explorers, at the time, it looked like only white men were eligible. NASA didn't exactly seem to be recruiting Black women astronauts. That world seemed closed.

Sian tried to be a realist, but her childhood dream never truly died. Many years later, someone emailed her to say that NASA was once again looking for astronauts. She knew the odds were comically low. When thirty-five hundred apply, they only choose nine. But Proctor looked at all the requirements and realized that she met almost every criteria, so she applied anyway.

In 2009, Sian Proctor made it to the final round—the top 1 percent of applicants—and all the way to a final yes/no phone call. The call was with astronaut Sunita Williams, who, at the time, held the record for most spacewalks by a woman.

Proctor received that fateful call . . .

. . . and the answer was no.

That childhood dream slipped away.

But Proctor realized that even if she couldn't personally go to space, she could still contribute to space exploration. She turned herself into an "analog astronaut," doing work on Earth that could help the frontiers of space.

For example, Proctor spent four months in a NASA-funded simulation of living on Mars. She focused on food strategies for long-duration spaceflight. Using freeze-drying technology, she experimented with different combinations and developed a program—and even a cookbook—called Meals for Mars.

Proctor's "space food" came a long way from the powdered beverages of the Gemini missions. The breakthrough was freeze-drying. Unlike normal "dehydrated" food (which Proctor admits tastes terrible), freeze-drying extracts the water from food under extreme conditions, and leaves the food with the same texture and taste. This isn't just about the taste of food for astronauts. And this isn't just about Mars. Proctor thought deeply about food and culture and sustainability, and she saw a connection between what's needed on Mars and the environmental problems on Earth.

"If we solve for space, we solve for Earth," Proctor once said in a TEDx Talk. "All the things that we need for space exploration to be efficient—food, water, energy, shelter—those things are the same things that we need to be able to thrive here on Earth."

Proctor's logic: If, hypothetically, we want to create future habitats on the moon or even Mars, then we need to think about food supply lines. "The food that we're going to be sending to them needs to be lightweight and shelf-stable," says Proctor. And if we can do that for the moon, then why couldn't we unleash that same tech on Earth?

She asks an even more provocative question: What if we collectively decide that when we eat fresh food, we eat only food that's locally grown? And if we need to import food, we only do it if it's freeze-dried. What would that look like? It would mean that in places like Arizona, say, the precious water would remain in the state.

"It would mean that we would no longer need huge refrigerators, because most of our food would be shelf-stable," Proctor said. "Let's stop the transportation of water around the world in the form of food. Let's take the water out of the food, leave it at its local source, and ship the nutrients." This would slash the costs. This would reduce food waste and spoilage. This would feed more people. This would make the planet more sustainable. And it wouldn't mean we could no longer eat fresh vegetables; you simply rehydrate the freeze-dried foods. It's easy. Before giving her talk, Proctor enjoyed a "Martian meal" of rehydrated chicken, rehydrated broccoli, and rehydrated peppers mixed with some spices and chow mein noodles. "It was totally delicious."

So even if Proctor couldn't be an astronaut, her role of "analog astronaut" could inspire others and help create real change. Food wasn't her only area of exploration. She's also a self-described "space artist," creating art with her drawing, paintings, and poetry. Her poems embrace the spirit of exploration, like these lines from "Seeker":

Why Go?
Because I can
It is what humans do
We explore, We observe, We learn

"It is what humans do." The poem caught the eye of Richard Garriott, president of The Explorers Club, who happened to be preparing for a dive to the bottom of the Mariana Trench.

Garriott and Proctor connected on Twitter, and Garriott was so inspired by the poem that he took it with him to the bottom of the sea, along with an Explorers Club flag. The poem would later travel with astronaut (and Club member) Scott Parazynski to the *Titanic*.

In a classic example of Explorers Club serendipity, Proctor was selected as part of the inaugural EC50. She asked Garriott to be her mentor. He happily agreed and the two became good friends. "She's an unstoppable force of nature," says Garriott, who could relate more than most to Proctor's lifelong dream of going to space.

Proctor's father had worked at NASA; Garriott's father, Owen, was the first astronaut to go into space who wasn't a pilot; he spent a then-record 59 days in space at Skylab in 1973.

Like Proctor, Garriott inherited his father's dream of going to space. But also like Proctor, it didn't seem possible. At thirteen he flunked his vision test and had no chance of making NASA's cut.

Then Garriott did something a little unusual. He said that if he couldn't go to space with NASA, he'd somehow find his own way. As a high school student in the 1970s, Garriott began writing computer games. (He's now credited as the inventor of MMORPG, or massively multiplayer online role-playing games, such as *Fortnite* and *Roblox*.) And when he sold his first original game and received his first royalty check, he realized it was larger than his father's annual income as a NASA astronaut.

He had a purpose for that money: space.

This was in the early 1980s, two decades before SpaceX or Blue Origin. Garriott helped to launch early private space companies like Space Adventures and Zero-G (which gave thrill-seekers a taste of zero gravity), and while it didn't get him into space, it led to him leading private expeditions to places like the *Titanic*, or using a nuclear icebreaker to reach the North Pole. (Nukes are the new sledge dogs.)

For more than half a century, there were only two ways to get to space: the United States or Russia. NASA told him no. Maybe Russia would say yes? Finally, after decades of trials and setbacks (including a risky surgery to remove part of his liver), he talked his way (and paid a fat check) to ride the Russian Soyuz shuttle. He spent two years training at a Russian military base with armed guards on the perimeter. And on October 12, 2008, roughly thirty years after he decided to will himself into space, Garriott blasted off to the International Space Station.

Richard Garriott met Sian Proctor at an interesting moment in her life. Everything seemed to click: Her work as an "analog astronaut" advanced space exploration; her art and poetry inspired a new generation; and her work on "Martian food" was a step toward solving sustainability problems here on Earth. She had just joined The Explorers Club. She might not be an astronaut—99.999 percent of people aren't—but she could take pride in what she had accomplished.

Then she heard about Inspiration4.

The idea was simple. As part of SpaceX's mission to explore Mars and make humans an interplanetary species, four civilian astronauts would fly into orbit. The first was Commander Jared Isaacman, an entrepreneur turned pilot who holds the aviation speed record for circumnavigating the world in a light jet. Isaacman used Inspiration4 to raise $243 million for childhood

Richard Garriott, the forty-fifth President of The Explorers Club.

cancer research (he viewed it as an "offset" to the money spent on space), and he launched an "entrepreneurship competition" for one of the four coveted seats—who could make a compelling pitch?

Proctor thought about how to apply. She could have positioned herself as a geologist or a scientist or a successful businessperson or an explorer—all of these things were true. But she focused on her poetry and her art. She shared a poem that's part of her concept called "Space2Inspire," which begins:

> You've got space
> I've got space
> We all have Space2inspire
> That's why we dream of going higher and higher

Proctor's poem encapsulates much of how exploration has evolved. It even articulates many of the themes from this book: shifts from exploitation to conservation, from conquering to collaboration, from exclusion to inclusion. Consider her next stanza:

> But what is space if you can't breathe
> Let's stop sucking out the air of our humanity
> We have a moment to seize the light
> Earth from space—both day and night

She doesn't see space exploration and environmentalism as mutually exclusive. She sees them as the same journey. And to promote inclusivity, she champions a concept she calls "J.E.D.I. space":

> We have J for justice to ignite the bold
> We have E for equity to cut past the old
> We have D for diversity to end the fight
> We have I for inclusion to try and make it right

Proctor's poem seemed to resonate. In three days it racked up seventy thousand views, including one from Jared Isaacman. He soon called her over Zoom and told her, "You're gonna go to space."

Consider how the very selection process of exploration has changed. Almost 140 years earlier, Adolphus Greely led a team of twenty-four men—most from the army, and funded by the US government—on a deadly

Sian Proctor

Christopher Sembroski

Jared Isaacman

Hayley Arceneaux

The crew of Inspiration4 checking out the Artemis Orion capsule mockup at the Johnson Space Center.

mission to the Arctic. (One suspects they would have been more successful if Henrietta had joined the expedition itself; then again they would have had no one at home to bail them out.) With the exception of two Inuit, they were all white. They barely trained and had no backup plans. If something went wrong, they would die.

This is no longer how exploration works. Proctor's qualifications, in contrast, were based on her own creativity and passion. And it was not lost on her that she would be the world's first Black female space pilot. "I feel very fortunate to be advancing women of color in space," she later said. "We have been overlooked, have not been supported as much as we could be. I would like to see that change."

Isaacman, Proctor, and their two crewmates—physician assistant and pediatric cancer survivor Hayley Arceneaux and data engineer Christopher Sembroski (both now Club members)—spent five months in training.

Every Monday night, the crew had mentorship calls from Richard Garriott and NASA astronauts. Early on, Garriott impressed upon them the importance of doing more training than they thought they'd need. "As an astronaut, you have to be trained to operate every system, and to be an expert on fixing at least one system," he says. The crew asked for more training; they got it. Isaacman looked forward to the simulations—the harder the better. "I liked the ones best where we died," says Isaacman. "I found those to be really instructive. You want to dig in and understand what's going on."

And the Apollo astronauts did more than just inspire the crew—they gave them mentorship and advice. (As Apollo astronaut Charlie Duke said of commercial spaceflight, "At first I was skeptical, but it's amazing what they're up to. This is opening up space travel to a lot of people who wouldn't have the opportunity.") They received a send-off call from Buzz Aldrin. The astronauts advised the crew to write two sets of letters to their family: one version for a good scenario, one version for the Greely scenario.

The astronauts were allowed to bring a few personal items, including Explorers Club Flag 218. Isaacman brought a stuffed animal to help reassure his two young daughters. It didn't take Proctor long to figure out what she would bring: her poetry, her artwork, and the autographed note from Neil Armstrong to her father, signed just over fifty years before.

On the morning of the launch, the crew stared up at Falcon 9, silhouetted in the night sky. The capsule was called *Resilience*—fitting, for Proctor—and it was the most beautiful thing she had ever seen. She called her family before the launch and told them, filled with tears, "I'm the happiest I've ever been in my life." Her father had passed away when she was nineteen and her mother when

The crew of Inspiration4 prepares for another parabola during a Zero-G flight.

she was forty-eight, but now she felt that "Mom and Dad are coming with me."

The crew also received a surprising call. "Good afternoon, this is Michelle Obama," the voice said from the other end of the line, to Proctor's delight. "You are making history, and I just want to thank all of you for your curiosity and your courage and your bravery."

They would lift off from Launch Pad 39A—the same one used for the Apollo missions. They took the elevator up 255 feet.

And as they traveled up, millions of people wondered . . . Is it worth it?

Is it worth the billions of dollars? Shouldn't those dollars be spent elsewhere? Is it worth the risk?

Isaacman gets the pushback. "Spaceflight is controversial," he says. "I completely hear the argument. It's so costly. How can you do all of that when we've got these problems here on Earth?" The way Isaacman sees it, the vast majority of resources should indeed be spent on the very real challenges at home, but at the same time, "we don't push the pause button on progress."

It doesn't always make the headlines, but scientific study remains the beating heart of space exploration. Jared Isaacman and Hayley Arceneaux perform an ultrasound of the eye during an experiment studying the effects of Spaceflight Associated Neuro-Ocular Syndrome (SANS).

"It's not always immediately apparent" how innovation will benefit all of humankind, says Isaacman, "but then down the road, everything changes." And he thinks certain questions deserve answers. "We know so little about our place in the universe. These are questions people have been asking since the beginning of time. 'Why are we here? Are we alone? What's our purpose?' "

But as Proctor, Isaacman, Arceneaux, and Sembroski slowly ascended the elevator on Launch Pad 39A, they weren't thinking about the ethics or philosophy of space funding. They had a job to do. They strapped into the cabin of *Resilience,* they said "go for takeoff," they felt the force of 3Gs thunder into their chests, and in the "Dragon 2" capsule, they soared into the sky to do what explorers have done for centuries—they left to chase the dragon.

Sian Proctor speaks at the 2022 Explorers Club Annual Dinner.

Several months after the launch, at the 2022 ECAD, Proctor was among the one thousand Club members who attended the annual gala. In keeping with the Club's long tradition, they wore black tie, and a few sampled unusual foods, such as tarantulas and python and alligator. They honored members like Rick Ridgeway (the legendary mountaineer), Dereck and Beverly Joubert (conservation icons), and Victor Vescovo (who had descended to the "Five Deeps"—the bottom of each of the five oceans).

Toward the end of the ceremony, the MC, Josh Gates, took the stage to introduce Sian Proctor. "I'm not sure that I can adequately sum up the work and accomplishments of Dr. Sian Proctor," he said. "She is a scientist and explorer. A poet and astronaut. . . . She brought her talents and her original poetry to space. And tonight, she brings them back to Earth for all of us."

Dr. Proctor took the stage, beaming. She looked out at the crowd. Then Proctor had a small request for her colleagues. "Raise your hand if you are on Twitter?"

Some nervous chuckles.

"Don't be afraid. Raise your hand!"

Plenty of hands shot into the air. Proctor explained that she won her seat on Inspiration4 thanks to her tweet going viral, and it's also how she connected with Richard Garriott. This seems fitting. The barriers to exploration have crumbled, and sometimes all it takes is a tweet.

Proctor then read aloud her poem "Seeker," which much like a Club flag has now been to the bottom of the ocean, to the *Titanic,* and to outer space. (She later donated the artwork of "Seeker" to the St. Jude Children's Research Hospital.)

As the dinner wound down and members shuffled to the makeshift dance floor—yes, explorers dance—Proctor mingled with her new colleagues: Laurie Marker, Asha Stuart, Mike Massimino, Nina Lanza, Richard Wiese, Brandi DeCarli, and a thousand other explorers who would be amused by the question "What's left to explore?"

It's true that much of the weekend honored the past, and young explorers marveled at artifacts like Matthew Henson's mittens, Roy Chapman Andrews's bullwhip, or the globe used to plan *Kon-Tiki.* And on the second-floor library, next to the rare and treasured books, it's impossible to miss that grim painting of an Arctic rescue—the Club still feels the ghosts of Adolphus Greely.

. . . kind of. The reality is that for most of the weekend, the explorers spent little time reminiscing over Shackleton or Greely or other dead men from a century ago. They were planning. Connecting. Brainstorming. On the Monday after ECAD, in a quiet moment when the crowds had thinned, Gino Caspari and Trevor Wallace once again visited the map room—not to dwell on the past, but to inspect the maps for clues that could help a secret new mission. Over closing ceremony cocktails on Sunday, a behavioral therapist who studies the trauma of indigenous cultures met an anthropologist who's focused on linguistics; the two women realized they had surprising overlap in their research, and they plotted a joint expedition. And the "two Callies," Callie Veelenturf and Callie Broaddus, realized that they could work together on "rights of nature" as an advocacy tool for conservation—one focused on the oceans, the other focused on the land.

These members did not join the Club to indulge in nostalgia. They joined to explore the future. And they can relate to what Club member Christopher Sembroski said after seeing the world from space: "This makes me want to explore the whole earth. It feels like the beginning of a much longer book."

Or as Jared Isaacman once said, "It feels like it's game on. . . . Humanity is just getting started."

"We shall not cease from exploration
And the end of all our exploring
Will be to arrive where we started
And know the place for the first time."

—T.S. ELIOT

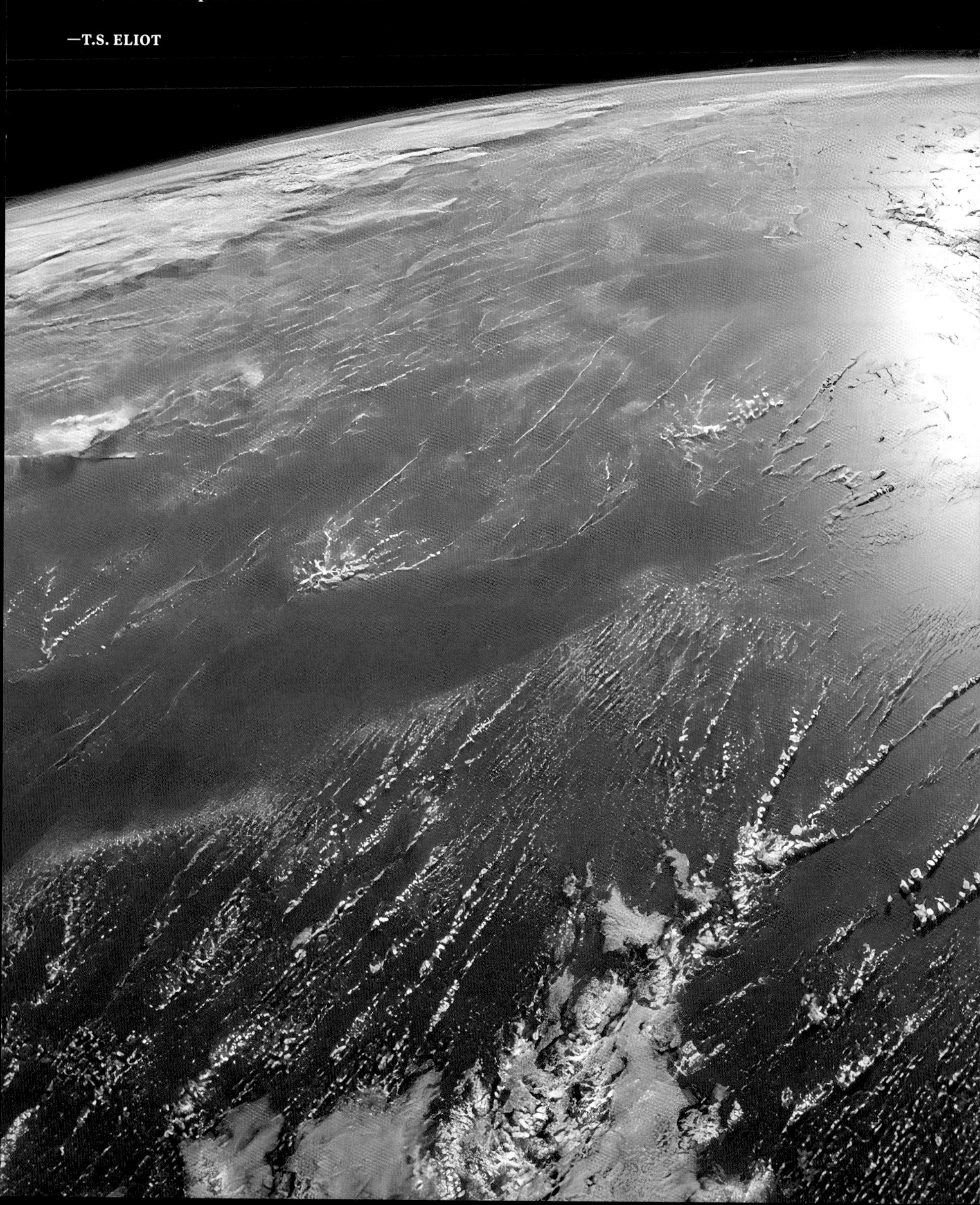

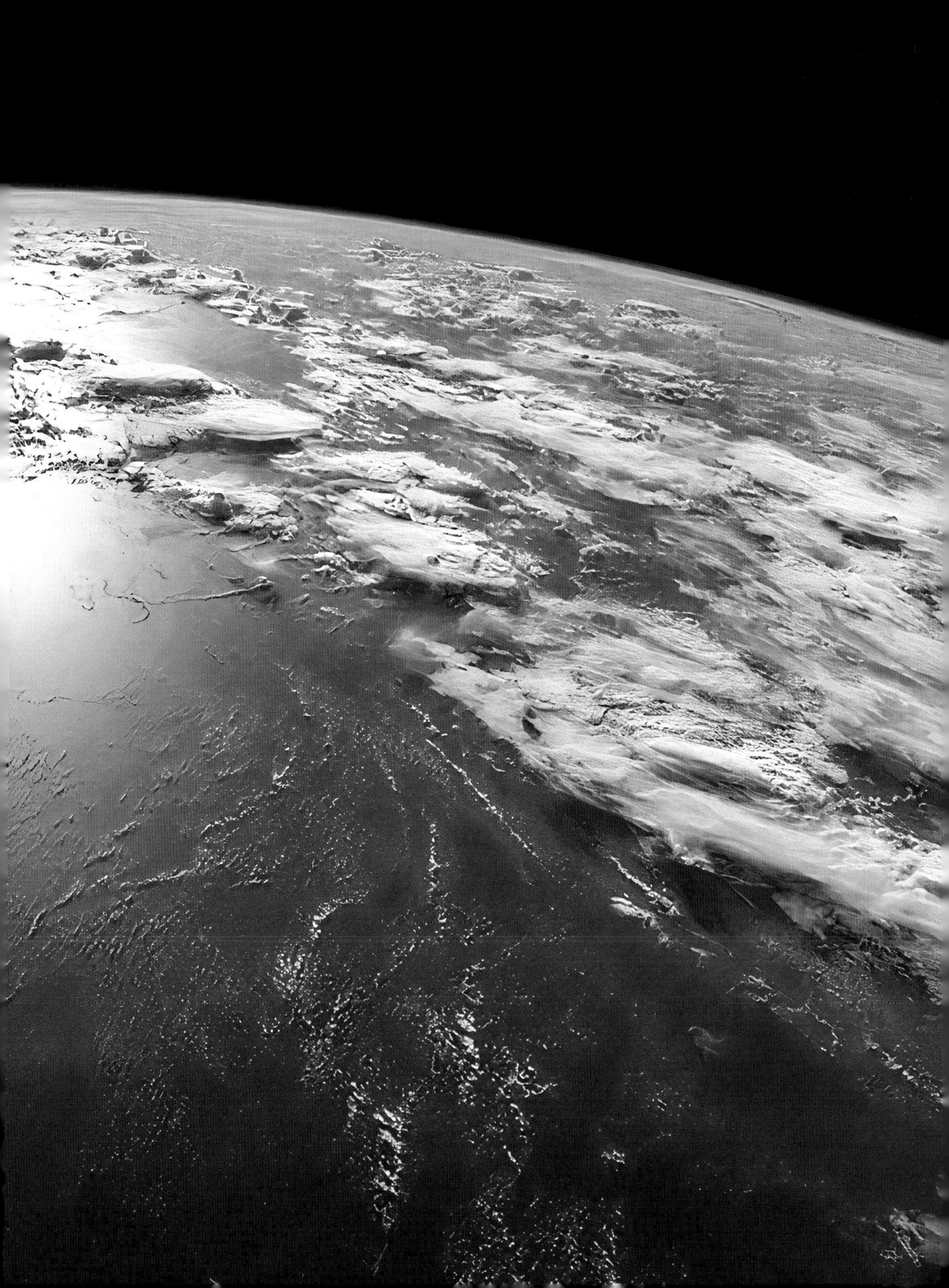

REFERENCES

**THE TWO GREELYS:
A TALE OF ARCTIC ANGUISH**

Much of what we know about the Greely expedition would not be possible without the primary sources that are safely stored in The Explorers Club research collection. The story in this book comes from a mix of those sources (particularly the letters from Greely and the crew), and also owes debts to A. L. Todd's *Abandoned: The Story of the Greely Arctic Expedition, 1881–1884;* Buddy *Levy's Labyrinth of Ice: The Triumphant and Tragic Greely Polar Expedition;* Paul Walker's *Adolphus Washington Greely: A Man of Indomitable Courage;* and Greely's own *Reminiscences of Adventure and Service.*

FIRST TO THE NORTH POLE . . . MAYBE?

In addition to The Club's considerable organic resources (such as interviews with ace archivist Lacey Flint), this section draws from Robert Peary's own book *The North Pole It's Discovery in 1909 Under the Auspices of the Peary Arctic Club;* Matthew Henson's memoir *A Journey Through the Ages;* and Bruce Henderson's *True North: Peary, Cook, and the Race to the Pole.*

**DOGS OVER PONIES—FIRST TO
THE SOUTH POLE**

Roland Huntford's *The Last Place on Earth* was indispensable for this section, along with Roald Amundsen's own work, *My Life as an Explorer: Autobiography of the First Man to Reach the South Pole,* and Robert Falcon Scott's posthumous *Scott's Last Expedition,* as well as Apsley Cherry-Garrard's memoir, *The Worst Journey in the World.*

TEDDY AND THE TABLE

Most tidbits were taken from interviews with Club members, prior Club journals, and prior editions of *As Told at The Explorers Club.* Candace Millard's *The River of Doubt: Theodore Roosevelt's Darkest Journey* is an excellent primer to Teddy's journey that we only hint at here.

THE LAST DRAGON CHASER

Alfred Lansing's *Endurance: Shackleton's Incredible Voyage* is the definitive text for this expedition, and for good reason—it's spell-binding. Also helpful were Shackleton's own memoir, *South (Shackleton's Last Expedition),* and in-person reporting from the 2022 ECAD weekend, where Mensun Bound shared his story of the *Endurance*'s recovery.

THE WINGS OF GREELY

In the largely overlooked *Adolphus Washington Greely: A Man of Indomitable Courage,* Paul Walker deserves credit for highlighting Greely's early role in aviation. Greely and Andrée's testy conversation comes courtesy of Alec Wilkinson's 2010 *New Yorker* article "The Ice Balloon." For the race between Byrd and Amundsen, we can thank the storytelling of a Club legend, Lowell Thomas, who shares a longer version of this tale in The Explorers Club book *Famous First Flights,* which he co-authored with his son.

FIRST TO SUMMIT EVEREST

This section draws heavily from the Norwegian legend himself, Sir Edmund Hillary, in his memoir, *View from the Summit.*

THE SOCIETY OF FORGOTTEN EXPLORERS

Interview with J. R. Harris, as well as in-person reporting from the 2022 ECAD weekend, form the basis for this section.

KON-TIKI

The foundation of this story comes from Thor Heyerdahl himself in his memoir, *Kon-Tiki: Across the Pacific in a Raft.*

**FIRST TO THE DEEPEST POINT
IN THE OCEAN**

The bulk of this story comes from an (awe-inspiring) interview with Dr. Don Walsh, as well as referencing a document he had written called "The Don Walsh Story."

FIRST TO THE MOON: APOLLO NIGHT AT THE EXPLORERS CLUB
This all comes from video footage of the 2019 ceremony in which The Explorers Club honored the Apollo astronauts.

"WHY ARE THERE NO GIRLS?"
Interviews with Faanya Rose, Lacey Flint, Milbry Polk, Rebecca Martin, and other Club members.

SEEING THE (UNDERWATER) LIGHT
Interview with Dr. Edith Widder.

DIVING AND MAPPING
Interview with Dr. Dawn Wright.

THE THRILL OF THE KRILL
Interview with Margaret O'Leary Amsler.

APOLLO'S ENGINES: LOST AND FOUND
Interview with David Concannon.

EXPLORATION AND SIDE HUSTLES: FROM OSCARS TO OCEANS
Draws heavily from Cameron's documentary *Deepsea Challenge*, as well as his speech at the 2013 Explorers Club Annual Dinner.

FROM APOLLO ROCKETS TO SOLAR WINGS
Interview with Dr. Bertrand Piccard.

THE TWO CALLIES: A TALE OF NATURE'S ANGUISH
Interviews with Callie Broaddus and Callie Veelenturf.

JANE GOODALL
Draws from her interview in *The Explorers Journal*.

EXPLORING BY STORYTELLING
Interviews with Asha Stuart and Jimmy Chin.

EXPLORING THE ROOTS
Interview with Mario Rigby.

EXPLORING THE SPACE VOLCANOS
Interview with Rosaly Lopes.

USHIRIKIANO
Interviews with Brandi DeCarli and Scott Thompson.

EXPLORING AS AN EXCHANGE
Interviews with Natalie Knowles and David Good.

SEEKING KNOWLEDGE THROUGH THE VISCERAL
Interview with Justin Fornal.

EXPLORING FOR TRUTH
Interview with Dr. Justin Dunnavant.

THE ASTRONAUT DEFENDING US FROM ASTEROIDS
Interview with Dr. Ed Lu.

CLUB CONNECTIONS
Interviews with Dr. Gino Caspari and Trevor Wallace.

EXPLORERS AS ALLIES
Interview with Billy Gauthier.

THE TRACK OF THE CAT
Interview with Dr. Laurie Marker.

EXPLORING FOR AGENCY
The core story draws from Sam Low's lovely *Hawaiki Rising*.

THE FIRST ENVIRONMENTAL LINGUIST
Interview with Dr. K. David Harrison.

EXPLORATION THROUGH ANTHROPOLOGY
Interview with Dr. Wade Davis.

EXPLORING THE RED PLANET
Interview with Dr. Nina Lanza.

FOOD, ART, AND THE JOURNEY TO MARS
Interviews with Jared Isaacman and Richard Garriott, the documentary *Countdown—Inspiration 4 Mission to Space*, and in-person reporting from the 2022 ECAD.

ACKNOWLEDGMENTS

As former Club president Ted Janulis said in one of the first interviews conducted for this book, "When you look at the 'Famous Firsts,' I now see them all as team sports. You don't get to the moon on your own." This is one of the book's core themes: The importance of collaboration in exploration.

So it's only fitting that the book is a true study in collaboration—a collaboration between explorers and editors and writers and designers and photographers and then more explorers.

Let's start with The Club itself.

Since its founding in 1904, there have been more than 8,000 members in The Explorers Club. This book, quite literally, would not be possible without them. So first and foremost, thank you to each and every member of The Club, past and present. You are the soul of this book.

Thank you to all of the Club members and officers who generously devoted their time to be interviewed, and who shared their extraordinary stories. Many are cited by name directly in the text, many more were not, but all were invaluable in shaping the book's context and spirit. In no particular order, thank you to Richard Garriott, Milbry Polk, Richard Wiese, Dr. Laurie Marker, Dr. Wade Davis, Ted Janulis, Rebecca Martin, J.R. Harris, Justin Fornal, Dr. Nina Lanza, Marc Bryan-Brown, Dr. Gino Caspari, Trevor Wallace, Dr. Kathy Sullivan, Sophie Hollingsworth, Dr. K. David Harrison, Asha Stuart, Dr. Rosaly Lopes, Dr. Margaret O. Amsler, Brandi DiCarli, Scott Thompson, Mario Rigby, Dr. Justin Dunnavant, Dr. Dawn Wright, Callie Broaddus, Dr. Ed Lu, Billy Gauthier, Dr. Don Walsh, John Houston, Dr. Bertrand Piccard, Craig Mattheson, Constance Difede, Mike Massimino, Callie Veelenturf, Lisandro Martinez, David Concannon, Kim Frank, Faanya Rose, Dr. Tom Paradise, David Good, Jared Isaacman, Jimmy Chin, Dr. Eddie Widder, and the many, many members who contributed through informal conversations.

Thank you, also, to the Club members whose incredible stories are *not* featured in this book. That might sound like an odd sentiment. But the truth is that there are, without exaggeration, thousands of worthy expeditions, stories, and projects that could and should be showcased, but there just weren't enough pages. The hardest part of this book was leaving out all this excellent and important work. There are titans of various fields, from astronomy to zoology and everything in between, who are not even been mentioned, much less featured. Robert Ballard, for example, the underwater archaeology icon who discovered the shipwreck of the *Titanic* in 1985 . . . his story is not in the book! There are painful omissions like this across the board. So thank you to the explorers whose stories are not covered, for your understanding and your grace. (Silver lining? There will be more books forthcoming from The Explorers Club . . .)

Thank you to The Club members and officers who read early drafts of the book and provided feedback and insights. The list includes J.R. Harris, Richard Garriott, Lindley Young, Ted Janulis, and all of the brilliant minds at HQ. Speaking of . . .

Thank you to the tireless, indomitable, and overlooked staff at The Explorers Club headquarters. To quickly peel back the curtain: I had hoped to include a brief section on the crucial role of The Club's HQ in the book itself, giving them the spotlight for once. The team at HQ, selfless as always, politely refused, so here's my chance to acknowledge their good work. Specifically: Thank you to The Club's 44th president, Richard Garriott, for that first inspiring tour of the building and for all of the illuminating conversations that followed. Thank you to The Club's longtime and beloved executive director,

Will Roseman, for championing the book since inception and for providing invaluable enthusiasm, direction, and leadership. Thank you to Lacey Flint, The Club's archivist, for the many, many hours spent with me and (patiently) educating me on its secrets and treasures. (Lacey, thank you for "shining the light.") Thanks to the director of communications, Kevin Murphy, for the many conversations that provided orientation, connections, and smart ideas. Thank you to Andrew McInerney for lending support in the form of encouragement and stellar imagery from the Club's bygone years—all that scanning really paid off! And thank you to Brooke Vahos, Coleen Castillo, Jenna O'Connor, Brittany Barbezat, Austin Raywood, Cristina Tranter, Gracie Almeida, Valerie Kilbridge, Heather Bain, Patryk Trzonkowski, George Shomo, Miguel Vasquz, Mimi Wlodarcyzk, Tomasz Trzonkowski, and Bonnie Wyper for all of your help, enthusiasm, and feedback. Enormous thanks to Liz Grady for rushing in to provide emergency assistance and expert guidance through the realm of image research and rights clearance. A huge thank you to Marc Bryan-Brown, Peter Aaron, Francis Dzikowski, and Christina Zhang for their skillful creation of the original photographs you see in these pages.

And a massive, Thor-Heyerdahl-globe-sized thank you to The Club's former membership and current grants director, Emerald Nash. The book wouldn't have worked without Emerald. The book wouldn't have happened without Emerald. I'm grateful for the hundreds (literally hundreds) of hours spent in our weekly meetings, arranging introductions to Club members, reading draft after draft after draft, giving smart feedback, tracking progress in spreadsheets, remaining relentlessly upbeat, and ultimately saving the day with the book's photographs. Thank you, Emerald.

One thing that has not changed since the days of Shackleton, Amundsen, and Henson is that when writing a book, a strong collaboration with the publisher is critical. So thank you to the wizards at Ten Speed Press, who somehow managed to create order out of all of the exploration chaos. Thank you to the brilliant and sharp-eyed editors, Matt Inman and Kimmy Tejasindhu, for all of the smart direction, for the structural guidance (Matt, an early conversation with you was foundational), for the much-needed questioning and pushbacks (Kimmy, you unfailingly knew *exactly* when to step in and set us straight), and for the consistent encouragement and guidance. Thank you, both. Thanks also to the ace team of designer Isabelle Gioffredi, production designer Mari Gill, production editor Mark McCauslin, production manager Serena Sigona, copyeditor Maureen Clark, indexer Jay Kreider, proofreaders Jacob Sammon and Andrea Peabbles, publicist Jana Branson, and marketer Allison Renzulli.

And a big thank you, of course, to everyone who helped make this book happen in the first place. Thanks to agent Albert Lee at UTA who spotted this book's potential, encouraged The Club to move forward, and worked his magic to bring it into the world. Thanks to agent Rob Weisbach (and his crackerjack team at Rob Weisbach Creative Management) for connecting The Club to its writer. You've been there from the very beginning and you are still there and have remained the book's fiercest champions—thank you all.

Thank you, finally, to those are who still out there in the field or the laboratory or in a submersible or space shuttle. Thank you for moving us all forward. Thank you for dreaming, for daring, for giving, for exploring.

—*Jeff Wilser*

CREDITS

COVER
Front: Andrés Ruzo on Boiling River Bridge, Boiling River, Peru; credit: Devlin Gandy. **Back:** The Gallery at The Explorers Club Headquarters, New York City; credit: Peter Aaron. **Endpapers:** *Saddle Between Karisimbi & Mt. Mikeno* by William R. Leigh—Kivu, Congo, 1926; photo by Marc Bryan-Brown.

FRONT MATTER
Half title: Page ornithologist James P. Chapin displays Flag 4 on expedition in the Ruwenzori Mountains, 1926–27; credit: The Explorers Club Research Collections. **Frontispiece:** The Apollo 11 lunar module *Eagle*; credit: NASA. **Epigraph:** The *Ra II*, 1970; credit: The Kon Tiki Museum. **Page viii:** The Explorers Club lobby; credit: Peter Aaron. **Page 2:** Charter members of The Explorers Club; credit: The Explorers Club Research Collections. Page 4: Lowell Thomas bust; photo by Marc Bryan-Brown. **Page 5:** Flag 32; credit: The Explorers Club Research Collections.

1: EXPANDING THE MAPS: CHASING THE DRAGONS
Pages 6–7: The Explorers Club, second-floor landing; credit: Peter Aaron. **Page 8:** Ship in the distance; credit: The Explorers Club Research Collections. **Page 10:** *Camp Clay* by Albert L. Operti; photo by Marc Bryan-Brown. **Pages 13 and 16:** Adolphus Greely; credit: The Explorers Club Research Collections. **Page 19:** Tidal readings; credit: The Explorers Club Research Collections. **Page 20:** Scorecard; credit: The Explorers Club Research Collections. **Page 25:** Greely team portrait; credit: The Explorers Club Research Collections. **Page 29:** Tent against Arctic landscape; credit: The Explorers Club Research Collections. **Page 30:** North Pole group; credit: Robert Peary. **Page 33 (left):** Robert Peary; credit: Robert Peary / **(right)** Matthew Henson; credit: Library of Congress. **Page 34:** Henson-Peary sledge; credit: Peter Aaron. **Page 35:** Henson mittens; credit: The Explorers Club Research Collections. **Page 37:** *Cape York* by Albert L. Operti; photo by Marc Bryan-Brown. **Page 38:** Josephine Peary and baby; credit: Explorers Club Research Collections. **Page 41:** Mathew Henson; credit: Matthew A. Henson. **Page 42:** Explorers Club flag prototype; credit: The Explorers Club Research Collections. **Page 43:** Lewis Cotlow Second Antarctic Expedition; credit: The Explorers Club Research Collections. **Page 44 (top):** Scott Expedition Party; credit: Henry Bowers (1883–1912) / **(bottom)** *As Useful as Horses* by Albert L. Operti; credit: The Explorers Club Research Collections. **Page 47 (left):** Robert F. Scott; credit: Henry Maull (1829–1914) and John Fox (1832–1907), Antarctica Images, Adobe Stock / **(right)** Roald Amundsen; photographer unknown. **Page 52:** Theodore Roosevelt; credit: Library of Congress. **Page 53:** The Board Room; credit: Peter Aaron. **Page 54:** The Map Room; credit: Peter Aaron. **Page 55:** Gertrude Bell; credit: Gertrude Bell Archive. **Page 56:** The *Endurance*; credit: Frank Hurley (1885–1962). **Page 58:** Ernest Shackleton; credit: Frank Hurley (1885–1962). **Page 60:** Shackleton's dogs; credit: Frank Hurley (1885–1962) / Library of Congress. **Page 62:** Shackleton Expedition, working to free the ship; credit: Frank Hurley (1885–1962). **Page 64:** The Explorers Club Bar; credit: Peter Aaron. **Page 67:** Mensun Bound with flag; credit: Mensun Bound / The Explorers Club Research Collections. **Page 68:** The Gallery; credit: Peter Aaron.

2: BREAKING THE BOUNDARIES: CLIMBING HIGHER AND DIVING DEEPER
Pages 70–71: President's Corner; credit: Peter Aaron. **Page 72:** Earth and lunar module; credit: NASA. **Page 74:** Maj. Gen. Adolphus Greely; credit: National Park Service. **Page 77:** Balloon inflation; credit: The Explorers Club Research Collections. **Page 78:** The Wright brothers, first flight; credit: John T. Daniels, Jr. (1873–1948). **Page 80:** Admiral Byrd; credit:

The Explorers Club Research Collections. **Page 82:** *Little America* by Anton Widlicka; photo by Marc Bryan-Brown. **Page 83:** Admiral Byrd and his dog, Igloo; credit: The Explorers Club Research Collections / Richard E. Byrd. **Pages 84–85:** ECAD 50th anniversary artwork and 64th and 68th Annual ECAD menus; credit: The Explorers Club Research Collections. **Page 86:** Tenzing Norgay and Edmund Hillary; credit: SuperStock / Alamy Stock Photo. **Pages 88–89:** Mt. Everest; credit: Natalia Maroz, Adobe Stock Photo. **Page 90:** Tenzing Norgay and Edmund Hillary at camp; credit: D and S Photography Archives, Alamy Stock Photo. **Page 91:** Tenzing Norgay; credit: Edmund Hillary, Royal Geographic Society. **Page 92:** J. R. Harris hiking in the Dolomites; credit: J. R. Harris. **Page 94:** Research Collections door; credit: Felix Kunze. **Page 95:** J. R. Harris; credit: J. R. Harris. **Page 96:** ECAD 1955; credit: The Explorers Club Research Collections. **Page 97:** J. R. Harris speaking at The Explorers Club; credit: Peter Domorak. **Page 98:** *Explorers Journal* cover; credit: The Explorers Club Research Collections. **Page 99:** Forgotten Four tiles; credit: Marc Bryan-Brown. **Page 100:** Planning the *Kon-Tiki*; credit: The Explorers Club Research Collections. **Page 103:** *Kon-Tiki*; credit: NASA Image Collection. **Page 104 (top and bottom):** Flag 123 and *Kon-Tiki* rope; credit: The Explorers Club Research Collections. **Page 107:** *Les Compagnons du Kon-Tiki* book cover; credit: private collection© Archives Charmet/ Bridgeman Images. **Page 108 (left):** Thor Heyerdahl Membership Certificate; credit: The Explorers Club Research Collections / **(right)** Thor Heyerdahl; credit: Library of Congress. **Pages 110 and 112:** *Trieste* illustration and diagram; credit: Don Walsh. **Page 115:** Walsh and Piccard; credit: Don Walsh. **Page 116:** Walsh, Piccard, and crew; credit: Don Walsh. **Page 118:** Man on the moon; credit: Neil Armstrong. **Page 121:** Michael Collins practicing in simulator; credit: NASA. **Page 122:** Buzz Aldrin descends from the lunar module; credit: NASA. **Page 126:** Earthrise; credit: NASA. **Page 131 (top):** Apollo astronauts at The Explorers Club; credit: Marc Bryan-Brown / **(bottom)** Framed Apollo Explorers Club flag; credit: The Explorers Club. **Page 132:** Kasha Rigby traversing above the clouds, Reddomaine Peak, China; credit: Jimmy Chin. **Page 134:** Amelia Earhart; credit: The Explorers Club Research Collections. **Page 137 (top left):** Margaret Meade; credit: Library of Congress / **(top right and bottom left and right):** Harriet Chalmers Adams, Ethel Tweedie, Josephine Peary with Inuit; credit: Explorers Club Research Collections. **Page 138:** Bessie Coleman; photographer unknown. **Page 140:** Kathy Sullivan and Sally Ride; credit: NASA. **Page 141 (top left):** Lhakpa Sherpa; credit: Lhakpa Sherpa / **(top right):** Sylvia Earle; credit: OAR/NURP/NOAA / **(bottom left):** Jane Goodall; credit: Everett Collection Historical, Alamy Stock Photo / **(bottom right):** Faanya Rose; credit: Faanya Rose. **Page 142:** Edith Widder in the Wasp; credit: ORCA. **Pages 146–147:** Bioluminescent plankton in the sea; credit: Aquir, Adobe Stock Photo. **Page 149:** The Wasp; credit: Edith Widder. **Page 150:** Jellyfish with neon glow light effect in Singapore aquarium; credit: Wei Huang, Adobe Stock Photo. **Page 151:** Clark Room fireplace; credit: Peter Aaron. **Page 152:** Dawn Wright preparing for the dive; credit: Dawn Wright. **Page 155:** Marie Tharp map; credit: Fiona Yacopino, Marie Tharp Maps, LLC. **Page 156:** Margaret Amsler on boat; credit: Jim McClintock. **Page 159:** Margaret Amsler with krill; credit: NHK-Japan. **Page 160:** Apollo 11 rocket; credit: NASA. **Page 161:** Apollo Engine Recovery Team; credit: Josh Bernstein. **Page 162:** *Deepsea Challenger*; credit: Charlie Arneson. **Page 164:** Cameron and team; credit: Dr. Joe Macinnis.

Page 167 (top): Cameron and team preparing; credit: Walt Conti / **(bottom):** James Cameron and Don Walsh; credit: The Explorers Club Flag Files. **Page 168:** Auguste Piccard; credit: © SZ Photo, Scherl, Bridgeman Images. **Page 170:** Auguste Piccard; credit: Keystone/Bridgeman Images. **Pages 172, 173, and 175:** Bertrand Piccard in flight; credit: Bertrand Piccard. **Page 176:** Bertrand Piccard and André Borschberg; credit: The Explorers Club Flag Files. **Page 177:** *Solar Impulse* over mountains; credit: Bertrand Piccard.

3: CURIOSITY IN ACTION: THE NEW GOLDEN AGE OF EXPLORATION

Pages 178–179: The Explorers Club Library; credit: Peter Aaron. **Page 180:** Elodie Freymann and Geresomu Muhumuza; credit Austin Deery. **Page 182:** Stream inside the Dracula Reserve; credit: Callie Broaddus. **Page 184 (top and bottom):** Dracula Transect Expedition and Dracula Expansion Expedition; credit: Callie Broaddus. **Page 187:** Green sea turtle; credit: Michael Ryan Clark. **Page 188:** Jane Goodall; credit: Danita Delimont, Alamy Stock Photo. **Page 190:** Andean cock-of-the-rock; credit: Callie Broaddus. **Page 191:** Callie Veelenturf with leatherback turtle; credit: Jonah Reenders. **Page 192:** Asha Stuart with Himba women; credit: Joseph Illonga. **Pages 196, 199, 200, and 200–203:** Mario Rigby; credit: Mario Rigby. **Page 205:** *Explorers Club 50* cover; credit: C G Venkatesh. **Page 206:** Jupiter's moon; credit: NASA/ JPL/ University of Arizona. **Page 209:** Map of Titan; credit: NASA/JPL-Caltech/ASU. **Page 210:** Rosaly Lopes with flag; credit: Rosaly Lopes. **Page 212:** Farmers working; credit: Brandi DeCarli. **Page 214:** Natalie Knowles and Takaknhoti; credit: Lucas Dezan. **Page 215:** Young Citizen Scientist in the forest; credit: Lucas Dezan. **Page 218:** Natalie Knowles; credit: John Meisner. **Page 219:** Justin Fornal; credit: Justin Fornal. **Pages 220, 222, and 223:** Justin Dunnavant; credit: Dr. Jennifer Adler. **Page 224:** Ed Lu in space suit; credit: NASA. **Pages 226–227:** Asteroid trajectory illustration; credit: B612 Asteroid Institute, University of Washington DiRAC Institute, OpenSpace Project. **Page 229:** Ed Lu at work in space; credit: NASA. **Page 230:** Gino Caspari–Trevor Wallace Expedition; credit: Trevor Wallace. **Page 232:** Billy Gauthier; credit: Kara Montague. **Page 234:** *Windspirit* by Billy Gauthier; credit: Spirit Wrestler Gallery. **Page 236:** Billy Gauthier; credit: Kara Montague. **Page 238 and 240 (top and bottom):** Laurie Marker; credit: Cheetah Conservation Fund. **Page 243:** Laurie Marker with Chewbaaka; credit: Christophe Lepetit, courtesy of Cheetah Conservation Fund. **Page 244:** Nainoa Thompson; credit: Polynesian Voyaging Society. **Pages 246–247:** The Polynesian Voyaging Society; credit: Wade Davis. **Page 249:** Nainoa Thompson and Dan Lin with Flag 124; credit: Dan Lin. **Page 252:** David Harrison with Nick Waikai; credit: Chris Rainier. **Page 254:** David Harrison with Tuvan consultants; credit: Sven Grawunder. **Page 257:** Wade Davis; credit: Chris Rainier. **Pages 258–259:** David Harrison, Gregory Anderson, and Charlie Mangulda; credit: Chris Rainier / Living Tongues Institute. **Pages 260, 262, and 264–265:** Mars photographs; credit: NASA. **Page 267:** Nina Lanza; credit: Nina Lanza. **Page 269:** Sian Proctor; credit: John Kraus. **Page 273:** Richard Garriott; credit: Gagarin Cosmonaut Training Center, via NASA. **Pages 265, 267, 268, and 279:** Inspiration4 crew; credit: John Kraus. **Page 280:** Sian Proctor at ECAD; credit: Peter Domorak. **Pages 282–283:** The Earth; credit: Inspiration4 Team. **Page 296:** Bagpiper Gilbert Kerr with penguin during the Scottish National Antarctic Expedition, 1902–04; credit: William S Bruce (1867–1921), Royal Scottish Geographical Society.

INDEX

Published in the United States by Ten Speed Press, an imprint of the
Crown Publishing Group, a division of Penguin Random House LLC, New York.
TenSpeed.com

Ten Speed Press and the Ten Speed Press colophon
are registered trademarks of Penguin Random House LLC.

Typefaces: Commercial Type's Druk and Graphik and Klim Type Foundry's Tiempos

Library of Congress Cataloging-in-Publication Data is on file with the publisher.

Hardcover ISBN: 978-1-9848-5998-3
eBook ISBN: 978-1-9848-5999-0

Printed in Malaysia

Acquiring editor: Matt Inman | Project editor: Kimmy Tejasindhu
Production editor: Mark McCauslin
Designer: Isabelle Gioffredi
Production designers: Mari Gill and Faith Hague
Production manager: Serena Sigona
Copyeditor: Maureen Clark | Indexer: Jay Kreider
Proofreaders: Jacob Sammon and Andrea Peabbles
Publicist: Jana Branson | Marketer: Allison Renzulli

Front cover: Andrés Ruzo on Boiling River Bridge, Boiling River, Peru; credit:
Devlin Gandy. Back cover: The Gallery at The Explorers Club Headquarters,
New York tCity; credit: Peter Aaron. End papers: *Saddle Between Karisimbi & Mt. Mikeno*
by William R. Leigh—Kivu, Congo, 1926; photo credit: Marc Bryan-Brown.

10 9 8 7 6 5 4 3 2 1

First Edition